on his own wide experience, first as a military trial lawyer and later as a civilian lawyer, West openly discusses command-approved fraud and command rigging of courts martial, and exposes high-ranking military officials as jury-fixers and conspirators. Among the many cases he considers here are the My Lai trials and those of Vietnam war-resisters and black militants. Finally, West argues that the operation of the military should be placed in the hands of civilian administrators, under the control of the attorney general of the United States.

West's book casts a clear, knowing light on the subtleties and cruelties of the American judicial system. *They Call It Justice* hits a nerve center of America.

Luther C. West served first as an enlisted man in World War II, then as a Regular Army judge advocate, in grades lieutenant through lieutenant colonel, for a total of more than twenty years. He is now a practicing civilian lawyer in Baltimore, where he specializes in conscientious-objector and military-criminal cases.

They Call It Justice

They Call It Justice

Command Influence and the Court-Martial System

Luther C. West

The Viking Press   New York

First published in 1977 by The Viking Press
625 Madison Avenue, New York, N.Y. 10022

Published simultaneously in Canada by
The Macmillan Company of Canada Limited

LIBRARY OF CONGRESS CATALOGING IN PUBLICATION DATA

West, Luther C
They call it justice.
Includes index.
1. Courts-martial and courts of inquiry—
United States.   I. Title.
KF7625.w48   343′.73′0143   76-24885
ISBN 0-670-69907-1

To Noah and Will

Contents

★

Introduction   ix

1   Blackmarket Coffee
    and the New UCMJ   1

2   Early Military Law,
    a Hyphenated System of Justice   15

3   World Wars I and II,
    a Breakdown of Justice   28

4   Korea, the Land of Morning Calm:
    The Boy in the Box   46

5   The Trial of Sergeant Adams:
    Keeping Counsel in Line   60

6   The First Ten Years,
    a Decade of Bad Law   75

7   The Powell Report,
    the Second Decade   92

8   Murder at Fort Bragg
and German-American Relations   108

9   The Claymore Mine Case: 125
Investigating Accidental Deaths

10   The Cooks-McGuire Case: 139
Injustice and Extraordinary Writs

11   The My Lai Trials: 154
Red and Green Lights

12   The Calley Conviction: 167
The Cover-Up

13   The Acquittal of Captain Medina: 182
The Ground Commander

14   The Trial of Colonel Henderson: 196
The Superior Commander

15   Louis Paul Font: 213
West Point Honor

16   Michael Daley: 229
The Trial of a War Resister

17   Captain Raymond Hopkins: 246
Black America in the Army

18   The Black Revolution: 261
Discipline and the Ku Klux Klan

19   Conclusion   278

Index   291

Introduction

Military justice provides for the discipline of the armed forces. If a soldier commits an offense—steals from another soldier, or refuses to fight in battle, or goes absent without leave, or commits a murder or rape—his immediate commander generally decides whether or not to punish him for this breach of discipline. If the offense might prove embarrassing to the military or to the individual commander, it may never come to trial at all. The Green Beret assassination and the My Lai cover-up for over a year are examples of this type of case. On the other hand, if a military commander decides that the best interest of the military dictates a trial in a particular case, and if he feels that the offense is provable, he might elect to try the offender by court-martial. If so, he may refer the charges to trial by a court-martial convened by himself, or he may refer the charges to a higher commander with a recommendation for trial by that commander. In either event the officer who refers the case to trial by court-martial would appoint counsel for both sides as well as the court members (i.e., the jury) from the membership of his own command.

If the commander concerned is honest, he will permit his court members to judge cases on their individual merit. If he is dishonest, or nervous, or frightened, or feels threatened in any number of ways, he may well usurp the independent judicial functions of the court-martial, and "influence" his court members to render a verdict and sentence designed to reflect his own wishes, regardless of the merits of the individual case. The commander (or even the commander in chief) might feel it necessary to effect a particular verdict or sentence in any case to protect what he considers the vital interest of his command, or of his career (or of the nation), whether he is honest or not. At an evening meal at the officers' club, a commanding general might drop the word to the president of the court-martial (i.e., the senior member of the jury), as to the type of verdict or sentence he wants in a particular case or series of cases. Under the guise of giving training in matters of military justice to the members of his command, he might have his staff judge advocate lecture his court members. Or he might have his chief of staff pass along the message more discreetly to key members of a military jury. If he is the president of the United States, he might have his secretary of defense or secretary of the army pass the word to appropriate military commanders.

These and a thousand and one other means are available: a raised eyebrow when a particular court-martial case is discussed, a frown, a fist pounding the desk. Obedience-trained officers do not find it difficult to fathom the wishes and desires of their commanding general (or of their president). Whether controls of this sort are necessary to protect the military mission, is, of course, a question that touches the heart of the democratic process. Defenders of things military have argued throughout the years that servicemen and women who are not subject to such controls may disrupt the discipline of an entire military organization.

Such advocates would cite the chaotic outbursts of racial violence aboard United States aircraft carriers in 1972 and 1973 as cases in point, and as indicators of the disaster that awaits the military commander who "loses control" of his men. The story of

Billy Budd must surface in the mind of many an old-line Annapolis graduate as he reads about roving bands of black sailors attacking white sailors on our carriers, and beating them unmercifully "just for being white." The tale of *Billy Budd* offers a packaged command solution. You string Billy Budd from the yardarm one morning at first light, and most of the sailors will get the message. It makes no difference that he may be innocent of any real wrongdoing, or that his court-martial was rigged by a kindly, well-meaning militarist who merely told the court members how to vote and what sentence to adjudge. Billy Budd's trial and execution were necessary (in his captain's mind) to preserve the state of discipline within the Royal Navy, and that was enough to seal his doom.

The modern Billy Budd thus may be a handsome black sailor, young in mind and body, and a respected and beloved leader of his race. He may also be an innocent, but when he hangs by his neck, literally or figuratively, the spectacle of his downfall may quiet the unsettled fear that beats in the breast of his commander that he was unable to control the "discipline" of his ship, just as it might still the violence that roams his flight decks at night. It would not be a "peace with honor," but it is what military justice is all about. It is designed to serve the ends of the military, and not necessarily the ends of justice.

In March 1951 I began a career that was to last for seventeen and a half years in the regular army's Judge Advocate General's Corps. When added to my enlisted service in the navy during World War II, my active duty totaled twenty years and eleven days. It was a career that gave me pause to think. At times I wondered why I was in a military organization posing as a lawyer. At times I wondered whether the lackluster mentality of senior judge advocates was the ultimate fate of all career military lawyers. I was startled and shocked at the willingness of younger judge advocates not to challenge these men. As a career army legal officer, serving in the ranks of first lieutenant through lieutenant colonel, and later as a civilian attorney I delved into almost every conceivable military offense—and into almost every facet of military criminal trial practice.

This book is about military justice as I saw it and still see it, as I practiced it and still practice it. I will also, at times, recount a brief history of the darker side of military justice, that which involves command-rigged verdicts and sentences and other legal atrocities committed in the name of military necessity. In an effort not to burden the reader with copious footnotes, I will at this time refer the more technical reader—and the professional who desires detailed case citations, law review articles, legal books, and chapter and verse of congressional hearings relating to the subject of command fraud in military justice, and particularly to the cases referred to in this book and to the historical data discussed in this book—to the author's article in the University of California (Los Angeles) *Law Review*, volume 18, number 1 (November 1970), pages 1 through 156, entitled "A History of Command Influence on the Military Judicial System." The article in question traces the command fraud involved in the trial of military courts-martial from 1775 until 1970. Otherwise, this book will omit formal citation of cases and other authorities.

They Call It Justice

1

Blackmarket Coffee
and the New UCMJ

In the year 1952, as a first lieutenant in the army's Judge Advocate General's Corps, I was assigned as military defense counsel for a young army private accused of wholesale theft and blackmarketing of GI coffee. The offense occurred in an American *Kaserne* in a small German town not too far from the headquarters of a U.S. Army infantry division. Throughout the alleged criminal act of the defendant, he had been closely watched by agents of the American military Criminal Investigation Division (the CID). The defendant had also been caught red-handed at the scene of the sale—and he gave a complete confession to the police after he was fully warned of his rights to remain silent. The division staff judge advocate reviewed the case in detail and recommended that the commanding general of the division refer it to trial by general court-martial. The commanding general concurred, and in due time the case was brought to trial.

At the trial, which lasted three days, both the judge and the opposing counsel were short-tempered. The case was the fourth in a series that I had defended against the same prosecuting judge advocate, with the same trial judge officiating. The first three had gone rather poorly for the prosecutor, and had resulted either in acquittals or in very insignificant sentences. But they had not been considered important cases. The most serious damage was done to the prosecutor's ego. The coffee case, however, was his on the evidence. It was an important case, and he was staking his all on winning it. But when it dragged on for three full days with the prospect of going into night session the last day, he was infuriated. Moreover, a flaw had developed.

The evidence revealed that on the day of the theft, the defendant, a cook's helper, was in fact ready to steal a one-hundred-pound bag of GI coffee from an American army mess hall. He was supposed to put the coffee into a garbage can, where his co-conspirators, the garbage men, were to load it onto a garbage truck and drive it to the home of the defendant's girl friend. A CID informer, posing as one of the co-conspirators, tipped off the police, and they were ready on the morning in question. But the flaw in the prosecutor's case, which he had not detected until the trial, had to do with the fact that on the morning of the theft, the defendant had overslept. With the garbage truck rapidly approaching the mess hall, and with the CID in place and ready, the failure of the defendant to appear would have been something of a minor catastrophe. So the informer supplied the necessary action. He simply directed two German KPs (who were not involved in the conspiracy) to load the marked coffee into a garbage can and carry it aboard the truck. Then the informer scurried to the defendant's barracks, awakened him, and suggested that he drive to his girl friend's home and retrieve his coffee. When he arrived he was arrested. The bag of coffee, which the informer had marked by jamming a handful of peas wrapped in a napkin inside, was recovered. The peas were found in place, and the defendant eventually gave a written confession.

In the early 1950s military counsel were permitted to argue law to military juries on motions for a finding of not guilty. Although the motions were technically addressed to the trial judge, the jury had the procedural right to overrule the trial judge on a motion for a finding of not guilty. The purpose of this procedural device was command-oriented. Legally trained judges in those days were almost brand new in military law, and were not overly trusted. Military juries, on the other hand, were completely trustworthy. They were usually commanders themselves, and had been handpicked by the convening authority. They were thus presumably far more in line with command interests than a legally trained military judge might ever be. An untrustworthy military judge might lean too much on legal technicality and, imbued with the liberal spirit of the newly enacted Uniform Code of Military Justice, erroneously grant a motion to acquit a defendant. By granting the military jury the procedural right to overrule the trial judge, the military provided a safety valve designed to prevent such erroneous rulings by military judges. It was in reality a paranoid arrangement to assure the military that legal officers were not going to take over the trial of military cases—not even if Congress had directed them to do so in the Uniform Code.

In the coffee case I knew there was no possibility however slight of our military judge granting my motion for acquittal. I wished to utilize the procedural device in reverse. I had carefully researched the law relating to the issue involved in the nearest American law library, some sixty miles from my office at division headquarters. I was reasonably sure that neither the trial judge nor the prosecutor had done so, and I thought with a little luck I could win the case. I was hoping that one of the jurors, looking at it from the viewpoint of justice and perhaps disgusted with the prospect of a pending night session, might object to the trial judge's ruling denying my motion, and thereby close the court and vote whether to sustain or deny my motion.

In my research I found there were no military cases on the precise point, but that in state cases, if an informer delivered the goods to be stolen to the associate of the defendant, the act of the informer could not be charged to the defendant. These cases held that where the trespass against the property was made by an agent of the state (the informer), the defendant could not be convicted of larceny. I also discovered that the same rule probably did not apply in federal cases, but I decided that that was a distinction that would have to be researched by the prosecutor. I prepared my argument solely on the basis of state law, and it was this law that I urged upon the court-martial members.

After the evidence was taken and both sides had rested, I made my motion for a finding of not guilty. The military judge, sensing that my point perhaps carried weight, stopped me several times, but ultimately let me proceed. I read long excerpts from state cases, cases that were on "all fours" with my own and which, of course, sustained my client's position 100 percent. I argued on until the hour grew quite late, and then submitted the matter. The prosecutor, red-faced and angry, realizing that he could lose the case, fumed a wrathful denunciation of my state cases. But as he had not researched the problem, his denunciation was wide of the mark. He terminated his argument quickly, and the military judge, just as quickly, denied my motion "subject to the objection of any court member." The trial judge then adjourned the court for the evening meal—when he noticed that one of the captains on the court had his hand raised. The captain politely informed the judge that he objected to his ruling. The court closed for a few minutes and then opened and announced that it had sustained my motion. The defendant was acquitted.

To me, there is no greater moment than this in the practice of law. This is what keeps our system of justice alive—but I sensed that my exhilaration was not shared by my judge advocate superiors. I feared that they would bitterly resent the verdict, and consider my actions in behalf of my client as disloyal to the military system.

★

I had taken my oath as a first lieutenant in the Judge Advocate General's Corps (JAG) on March 1, 1951. As a young lawyer recently graduated from George Washington University's Law

School, I had mixed emotions about making the army my career. During World War II I had served as an enlisted man in the navy, and I still held a resentment against the officer corps generally. I also sensed that some career military officers were World War II misfits who chose to remain in military service rather than join the competitive world of civilians. But my family was growing, the pay inducement was good, and I was attracted by the offer of immediate trial work. Thus I rationalized my doubts and convinced myself that I would still be a lawyer, but would simply wear a uniform. I was bored with my job as a beginning attorney in the Federal Power Commission in Washington, D.C., and I longed to try cases. Thus I applied for active duty as an army lawyer, and when I was tendered a commission in JAG I joined the regular army.

Prior to shipment to Germany, I attended the Judge Advocate Basic Officers' Class at Fort Myer, Virginia. It was here that I began hearing strange legal concepts from military lawyers. Our instructors hammered home to us that we were army officers first, and lawyers second. We were instructed that our commander was our client twenty-four hours a day, seven days a week, and never to forget it. All other clients were secondary. We also learned that the basic purpose of the army consisted of only one word: FIGHT!

Trial duty, however, was reassuring, and after joining the infantry division I turned myself to it with zeal. There were five trial attorneys in the division, one trial judge and the staff judge advocate, all of whom worked out of the legal office at division headquarters. In the early 1950s there was no "guilty plea program" in the army. This meant that every case tried, at least in our division, was a contested jury trial, and in the event of a guilty finding, whatever sentence was adjudged was the sentence that prevailed. Our case load was extremely heavy. There was precious little time to prepare for trial, there was no one to ask for advice because our superiors were as inexperienced as we, and our cases ranged from mild reprimand situations to potential death sentences. As trial attorneys we could either sink or swim—and we tried contested jury trials, one after the other, week after week, month after month.

The counsel in these cases also tried each other. All trial attorneys in the division were young judge advocate officers, fresh out of law school, and all but me were reserve officers. All, except me, were serving involuntarily in the army, and none of us had any sense of fierce loyalty to the military. The closeness of the office, the day-after-day contest, and the intrigue of trial work set the stage for us. Most of us developed a marked degree of competitiveness among ourselves, an eagerness to fight that was quickly and easily carried over to our work. We litigated not only to win but to humiliate opposing counsel. Also, I was never able to forget our army-oriented instructors at JAG School at Fort Myer. I resented the slanted instruction I had received there—and I hoped to prove it incorrect in practice.

In the early fifties there were three regiments in an infantry division. In our division each trial attorney's work load was arranged so that he prosecuted cases in one regiment, and defended cases in two regiments. The army prosecutor, circa 1950, was confronted with a tangle of legal administration. It was his responsibility physically to set up the courtroom, notify the court personnel of the place and time of the trial, summons all witnesses for both the government and the defense, arrange for necessary transportation, flights, trains, automobiles or boats, pay all necessary witnesses and other fees connected with the case, arrange for the presence of the defendant and guards—and to catch all kinds of hell if anything went wrong. Thus the prosecution-defense assignments, with a two-to-one ratio in favor of defense duties, were a concession to reality. At least in our division, the prosecution of military cases under these circumstances was a hair-raising experience. There was a multitude of possibilities for slip-up, and the unwary prosecutor could quickly lose a series of cases through administrative hassle. Some counsel were so destroyed by this initiation process that they never fully recovered.

The staff judge advocate (SJA) of the division was a quiet, mild-mannered lieutenant colonel, a loner, who had elected to remain on active duty following World War II. His executive officer, a major, also a holdover from World War II, was far more aggressive. The SJA appeared to be totally inexperienced in legal work, and the major had had a year or two of civilian experience as a practicing attorney. By assignment, the major was the trial judge in every general court-martial case tried in the division. In my opinion both men were unequal to the task of running a smooth judge advocate office. Both officers were honorable men, and both were my friends. They were also my superiors and they wrote my efficiency reports upon which my promotion potential was judged by army promotion boards in the Pentagon.

Prospective cases in the division, such as the coffee case, were first reviewed by the staff judge advocate, after they had been investigated by military criminal police agencies. The SJA would make a written recommendation to the commanding general of the division. The division commander (a major general) in turn either referred the case to trial by general court-martial, or disposed of it through other channels. He could return it to a lower command for trial by inferior court—that is, by either special or summary court-martial. Or the general could dismiss the charges himself, or take administrative or nonjudicial action in the case. The general was the "convening authority" and his was the very widest choice. Most of the time, if the staff judge advocate recommended trial by general court-martial the cases were disposed of in just that manner.

In such cases the division commander, as the convening authority, picked the court-martial jury, or court-martial members, from his own command, usually from the battalion of the defendant. Each juror almost always was a career officer, whose future was nearly 100 percent subject to the continued favor of the division commander. Any division officer who received a bad efficiency report from a general court-martial convening authority, or who otherwise displeased him, was in serious trouble. He could find himself passed over for promotion, or "nonselected" for advanced service schools, or both. Thus, when an officer found that he had been selected by his commanding general to perform jury duty, in the trial of a criminal case that the general thought serious enough to warrant a general court-martial, he was in something of an ethical bog right from the start.

The new, civilianized Uniform Code of Military Justice enacted into law by Congress became operable in all branches of the military service on May 31, 1951. Sweeping reforms had been written into this law. Under the statute the inequities of military justice as it was practiced in World Wars I and II were supposedly outlawed. Military trials would be fair; legal counsel were required to be employed on both sides; a military lawyer would serve as judge (or as law officer) in all general courts-martial; and the entire system would be supervised by the United States Court of Military Appeals, a three-judge *civilian* court appointed by the president.

Moreover, command influence was officially outlawed in Article 37 of the Uniform Code. The article prohibited anyone from "coercing" by "any unauthorized means" the action of a court-martial in reaching its decisions, or the action of a court-martial convening authority in matters of military justice. The new article also prohibited the time-honored right of the military commander to censure a court member, counsel, or military judge for the performance of his judicial duty.

The beauty of this system of military justice lay, in my opinion, not so much in its fine-spun language, which on paper was almost flawless, but in the simple fact that it worked at all. How any defendant could receive a fair trial in an environment where one man—the convening authority—exercised so many different police and judicial functions was a marvel. Add to the various functions (i.e., police, investigative, grand jury, and selection of trial jurors, judge, and counsel) that were entrusted to one man the fact that at every stage of the way, every individual involved in the entire process was subject to the career veto of the same person (the convening authority), and the prospect of objective justice becomes even more dim.

I found in practice, however, that given a number of favorable conditions, it was possible to achieve justice in military trials. If the case being tried was not controversial; if it posed no threat to the well-being of the division commander, assistant division commander, the division chief of staff, or the staff judge advocate; if the same officials refrained from making their views or desires known to court members; if there was no drive on in the command concerned to increase the general court-martial conviction rate, or to increase the severity of court-martial sentences generally; and if trial defense counsel were unshackled and reasonably competent and determined to win, it was *possible* that army officers could fairly judge military cases and impose just sentences. But if the scales were tipped anywhere along the line, and command emphasis was brought to bear on the case involved or on the judicial process generally or on the defense counsel, through whatever covert or overt channels were available, the chances of a defendant receiving a fair trial were drastically reduced. Command influence, despite the formal language of Article 37 of the Uniform Code of Military Justice that outlawed it, was a very slippery thing. Like an iceberg, it often existed mostly beneath the surface. If the command were dishonest, or chose to ignore Article 37 (as some did in selected cases) and exerted illegal influence upon their military courts or defense counsel, this was very difficult for a young, relatively inexperienced military trial defense counsel to prove in a court of law.

In our division we were never told to ease our pace, or not to litigate issues that might embarrass our command. Our staff judge advocate was withdrawn and shy, but he had the integrity not to overreach his subordinate legal officers. He did not seek a showdown with recalcitrant counsel, and he obviously chose to weather any embarrassment that our conduct might have caused with his superiors. Most of the flak that counsel received in the trial of cases during my nearly three years in the division came from other counsel within the office. We were jealous of our records, and we moved to further our own image as trial attorneys. And at times the staff judge advocate was caught in the middle—as he was on the coffee case. It was he who had assured the convening authority that the case was a solid case, and that the defendant should be tried by general court-martial. Thus the commanding general would tend, or could easily tend, to hold the staff judge advocate responsible if the case were tried and lost.

But if our staff judge advocate took a beating from his superiors because of trial counsel's conduct, he suffered in silence. His executive officer, the military trial judge, was more vocal in his dissatisfaction, but he fought a losing battle. He had his own ego and ethical problems to contend with. He frequently lost the command viewpoint himself, and injected himself into our cases more and more, first on one side and then on the other. But he too was unable to keep the trial attorneys in line. The staff judge advocate quietly withered away and made more and more errors in the referral of charges to trial. Necessary oaths were missing from charge sheets, or charges were not signed at all, or the SJA improperly advised police investigators. He furnished us fuel and we litigated his errors, sometimes for days on end. The only saving feature was that the case load was extremely heavy, and the winners and losers were all tossed into the same gristmill.

At the completion of my three-year tour in Germany I felt I had done a creditable job as a military criminal trial attorney. Our cases were mostly well tried from both sides, with no holds barred. Opposing counsel slugged each other in our cases, and we fought to win, and the overall effect was good advocacy. When my tour of duty in Germany was over I was ordered to a new military assignment in Washington, D.C. My co-counsel, of course, all returned to civilian practice. Efficiency reports would mean nothing to them. But as a career army lawyer, I had to live with mine.

When I returned to the United States in November 1954, I had never seen any of my efficiency reports. In Washington I had the right to visit the Pentagon and read these reports, but I neglected to do so for many months. Finally, I read them and then, for the first time, I saw what my superiors—actually, my friends—had

had to say about my performance of legal duties in Germany. I was dismayed as I translated the numerical ratings, and saw that in effect I had been rated as a "marginal" officer, and that I stood near the bottom of most regular army career legal officers of my rank and experience in the army. Without once criticizing me for being too aggressive or outspoken as a military defense counsel (for criticism of this nature was outlawed by Article 37 of the Uniform Code) I was branded as a mediocre lawyer. My indignation was near the boiling point, but I understood the message. It came through loud and clear. The coffee case, and cases like it, came flashing back to my memory. My fear of command retaliation was realized. My friends in the division, my SJA and my trial judge, were informing me in the only effective manner they knew —via poor efficiency reports—that you don't play games in the trial of military cases. Not if you are a regular army career legal officer. Staff judge advocates and military commanders expect convictions. Effective trial work that results in too many acquittals or other embarrassments to the command or the staff judge advocate is not placed very high on the military scale of judicial values.

During the next three years of my military career I tried to live down my poor ratings in Germany. During these years I was not directly faced with military trial work. As a freshly promoted captain (apparently even marginal officers were promoted to captain), I was assigned as legal adviser to the commanding general at Walter Reed Army Medical Center in Washington, D.C. My duties were mostly civil in nature, and I found the ethics of army medical officers considerably higher than those of my JAG superiors in Germany. I soon was receiving maximum efficiency reports at Walter Reed, and upon my departure in late 1957 I was awarded the army's Commendation Medal (the only one I was to receive in the army) for my service at the Medical Center. After nearly seven years in the Judge Advocate General's Corps, at age thirty-four, I finally neutralized the near-paralyzing effect of my low efficiency reports from Germany. Upon my assignment to Korea in December 1957 I was in fairly good standing, professionally, within the army's legal corps.

During my three-year tour of duty at Walter Reed, I had read extensively on military justice and its controversial history. I also read an increasing number of cases that were handed down by the United States Court of Military Appeals on the subject of command influence. My reading convinced me that commanders and staff judge advocates historically had been grossly dishonest in the administration of military justice—and that they were not reform-minded, nor did they accept the reforms that were intended in the enactment of the Uniform Code of Military Justice, especially as they related to the eradication of command influence from military practice.

The feeling that I had been victimized for aggressive trial defense work in Germany, of course, never left my mind. I realized that my reaction was exactly what was intended. The insult of low efficiency reports for this "delict" is not aimed necessarily at the individual in his personal capacity as much as it is intended to teach him a lesson in military manners. Namely, such reports are intended to teach the young career judge advocate that he is a military officer first and a lawyer second. I comprehended my efficiency reports from Germany as merely a warning to get in line, to shape up, and to reorient my thinking along command lines, along lines of unswerving loyalty to my superiors. The army was still willing to live with me. I *had* been promoted to captain, but the handwriting was on the wall: I would either reform or I could get out of the army.

My review of military legal history at Walter Reed also convinced me that I had been used as a tool to influence illegally military jurors in Germany. I was required in Germany, along with all other trial attorneys in our division, to give canned lectures on military justice to battalion and company officers, to include mention of the soothing effect of speedy convictions and "appropriate" sentences (i.e., severe sentences). I despised these lectures, and my judge advocate superiors were frank to tell me that my lectures were wide of the mark, not clearly delivered, and not sufficiently to the point. Once when I digressed, and recounted a matter that cast a different light on the subject, I was frantically waved down from the back of the classroom by my superiors. But I was also present when very different, more to the point lectures were given on the same subject. On more than one occasion I was ushered into a regimental commander's office and made to stand at attention, along with opposing counsel, the military judge, and every member of an assembled general court-martial jury, and ordered to listen as the regimental commander intoned last-minute instructions from U.S. Army headquarters, Heidelberg, Germany, to the effect that the state of discipline within the European command was exceedingly bad and that convicted felons should receive maximum sentences and dishonorable discharges.

Following such séances, everyone (including the assigned military defense counsel) would dutifully salute the regimental commander and file back to the courtroom, usually in a converted mess hall, to commence the trial of the day. It was with a sense of shame that I recalled that as hard as we fought our cases in Germany, we missed the real point of command influence. We never challenged insults like these. We never challenged the appointment of the assistant division commander as a court member on important cases, nor did we challenge the appointment of the division chief of staff as a court member, or the appointment of a regimental commander—or in some instances the appointment of all three of these officials to the *same* case. In cases where the jury was loaded with rank of this nature, the defendant was hanged before the case started.

I arrived in Korea in midwinter of 1957–58 with many of these bleak thoughts in my mind. The temperature was 15 degrees below zero and my ankles nearly froze as I carried my baggage from the belly of our troop transport, a plane that was so badly overloaded we made three take-off attempts from Japan before we were airborne. That night I slept in a "wind tunnel," a quonset hut that had cracks beneath the doors and windows large enough for a hand. The lights were left on to deter the rats, and we slept fully clothed because of the cold, but I was glad to be there, for I was hoping to return to trial work in Korea.

2

Early Military Law,
a Hyphenated System of Justice

Military justice technically is that system of law that provides for the punishment of servicemen and women who offend against military regulations or custom. We speak of *military* justice, to distinguish it from Alabama justice, or California justice, or Chinese justice. The term does not necessarily designate a second-rate, substandard, *hyphenated* system of justice. Ideally, military justice relates to the rule of law, as opposed to the rule of a particular class, interest, or group. It is not supposed to be corrupt, dishonest, or subject to the manipulation of a privileged few.

But military justice has a more complex side. It is interwound with certain values that are not present in civilian societies. Specifically, military justice must support discipline at the same time it enforces the rule of law in the military community. Only well-disciplined armies obey orders, and only well-disciplined armies win wars. Military necessity and national security demand a disciplined and topflight armed force.

The enforcement of discipline within the American armed forces historically has been recognized as the exclusive prerogative of the military commander. A high state of discipline has always been viewed as vital as food and bullets to the successful outcome of a military mission. While there may be social values that dictate contradictory approaches to the question of discipline within our armed forces, there is no doubt about the position held by the military establishment. We are told that if armies are to win wars, discipline must be rigidly enforced, offending soldiers must be quickly and harshly dealt with. If necessary, verdicts and sentences in military trials must be reached without regard to the niceties of civilian justice (i.e., the rule of law).

If we are to win wars and to escape defeat in battle, the individual soldier must be prepared to fight to his death, and die if ordered to do so. If he elects not to fight, or to disobey orders, the consequences of his actions must be absolutely predictable. While the soldier can always allow himself a slim chance for survival on even the most desperate battlefield, he must not be able to anticipate any chance for acquittal or a light sentence at his court-martial if he refuses to fight. As viewed by the military commander, this is the meaning of military discipline, and this is the meaning and purpose of military courts. The rule of law must give way where discipline is at stake, or where the military commander fears it is endangered. Thus the commander feels he must be permitted to govern the outcome of military courts if need be; he and he alone must be in charge of the discipline or punishment of his soldiers because he alone is charged with the responsibility of success or failure in battle. If the commander is not permitted to punish his soldiers, the nation is severely handcuffing the commander—and a handcuffed commander might come out second best in battle.

It is for these reasons that our nation has always maintained a separate jurisprudence for military courts-martial, and it explains why military law has never been subjected to the review power of the United States Supreme Court. From the founding of the nation, the American military has had almost unlimited control over almost every facet of military justice. The military commander has traditionally controlled the independent judicial functions (i.e., verdict and sentence) of the court-martial whenever he felt it was necessary for the discipline of his command. Ultimately such practices shocked Congress into outlawing certain prerogatives of military commanders.

Congress attempted to overhaul the system following World War II. The Uniform Code of Military Justice, enacted into law in 1950 and made effective in May 1951, was intended to introduce sweeping changes in the administration of the court-martial system. Military defendants were to have defense counsel who were certified lawyers. Military judges who presided at all general courts-martial were required to be legally trained. These were startling changes and they were bitterly resisted by the military, but the most profound change was in the creation of the United States Court of Military Appeals, which was authorized to supervise the administration of military justice within the armed forces. The court was to consist of three *civilian* judges, appointed for fifteen-year terms by the president of the United States. This was the first time in our history Congress has subjected military case law to review by a civilian court. And there was yet another change—on paper at least. Congress outlawed the military commander's right to control the judicial functions of military courts.

There had been earlier efforts to achieve justice in military law following the close of World War I. In 1920 military commanders were stripped of their right to reverse acquittals or to return inadequate sentences to trial courts for an increase in sentence. For the first time commanders were required to provide military defendants with a defense counsel who did not have to be a lawyer, and judges were also required in general courts (but they too did not have to have legal training). These "reforms" were some of the conditions that occasioned the enactment of the Uniform Code of Military Justice in 1950. But the major catalyst for change was the maladministration of millions of court-martial cases in two world wars, the imposition of sentences that shocked the conscience of the nation, and the callous disregard of civilian concepts of justice by military commanders.

But even so, as late as 1950 Congress still attempted to compromise between the dictates of justice under the rule of law, on one hand, and the dictates of discipline and military necessity, on the other. To balance the 1950 reforms, Congress provided that the military establishment was to continue to administer the system. The military commander was still in charge. He still decided what charges to prosecute, what offenses were to be investigated, and what offenses were to be covered up. He still picked military juries from his command. Usually he also picked the prosecution and defense lawyers as well as the military judge—all of whom were military officers or high-ranking noncommissioned officers and, as such, subject to military orders and to military pressures.

These operational controls were considered by Congress to be sufficient to satisfy the legitimate needs of the military. And the reforms embodied in the Uniform Code of Military Justice were considered sufficient to assure fair trials for military defendants.

A military organization, however, is not a democracy, nor is it devoted to such ideals. It is singularly devoted to achieving the goals of commanders, regardless of the legalities at stake. Under these conditions, if a military commander, post-1950, were to pass the word to his subordinate commanders that he wanted a much higher conviction rate in his court-martial trials and more severe sentences, there is every likelihood that such results would be obtained immediately. Such is the nature of military organizations. Command influence may have been outlawed by the Congress, but the military mentality was not subject to statutory change. The military commander was still charged with the "discipline" of his troops. He might eventually be forced to greater circumspection in the administration of military justice, but it was still *his* command, and if he chose to impose illegal restraints he would run little risk of harm to himself or chance of exposure.

Subordinates tend to protect their superior military commanders, even if their actions are illegal. If a military commander were exposed in jury rigging, and if such fraud were brought to light, the worst that would happen to him would be the reversal of the particular conviction involved. No adverse or disciplinary action would be taken against the commander for "fixing" court-martial verdicts, for a simple reason: the punishment of military commanders who violate the law in this respect has been entrusted to other military commanders. Military commanders do not punish each other for "maintaining discipline" within their commands; this would violate the unwritten law of military commanders. Also proof of such influence more than likely would be exceedingly difficult to establish, depending upon the secrecy or subtlety involved.

If a military commander were experiencing extreme racial unrest in his command, for example, and if he were to mutter to his subordinates at his dinner table one night that "this racial trouble has got to stop!" and if he were to follow up this statement with a pronounced glare at his commanders, it would take little imagination on the part of his officers to gather what he was talking about. If a racial incident were to occur on post shortly thereafter, and if it were referred to trial by general court-martial, there is a good possibility that the charged offender would be easily convicted and given a jolting sentence.

In a case that occurred at Camp Lejeune, North Carolina, in 1972, a young black militant marine was charged with committing sodomy by force upon a white marine. For several days preceding the event, there had been racial trouble in the unit concerned, and for several years preceding the incident there had been almost unbroken racial discord at Camp Lejeune. On the night of the alleged offense, the accused black marine and several of his buddies openly attacked a group of white marines who were asleep in their barracks. There had been no provocation, and the obvious intent of the attack was to create further racial friction at the camp. The following morning a physically small white marine, who had been in the barracks at the time of the assault, reported for the first time that he had been sodomized by force by a black marine. Although there were many white and black marines in the barracks at the time, the victim had not cried out, and no one else saw the sodomy taking place. Nevertheless, general court-martial charges were lodged against the black marine on the word of the victim.

Whether or not the commanding general at Camp Lejeune had previously taken an open stand against racial discord, would not every member of his all-white general court-martial know what his feelings were on this particular case? Wouldn't every member of the defendant's all-officer jury know exactly what their commanding general expected of them by the mere fact that he had referred such a weak case to trial by general court-martial in the first place? Would they have to be told, specifically, what the general wanted? Would it be reasonable to assume that this jury of military officers might resolve this case against the defendant because, if they failed to do so, they would be letting their commander down? Would not the conviction of this black marine instill fear in the hearts of black-militant marines at Camp Lejeune? Isn't this the meaning of discipline?

Consider another example, the case of a war resister, a conscientious objector to the Vietnam war. The defendant, who had been AWOL for over a year from the army, surrendered at Fort Devens, Massachusetts, in the fall of 1971. While awaiting disposition of his court-martial charges, he was placed in the Personnel Control Facility (PCF) barracks at Fort Devens, a dismal place where overflow from the stockade was kept (but not under guard or other restraint) while the military decided what action to take in their cases. Once in the PCF barracks, the young conscientious objector complained about the lack of heat in the barracks, the absence of hot water, inadequate toilet facilities, the presence of roaches and rats, and general unsanitary conditions.

In December and January, distressed over the lack of attention paid to his complaints about the barracks, he enlarged his sights to include protests against the racist attitude of the command in the court-martial of black soldiers at the post, and publicly demanded an end to the Vietnam war. He organized protest demonstrations to this effect outside the main gate at Fort Devens. The demonstrators included scores of soldiers from Fort Devens and civilians from adjoining communities. The fourth demonstration was the largest; it lasted continuously from Friday evening to Saturday evening and was conducted less than forty feet from the Fort Devens main gate.

If this soldier's AWOL charges were suddenly referred to trial by court-martial following his fourth demonstration, while many other AWOL offenders with similar absences were simply handed administrative discharges by the command and escorted off the post without formal trial, some inevitable questions would occur. Wouldn't reasonable men conclude that the commanding general wanted to try this dissenter by general court-martial for protesting rather than because he had been AWOL? If charges of this nature were referred to trial by general court-martial, would the presiding military judge feel free to dismiss the charges on preliminary motion if he found that the general had acted illegally? Would the defendant have any real chance of getting a fair hearing from a military judge on a motion of this nature, at Fort Devens?

Take another situation, the case of Lieutenant William Calley. Did the military place any obstacles in Calley's path when he tried to prove that he was acting under military orders when he killed the women and children at My Lai? Did the military attempt to cover up the guilt of higher-ups in the My Lai trials? Was Calley's company commander, Captain Ernest Medina, vigorously prosecuted? Would any military jury in the United States Army have convicted Colonel Oran Henderson, the brigade commander at My Lai? Did Lieutenant Calley get a fair trial, or did his conviction have the taint of command influence? Specifically, were the My Lai trials utilized to implement the desired goal of the military, namely (1) to keep the guilt at the lowest command level possible, and (2) to prove that Calley was an aberrant, murderous officer, a misfit who besmirched the good name of American fighting men in Vietnam?

It can be argued from the foregoing cases that while command fraud may appear to exist in many military cases, one would be hard put to actually prove the existence of such fraud. It is very difficult to prove fraud in any case—military or civilian—and to prove judicial fraud is even more difficult, especially in isolated cases. If there exists a long-standing history of fraud the quest becomes easier. If one approaches the question of exposing command influence in particular cases, the history of military justice thus becomes pertinent. The history of military justice is replete with fraud.

For years, in both the United States and England, military justice was tolerated on the convenient basis that it pertained to a "separate society," to a second-class citizenry. By their act of voluntary enlistment soldiers had contracted away their right to fair trials and civil liberties, and submitted themselves as a body of subjects to be governed not by the law of the realm, but by the law of "military necessity."

Court-martial law, of course, was vastly different from English and American common law. Strange doctrines abounded in military practice, such as the "Court-of-Honor" concept. The practice developed that the soldier was subject to a code of "honor" and ordinary legal concepts did not apply. It was a gentlemanly code and it worked extremely well in most officer cases, where an officer might be tried for striking another officer while his face was turned or for challenging a fellow officer to fight a duel over a point of honor.

But the Court-of-Honor theory wore thin in the trials of enlisted men, where a defendant might be sentenced to a thousand lashes on his bare back for stealing a brass article from a native hut, or to have his tongue burned through with a red-hot iron for blasphemy, or to be hanged by the neck for stealing two regimental standards. Under the Court-of-Honor concept ordinary rules of judicial due process simply did not apply. Most important, lawyers for the accused were not permitted to belittle the proceedings. In England defense lawyers could attend military trials, but they were not allowed to speak. In America defense lawyers were totally excluded from military trials from 1775 until about 1825. From

1825 until the close of the century, defense counsel were permitted in American military courts, but could not participate in the proceedings. If they wished to ask a question of a witness, they had to write it down and pass it to the prosecutor. Legally trained lawyers were not required to represent defendants in American general courts-martial until 1950—and in military special courts-martial until 1969.

The agency concept of court-martial law was another interesting historical idea that died rather late. Under this approach a military court-martial was not viewed as a court of law at all, but only as an agent of the executive authority, as an instrumentality of the military commander for the enforcement of discipline within his command. Thus the military court was governed by the commander who appointed it. As the agent of the commander, the court-martial looked to the commander for its orders, and for its rules.

The Blackstone of American military law, Colonel William Winthrop, aptly described the American court-martial system in 1886 as follows:

> Courts-martial are not courts, but are in fact, simply instrumentalities of the executive power . . . to aid him in properly commanding the army and enforcing discipline therein, and utilized under his orders or those of his authorized military representative; they are indeed, creatures of orders and except insofar as an independent discretion may be given them by statute, they are as much subject to the orders of a competent superior as is any military body of persons.

The substance of Winthrop's definition of military law was closely followed in the American armed forces. It was this feature of military law that critics found so highly objectionable. Professor Andrew A. Bruce of Minnesota University wrote of the system in 1918:

> A court-martial is merely an agency "appointed" by the commanding officer for the training of the soldiers in disci-

pline, and though one is sentenced by such a tribunal to death or to a long term of imprisonment, he is not deprived of life or liberty or in fact punished at all, but merely trained and educated and disciplined. A criminal sentence in the army, in short, serves the same purpose as the manual of arms or the setting up exercises.

Professor Edmund Morgan of Harvard Law School, and one of the foremost authorities on military law of all time, wrote in 1918: "The control of the appointing officer over the court and its findings is to the civilian the most astounding characteristic of military law." The same point was made by Delmar Karen in 1946 in the *Wisconsin Law Review*: "The system is so flexible that it is almost entirely up to the commanders to determine not only who shall be tried, for what offense, and by what court . . . but also what the result shall be in each case."

These features of military law, inherited from the British court-martial system at the time of the American Revolution, could not, of course, have long sustained without the approval of the United States Supreme Court. In 1858 the Supreme Court first ruled that sentences of regularly constituted courts-martial were not reviewable by civil courts, except on specific jurisdictional grounds: where the court-martial tried a person who was not subject to military law, or adjudged a punishment not authorized by military law, or assumed jurisdiction over an offense that was not ordinarily triable by military courts.

The Supreme Court reiterated its ruling on this matter in 1863 and again in 1867. In 1879 it refused to review a case where the defendant had originally been given an "inadequate" sentence, and the case was returned to the court-martial by the appointing authority for an appropriate increase in punishment. The second time around, the sentence was increased to include discharge and imprisonment. The Supreme Court ruled that a court-martial verdict could not be impeached in civil court proceedings for a "mere error or irregularity." In *Keyes* v. *United States* the Supreme Court in 1883 refused to review a court-martial proceedings where the defendant's commanding officer—who had preferred one of the charges against him—sat as a member of the court-martial jury that tried and convicted him, and also appeared as a witness at the same court-martial and testified against him. The Court ruled that regardless of the "irregularity," court-martial verdicts were not reviewable on their merits by civil courts.

In 1897 the Supreme Court refused to review the appeal of army Major General David G. Swaim, who had been the judge advocate general of the army. He was ordered to be court-martialed for a fraudulent transaction in a private financial matter, and for thereafter making a false statement about the occurrence to the president of the United States, Chester Arthur. General Swaim was convicted and sentenced, but the sentence, in the opinion of the president, was inadequate. The case was returned to the court-martial for "revision" of sentence. The sentence was duly increased but the president still felt it was inadequate, and the case was returned to the court-martial once again. The third sentence, more severe than the second one, satisfied the president, who promptly approved the proceedings. General Swaim was to be suspended from duty for twelve years, and to forfeit half of his pay each month for the same period, but he was still entitled to "allowances" for food and quarters. When the general applied for his allowances, however, he was advised that as he was performing no duty, he was not entitled to them.

General Swaim, no longer enamored with the Court-of-Honor concept, sued the United States for that portion of his back pay representing allowances for food and quarters, which he contended he was entitled to under the third sentence of his court-martial. His claim was denied by the Court of Claims, and he appealed to the United States Supreme Court. The Supreme Court rejected his appeal, stating:

> As we have reached the conclusion that the court-martial in question was duly convened and organized, and that the questions decided were within its lawful scope of action, it would

be out of place for us to express any opinion on the propriety of the action of that court in its proceedings and sentence. If, indeed, as has been strenuously urged, the appellant was harshly dealt with, and a sentence of undue severity was finally imposed the remedy must be found elsewhere than in the courts of law.

The Supreme Court affirmed this principle once again in 1901 and again in 1911. In 1911 the Court ruled that due process is determined by circumstances, and that to "those in the military or naval service of the United States the military law is due process." The decision, therefore, of a military tribunal acting within the scope of its lawful powers was not to be reviewed or set aside by civil courts.

On the eve of World War I the American military court-martial system was completely dominated by military commanders. Reversal of acquittals and "revision" of inadequate sentences were time-honored concepts. The accused was not entitled by law to a legal or nonlegal defense counsel. The prosecutor could serve both as the prosecutor and as defense counsel in the same case. There was no judge in military proceedings. The president of the court-martial or the prosecutor served as the judge. There was no appellate system worthy of the name. Military lawyers could only *advise* a military commander that any given conviction might be illegal as a matter of law. It was up to the commander concerned, the appointing authority, whether to accept the opinion of his lawyers. If he chose to affirm the conviction, even the president of the United States could not legally reverse it on a point of law.

These were the "safeguards" military commanders felt were necessary (in 1916) to assure that all was well with the state of military discipline. But even so, the military command was uneasy. The servicemen still enjoyed one judicial protection: courts-martial customarily followed rules of judicial procedure and evidence that were observed in state and federal courts insofar as they followed anything at all. But in 1916 the judge advocate general of the army effected a change in the Articles of War, thereby eliminating this safeguard. Endorsing the change, Congress authorized the president of the United States to draft rules of procedure and evidence to be followed in military trials, a provision of military law that has persisted until this day. In essence it means that military commanders may urge rules of procedure and rules of evidence upon the president, who, in turn, may promulgate them in presidential Executive Orders that are then legally binding on military courts.

Thus, on the eve of American entry into World War I, the screws of military justice were turned even tighter, and the noose of military justice was drawn even more securely about the neck of every American citizen called upon to fight.

3

World Wars I and II,
a Breakdown of Justice

Once the United States entered World War I, examples of judicial outrages were not long in coming. The absence of a meaningful appellate system was one of the first judicial faults that were exposed in military law. The case involved a group of noncommissioned officers who were placed in arrest of quarters for shooting craps on a company street. Under time-honored concepts of military law, persons in arrest of quarters are not required to perform military duty. Thus, when the noncommissioned officers were ordered to drill the following day, they refused.

They were charged with mutiny. Their defense was overruled and they were convicted and sentenced to periods of confinement ranging from ten to twenty years in jail. Upon review, appellate lawyers agreed that their defense was valid and their convictions illegal. But because the appointing authority affirmed the convictions and refused legal recommendations to reverse the convictions, the machinery of military appellate agencies was blocked. However, the *acting* judge advocate general of the army disapproved the convictions and ordered the men restored to duty. Two days later he was himself relieved from duty, and the sentences were reinstated. The secretary of war upheld the judge advocate general of the army, who had returned to duty in the nick of time to save the day for army discipline. The convicted sergeants were ultimately restored to duty through the clemency powers of the president, but their general court-martial convictions stood.

The 1917 case of a military policeman (MP) at Fort Gordon, Georgia, was even more graphic. The MP while on duty in Augusta was checking commercial shops one midnight. Finding a jewelry store unlocked and suspecting burglars inside, the MP entered the store. A few minutes later he was arrested himself by civilian police for being inside the jewelry store. He was tried by general court-martial at Fort Gordon and acquitted. His commanding general, displeased with the effect the acquittal might have on the state of discipline at Fort Gordon, ordered the military court-martial to take a second reading on the matter. The second time around, the court-martial found the MP's story less believable and he was convicted and sentenced to a dishonorable discharge and five years' imprisonment.

Upon appellate review of this case, the judge advocate general of the army found as a matter of law that the conviction was not supported by the evidence, and recommended to the Fort Gordon commander that he reverse the conviction. The Fort Gordon commander obligingly reconsidered the verdict, but after reconsidering the matter refused to change his opinion, and the conviction was affirmed. Like thousands of others of a similar nature, the conviction record was quietly filed away in the office of the judge advocate general of the army.

In another instance, a young Italian-American recruit refused to sign an enlistment and assignment card at Camp Upton, New York, in 1917. Ordered to do so, he refused. For unknown reasons, at his trial by general court-martial he was acquitted. The commanding general at Camp Upton returned the case to the court-martial and directed it to reconsider its findings of guilt and innocence in the case. He further advised the members of the court-martial:

The reviewing authority does not intend to give the impression that he personally believes that the accused must be required to serve a long period of confinement for this act, but rather he desires the court to understand that the commission of this act should be met by severe punishment, and then, if in this case there are reasons why the sentence should be reduced, such reduction should be ordered on the action of the reviewing authority rather than in the inadequate sentence awarded by a court appointed as an *executive agency* in the administration of discipline. [Emphasis added.]

Upon reconsideration of the case the trial court convicted the defendant and sentenced him to a dishonorable discharge and five years' imprisonment.

The practice of returning inadequate sentences to trial courts for increased sentences in World War I was prevalent. Thousands of such cases were affirmed in this period. For example, Private Ernest D. was convicted of stealing a shirt and a pair of shoes at Fort Riley, Kansas. He was sentenced to six months' confinement. Upon reconsideration during revision proceedings, he was sentenced to a dishonorable discharge along with six months' confinement. In another World War I case of this kind, Private Alexander K., Company B, Fifty-fifth Infantry, was convicted of stealing a five-dollar gold piece, and was sentenced to confinement for six months and partial forfeiture of pay for a like period. On revision, his sentence was increased to total forfeiture of pay, confinement at hard labor for two years, and dishonorable discharge.

The trials of blacks during World War I reveal military justice at its lowest ebb. In 1917 a company of black soldiers stationed at Fort Sam Houston, Texas, mutinied. They stormed their arms' room, secured their rifles and approximately fifty thousand rounds of ammunition and marched into Houston. Before they were brought under control by federal troops some four hours later, they had killed seventeen or eighteen white civilians. Sixty-three blacks were court-martialed. Fifty-five were convicted and thirteen were sentenced to be executed. *Two days* after the completion of the trial, and some four months *before* their records of trial were received in Washington, D.C., for "appellate" review, the thirteen blacks sentenced to die were executed.

Sentences adjudged in World War I cases were shocking in their severity. A KP on duty at Fort Dix, New Jersey, who refused an officer's order to surrender his cigarettes was sentenced to twenty years' imprisonment. A man who was AWOL for twenty-seven days and escaped from confinement at Fort Dix received a forty-year sentence. A soldier's refusal to drill at Fort Dix and his subsequent escape from confinement warranted a sentence to thirty years' imprisonment. Two rear-line soldiers in France refused to drill, contending they were sick. They were sentenced to death. Two front-line soldiers found asleep in the trenches while on guard duty, who had gone without sleep for several days, were also sentenced to death. The defense counsel in the four French cases were all second lieutenants; none of them was a lawyer. None put up any defense of his client. Fortunately, the president of the United States refused to approve the execution in the French cases, and the sentences were ultimately commuted. (Under military law during World War I, the execution of soldiers convicted of military offenses required the confirmation of the president, whereas the execution of soldiers convicted of murder did not require the approval of the president, thus distinguishing the French cases from the execution of the black soldiers at Fort Houston.)

Following World War I, the press attacked the military establishment for its handling of such cases, and there were prolonged hearings in Congress. Because of this unprecedented publicity, judicial atrocities committed during World War I were documented and defended by military advocates. Their justification was almost as outrageous as the cases. The judge advocate general of the army, Major General E. H. Crowder, assumed this task almost single-handedly, which simplifies the task of historians. General Crowder commented favorably on the conviction of the MP at Fort Gordon who had been arrested in the jewelry store. Despite the fact that the MP was first acquitted by a duly constituted court-martial and then, upon reconsideration, convicted and sentenced to five years' imprisonment, and despite the fact that the judge advocate office found that the conviction was not supported by evidence showing guilt beyond a reasonable doubt, General Crowder felt it was particularly praiseworthy that the Fort Gordon commander *twice* considered the matter of affirming the case. In most civilian cases, a trial court's sentence is reviewed only once. He therefore hailed the case as a "good illustration of a feature in which the system of military justice sometimes does more for the accused than the system of civil justice."

As justification for his recommendations supporting the execution of the four soldiers in France, General Crowder stated:

[It] is enough here to say that General Pershing especially urged the importance of adopting this policy [the execution of the soldiers] for the protection of his Army's welfare, and his chief law officers concurred in this message; and that under the circumstances no one could have been criticized for acceding to this urgent request and adhering to the principles handed down by all fixed traditions of military law.

As for the matter of permitting second lieutenant nonlawyers to defend capital cases, General Crowder in a lengthy letter to the secretary of war assured him that all was well with military justice because of the "automatic appeal" system that operated in his Washington office. Crowder explained:

Virtually this appellate review performs over again the functions of counsel for the defense, and not only in technical duty but in actual spirit, this appellate review seeks to make good those deficiencies of defense counsel which may become obvious to the experienced scrutiny of the appellate officer. It is in this appellate review that I find the most satisfactory assurance that such deficiencies as may have from time to time occurred through the inexperience of officers for the defense have been adequately cured.

General Crowder admitted that some military sentences in excess of twenty-five years were too harsh, but again he relied on his "appellate review" section to cut these sentences to a proper level. He also justified the time-honored right of military commanders to reverse acquittals. Speaking from his own experience he recalled "more than one case in which the verdict of acquittal was notoriously unsound and in which the action of the commanding general in returning the case furnished a needed opportunity for doing full justice in the case." He also had to admit that his "appellate review" section had no real appellate function and could not reverse convictions on matters of law, but could only recommend clemency to commanders, who might or might not see fit to follow the recommendations. After the war was over Crowder grudgingly conceded that proceedings in revision, wherein acquittals and light sentences were reconsidered, should be abolished by statute. He also conceded that a true appellate agency should be established in his office to review military cases on matters of law to include the power to reverse illegal convictions.

Crowder's chief antagonist and all-time champion of reform of the military judicial process was his chief assistant, West Point graduate Brigadier General S. T. Ansell. It was Ansell who figuratively held Crowder's feet to the fire during World War I by feeding a constant stream of information to critics of military justice. Ansell also was an activist. It was Ansell who publicly demanded that the secretary of war reverse illegal wartime convictions and create true appellate courts for that purpose in World War I. It was Ansell who reversed cases of this nature and who was relieved of his job for doing so. It was Ansell who kept the pot boiling, who kept a black book of judicial atrocities, and who reported the atrocities to the press and to Congress throughout the war. It was Ansell who leaked the details of the four French death cases to the president of the United States behind Crowder's back, and who effected the commutation of the death sentences. It was Ansell who, without the knowledge of the judge advocate general or the secretary of war, actually established boards of review in Washington and France and attempted to give them true appellate power over military cases.

Again, it was Ansell who in 1919 wrote one of the most brief but classic denunciations of military law ever written, as follows:

Errors committed in such trials by men ignorant of law are not likely to be untenable and idle. . . . There are likely to be, indeed there are, ridiculous blunders with tragic consequences. . . . Frequently they are wrong from beginning to end; wrong in the findings, wrong in the "advice" given by compliant and impotent law officers, who recommend approval of such proceedings, wrong in everything. And yet of such errors there can be no review.

The system may well be said to be a lawless system. It is not a code of law: it is not buttressed in law, nor are correct legal conclusions its objective. The agencies applying it are not courts, their proceedings are not regulated by law. . . . The system sets up and recognizes no legal standard, and has no place for lawyers or judges. Whatever is done with the final approval of the convening commander is done finally beyond all earthly power of correction. Setting up no legal standard— in a word, being a system of autocracy and not law—it contemplates no errors of law and makes no provision for the detection and correction of errors that under the system can never occur. Accordingly, questions of law as such cannot arise, and such questions as do arise are presented to the commander for determination, not as questions of law to which he is bound to defer, but as questions to be disposed of by him finally and in accordance with his ideas, first, as to the requirements of discipline, and secondly, of right and justice. The system, which is one of absolute penal government of every person subjected to military law, and which results in an almost incomprehensible number of courts-martial annually, is perhaps most remarkable in that it has no place for a lawyer. The military commander governs the trial from the moment of accusation to the execution of the sentence, and such law adviser as he may have on his staff is without authority or right to interpose. . . . At every point the decision of the commanding general is final and beyond all review. All the legal reviewing machinery designed to "advise" commanders in the administration of justice is *extra legal*, is not established by law . . .

Ansell lost his magnificent battle to reform military law, and following the war he was reduced in rank to lieutenant colonel and retired. Ansell's proposed legislation to reform military law, the last of his great efforts to improve the military judicial system, was largely rejected in 1920. But long after Ansell's death his proposal was adopted almost *in toto* (in 1950) with the enactment of the Uniform Code of Military Justice. A junior officer on Ansell's wartime staff, Edmund Morgan, who supported Ansell in his bitter struggle with General Crowder and the secretary of war, was later to become a professor at Harvard Law School and one of America's foremost authorities on evidence. He also headed the governmental commission that drafted the Uniform Code of Military Justice in 1949 and 1950, and he named the civilian court created by that Act in honor of his friend, Ansell, a name and court that Ansell first urged upon Congress in 1920. The United States Court of Military Appeals thus owes its name and much of its heritage to Ansell.

Ansell's criticisms of World War I military court-martial practice resulted initially in a watered-down reform. In 1920 and 1921 the Articles of War, as previously noted, were amended to outlaw revisionary powers in military commanders, in both the findings and sentence stages of the trial. Nonlegal defense counsel were provided to accused; nonlawyer judges were to serve as judges, with a provision that legal officers were to serve as judges in general courts-martial "if available"; and boards of review, consisting of military lawyers, were established in Washington, D.C., and given appellate power over military convictions. One of Ansell's last public services was to note in 1922 that the military generally saw fit to find a legal officer "available" to serve as prosecutor but not as judge in general courts-martial. He pleaded that this failure in the administration of military justice be corrected administratively by the military before the "exigency that necessitates legislative action" occurred. The explosion of public wrath in 1946 against the administration of military justice during World War II shows how seriously the military took Ansell's last warning.

The maladministration of military justice in World War II was of gigantic proportions. Although the 1921 *Manual for Courts-Martial* was changed slightly in 1928, command control of the military judicial process weathered the reform movement with hardly a hitch. The military commander lost his right to reverse acquittals and to return inadequate sentences to courts for "revision," but in World War II he made up for this loss in other respects. Primarily, he reserved to himself the right to reprimand court members, counsel, or judge who displeased him in the performance of their judicial functions. He also reserved the right to advise court members of "appropriate" sentences, which were usually near the maximum. Ultimately, the War Department published confidential documents setting forth minimum acceptable sentences which were read to court members immediately before they adjourned to vote on the findings and sentence. Military commanders still supervised the administration of military justice. They decided which offenses were to be tried; they picked the counsel, judge, and jury from the officer ranks of their command; and they quickly and repeatedly let it be known to their courts that they could not increase sentences or return findings of not guilty to trial courts, but that they *could reduce sentences* if reduction was warranted.

An example of this obnoxious characteristic of military justice was graphically reported by Arthur John Keeffe, chairman of a World War II investigating committee that investigated naval injustice. Keeffe reported:

[I]n a series of thirty-seven courts martial trying desertion cases at Norfolk, the general court imposed a sentence of fifteen years in each. Then the Admiral at Norfolk who acted as the Convening Authority reduced each of the thirty-seven mentioned cases from fifteen to three years.

Keeffe pointed out that this series of cases was in line with the age-old "agency" concept of military law. The court-martial was an instrumentality or agent of the commander; it did his bidding and followed his orders. Thus, despite what reforms were made in 1920 and 1921 in military law, the agency concept survived. The commander couldn't reverse acquittals, and he couldn't direct his court-martial members to increase an adjudged sentence, but he could direct his courts to impose a designated *severe* sentence for a particular type of case, and then, in turn, reduce it to whatever term he felt was appropriate. In other words, as Keeffe pointed out, the World War II commander still fixed the sentences that were adjudged in his courts.

Another World War I snag was eliminated at the beginning of World War II. Branch boards of review were established in overseas theaters. Once these boards affirmed a sentence, and it was approved by the theater staff judge advocate, the sentence, including the death penalty, could be carried out immediately. Thus, there would be no more embarrassing "French death cases" that would go unexecuted because of timid action by the president of the United States or because of the interference of a reform-minded general officer who might be lurking in the War Department. But there were no Ansells of World War II, nor have there been any since. The criticism of World War II military justice did not come from within the ranks of the judge advocate general's office, as it did in World War I. It came from millions of GIs, from the press, from discharged lawyer-soldiers, from bar associations, and from lower federal courts—and it came in great abundance.

One of the major evils that triggered the criticism was the establishment of minimum acceptable sentences. Some convening authorities expressly advised each of their court members in writing what sentences would be adjudged in the event of any given conviction. Court personnel were bluntly told that the appointing authority could reduce sentences where a sentence was excessive, "but where an inadequate or inappropriate sentence is adjudged, no remedial action can be taken and the end sought to be obtained in the administration of military justice has been thwarted." Military appellate "courts" made a pretense of combating such directives, but in essence encouraged these practices by carefully spelling out to commanders exactly how far they could go in sentence fixing, as seen in the following excerpt from a 1944 board-of-review decision:

It is fundamental that courts-martial have the right and duty to take into consideration, in arriving at proper sentences, general policies announced by the War Department and commanding officers relative to the enforcement of discipline and uniform sentences. An important consideration in determining the punishment to be imposed in a given case is "its effect upon military discipline" (Winthrop's *Military Law and Precedents* [reprint] p. 397). Indeed it is fundamental that courts-martial are "instrumentalities of the executive power to aid him in properly commanding the Army and in enforcing discipline therein." (Winthrop's Military Law and Precedents [reprint] p. 49). While the functions of a court-martial and the reviewing authority should remain separate and distinct, it is equally essential to the enforcement of military discipline that members of courts-martial be made aware of the gravity of certain offenses and the need of drastic punishment to deter commission thereof. For a commanding officer to inform his court-martial of offenses that are impairing the efficiency and discipline of his command and to suggest to them his opinion of appropriate sentences, the ultimate decision in each specific case being left, of course, to the wisdom and judgment of the court is consistent with all our principles of military justice.

In the foregoing case, a letter from the convening authority was read to the assembled court members immediately before the court retired to vote on its findings and sentence. In essence the letter stated that there was an increasing amount of intentional, hazardous flying in the Army Air Corps, and that such flying "must be stopped and stopped now." It concluded with a statement that dismissal from the service was considered "appropriate" for persons convicted of intentional flight violations.

The defendant pilot was charged with buzzing Long Island at less than a thousand feet. He was convicted and sentenced to dismissal. Eight of the ten members of his general court-martial signed a recommendation for clemency, urging the convening authority to commute the defendant's dismissal to a $200 fine. But the jury's recommendation was rejected. Upon appeal, the board of review affirmed the sentence on the basis that the convening authority's sentence was not couched in "mandatory" terms. Thus, despite the fact that eight of the defendant's ten-member court-martial board were pulling for him, the dismissal stuck, and the defendant was ultimately "dismissed" from the air corps, a euphemism for dishonorable discharge.

The bizarre court-martial of Second Lieutenant Sidney Shapiro furnishes another insight into World War II military justice. Shapiro, an attorney, was charged with the defense of general court-martial cases. One of his clients was a Mexican-American soldier, accused of sexually assaulting a young lady. At the trial Shapiro seated a different Mexican-American GI at the counsel table, without notifying court authorities. After the victim and other prosecution witnesses had identified the impostor as the man who had committed the assault, and the prosecution had rested its case, Lieutenant Shapiro announced that the prosecution had convicted the wrong Mexican-American. The proper defendant was quickly rounded up, and the trial began anew. The real defendant was convicted and given five years' imprisonment amid much "embarrassment to the court."

A few days later Shapiro was himself arrested by military authorities for his unorthodox defense tactics. Two days later, at 12:40 p.m., he was served with court-martial charges and advised that he was to be court-martialed at 2:00 p.m. that afternoon at a place forty miles distant. He was told to select a defense counsel and drive himself to the scene of the court-martial. The first officer Shapiro selected was not available; he was an attorney and Shapiro was told that he would serve as the prosecutor. Lacking alternatives, Shapiro obtained the services of two nonlawyer lieutenants and drove to his court-martial. His request for a postponement for the purpose of preparing his defense was denied. By 5:00 p.m. that afternoon the case was over. Shapiro was convicted and dismissed from the service.

Two years after the war was over Shapiro sued the United States in the Court of Claims for his back pay as a lieutenant, alleging that he had been illegally discharged from his commissioned status. In one of the few court-martial decisions out of World War II that were ever reversed by a federal court, the Court of Claims ruled in favor of Shapiro. The court held that "[a] more flagrant case of military despotism would be hard to imagine." The court proceeded to state: "It was a case of almost complete denial of plaintiff's constitutional rights. It brings great discredit upon the administration of military justice." The government did not appeal the decision to the Supreme Court, and Shapiro emerged a winner —one of less than five or six servicemen during all of World War II who were freed or otherwise vindicated by lower federal courts.

The trial of a young soldier named Benjamin L. Beets illustrates another aspect of World War II justice. Beets was convicted of rape by court-martial in 1945. His defense counsel was a nonlawyer who initially refused to defend him. The day before Beets's trial his nonlawyer defense counsel was handed his charge sheet and *ordered* to defend him the following day. After Beets's conviction, and after his sentence was affirmed by military appellate agencies, Beets brought suit in federal district court on a writ of habeas corpus alleging that his conviction and sentence were in violation of basic due process. The United States District Court denounced the verdict as follows:

> The Court has no difficulty in finding that the court which tried this man was saturated with tyranny; the compliance with the Articles of War and with military justice was an empty and farcical compliance only, and the Court so finds from the facts and so holds as a matter of law.

Beets was freed but his freedom was of short duration. The government appealed the district judgment to the Circuit Court of Appeals and that court saw fit to return Beets to federal prison on a technicality. During the interval between the decision of the district court granting him his freedom and the government's appeal to the Circuit Court of Appeals, the Articles of War were amended, granting military prisoners an administrative appeal to the judge advocate general of the army. As such, the circuit court ruled that Beets would have to return to prison and file his "administrative appeal" prior to seeking habeas corpus in federal court. Thus Beets returned to prison. The last that the federal court index shows in Beets's case is that the judge advocate general of the army ultimately *rejected* his administrative appeal and ruled that he had been accorded "due process of law." A trial that was found to be "saturated with tyranny" by a federal district court was translated into "due process of law" by the military, and the case was closed.

One of the most outrageous of all World War II court-martial cases to reach the federal courts was that of a young soldier named Eugene P. Brown who was convicted of murder by court-martial in Mannheim, Germany, in 1947 and sentenced to life imprisonment. The accused was convicted of murder while he was on sentry duty because he did not *retreat* prior to firing the fatal shot that killed his victim. Evidence of malice was also lacking, since the entire affair took only two minutes. After unsuccessfully running the gauntlet of military appellate agencies, Brown sued for his freedom in United States District Court in Georgia. The court granted his writ and freed him. The government appealed to the Fifth Circuit Court of Appeals, and once again the decision was in Brown's favor. What was at issue were basic guarantees of due process. The trial defense counsel was a nonlawyer. The military judge was also a nonlawyer who failed to recognize or properly instruct on legal issues in the trial of the case, and the military review of the case, in the words of the district court, revealed a "total misconception" of applicable law by military appellate agencies.

There was one additional error of almost monumental proportions. At the time Brown was tried the Articles of War expressly stated that the judge of general courts would be a lawyer "if available." (It will be recalled that Ansell's last charge against the military in 1922 was that the military was making lawyers available as prosecutors but not as judges, in contradiction to the 1921 amendment.) There was only one military lawyer assigned to the Brown case, and he was assigned as an assistant prosecutor. It was this circumstance that prompted the district and circuit courts to free Brown.

But the government appealed, and the Supreme Court ordered Brown returned to prison. The Court ruled that the availability of legal officers to serve as prosecutor or as judge was a question for military discretion only, and not for federal courts. Had the Court stopped at this point the decision would not have reached the absolute nadir in military law that it was soon to reach, but unfortunately the Supreme Court proceeded to further issues. The Court ruled that questions concerning the quality of due process accorded to Brown at his trial—such as the failure to provide him with a legally trained defense counsel, the failure to appoint a legally trained judge, and the misapplication of legal principle by counsel, the trial court, and military appellate agencies—were *beyond* the scope of civil review. The Court cited principles of law it had reiterated over a half century before, holding that only military authorities could correct errors that occurred in military trials. The Supreme Court in 1950, long after the public outcry against the wartime administration of military justice had reached gigantic proportions, reversed the decisions of the district and circuit courts and remanded Brown to jail. And with the return of Brown to prison, the hope of judicial reform of military law was shattered.

Despite the Supreme Court decision, other segments of American society were not so reluctant to act. A committee appointed at the conclusion of World War I to investigate the maladministration of military justice during World War I had endorsed the system as honest by a split decision. But the military was not so lucky the second time around. The prestigious Vanderbilt Committee, composed of leading jurists and law professors, and appointed by the American Bar Association in 1946 at the request of the War Department, served as a major impetus to reform. After conducting hearings across the United States, and after interviewing hundreds of servicemen and former servicemen, and after reviewing countless court-martial cases, the Vanderbilt Committee rendered a stinging condemnation of World War II military justice.

The committee found that a breakdown in military justice had "definitely occurred." The first cause for the breakdown was that commanding officers did not follow the system as laid down in the *Manual for Courts-Martial*, but found it their duty to interfere with the court-martial process for "disciplinary purposes." The second cause was that sentences were "frequently excessively severe and sometimes fantastically so." The committee found that in "many instances the commanding officer who selected the members of the court made a deliberate attempt to influence their decisions." The committee further noted that this practice was not necessarily even denied by military commanders, "and indeed in some instances was freely admitted." Court members were led to believe that they were to impose the maximum sentence in order to permit the commander who appointed the court to "adjust" the sentence downward to whatever level he felt was necessary to "effect discipline" within his command. Even the War Department had engaged in this practice and had published classified documents setting forth approved *minimum* sentences for designated offenses.

The Vanderbilt Committee further declared that the War Department had not only made no effort to check the illegal control of the court-martial system by its overzealous commanders and legal officers, but that it had in fact condoned the entire operation on the convenient basis "that discipline is a function of command." The committee concluded its report, which included some 2,519 pages of recorded testimony, with the following comment:

> Undoubtedly there was in many instances an honest conviction that since the appointing authority was responsible for the welfare and lives of his men, he also had the power to punish them, and consequently the courts appointed by him should carry out his will. We think this attitude is completely wrong and subversive of morale; and that it is necessary to take definite steps to guard against the breakdown of the system at this point by making such action contrary to the Articles of War or regulations and by protecting the courts from the influence of the officers who authorize and conduct the prosecution.

The military had no real answer to the Vanderbilt report. But an array of witnesses, pro and con, paraded through various congressional hearings in the late 1950s. There were additional reports from investigative committees, the great majority of which were seething denunciations of military justice. But the demand for reform was not necessarily antimilitary in tone. World War II leaders were carefully hailed as heroes, and the letter of the *Manual for Courts-Martial* was proclaimed generally as being well intended. It was only in the *operation* of the *Manual* where the breakdown occurred; military commanders unfortunately did not follow the *spirit* of the *Manual*. The demand thus was for judicial reform, not for the destruction of the system. Congress met this demand in the enactment of the Uniform Code of Military Justice, designed to maintain discipline within our armed forces through the *fair trial* of accused servicemen. The legislation also, at least in part, was an effort to atone for the millions of wartime court-martial convictions which systematically deprived American soldiers and sailors of their basic guarantees of due process by well-motivated but overzealous military commanders.

The chairman of the committee that drafted the Uniform Code, Professor Edmund Morgan, writing in the *Vanderbilt Law Review* in 1953, issued a stern warning to the military and to the American people:

> If experience under the Code shows that the influence of command control has not been eliminated, it may well be that a new system will have to be established in which the military will have control only over the processes of prosecution, and the defense, trial and review be under the exclusive control of civilians. The services have the opportunity of demonstrating to Congress that the concessions made in the Code to the demands for effective discipline do not impair the essentials of a fair, impartial trial and effective appellate review.

4

Korea, the Land of Morning Calm:
The Boy in the Box

Prior to my arrival in Korea in the early winter of 1958 I had written to the Eighth Army staff judge advocate, requesting that I be assigned to an infantry division. I knew my days in the army as a trial attorney would be mostly back of me once I was promoted to major. But when I got to Korea I discovered that another fate awaited me. As a regular army officer I was told that I should serve a tour of duty as an adviser with a foreign army. Thus I was assigned to a two-man judge advocate office in Seoul, part of the Korean Military Advisory Group headquarters of the United States Army (KMAG).

According to my orders I was to serve as a legal adviser to the Korean Army judge advocate general and his staff on matters of military law. In actual practice the duties were somewhat different. For several weeks I dutifully reported to General Kim's office each workday morning, and he and I and his staff would discuss, in English, any topic that struck the general's fancy. I enjoyed these conferences, but we never spoke about military justice or military law as such. The conversations were intimate, warm, friendly discussions about the cultures of America, Europe, and Asia. I learned that General Kim and most of his staff had been educated in Japan, that they were far more versed in classical music and literature than I was, and that they looked down on most things Korean. They were loyal, affluent supporters of the Korean dictator Syngman Rhee. I estimated that their military salaries ranged between $40 and $100 a month in American dollars, and that the remainder of their wealth came from other sources. I was astounded to learn that the role of civilian attorney was suppressed in Korea. I was told that only about 3 to 4 percent of the graduating law students who took the bar examination each year passed it. Most disputes between average citizens were settled by the police. Disputes of greater magnitude were settled at higher levels of government through the intervention of influential office holders. To my surprise, I also learned that I was financially responsible for all of the office furniture in the Korean judge advocate headquarters, and that it had not been inventoried in years.

My visits to the judge advocate general's office of the Korean Army also showed me the "close parallel" between the United States Army and the Korean Army. It was a similarity that existed primarily on paper. The U.S. judge advocate general's office, for example, had a Lands Division. So did the South Koreans. We had a Board of Review Number One. So did General Kim. We had a Military Affairs Division. So did the Koreans. Our judge advocate functions, however, were housed in the air-conditioned Pentagon in Washington, D.C. The Koreans, unfortunately, made do with far less. Their judge advocate headquarters was housed on the top floor of a dilapidated, ill-repaired, dust-ridden stucco-and-wood-frame building. You reached General Kim's office by walking up four flights of badly sagging wooden stairs, and through a short, dimly lighted narrow corridor. The scene was dismal.

Small wooden signs, with hand-printed letters in both Korean and English, jutted into the corridor at about head height from the various doorways that I passed along that short corridor. These signs read LANDS DIVISION, BOARD OF REVIEW NUMBER ONE, MILITARY AFFAIRS DIVISION, etc. In the Pentagon, sections such as these would have housed scores if not hundreds of employees, but the rooms behind these doors in General Kim's corridor were exceedingly small and dark. The entire judge advocate staff for these offices consisted of the handful of Korean officers who conducted the daily English classes with me in General Kim's office. We would discuss, with tongue in cheek, how Colonel Ko would double as the Lands Division in the morning and sit as Board of Review Number One in the afternoon. Major Park would do the same thing with Military Affairs and Claims and so on down the line. This, then, was the "similarity" between the physical organization of the American and Korean judge advocate functions.

Again to my surprise, I discovered that the similarity did not end at this point. Someone had made an effort to pattern a great deal of Korean court-martial law and procedure after American practices. Although the Korean legal system was based on civil law jurisprudence, their court-martial system apparently was patterned after our 1928 *Manual for Courts-Martial*, which was based on common-law doctrines of law and procedure. The two methods of jurisprudence are largely distinct and separate, and each rules supreme within its geographic area. Yet the South Korean Army, the fourth largest in the world, had adopted out of hand our 1928 *Manual for Courts-Martial* as the basis for its courts-martial jurisdiction. My doubts really soared when I learned this. I was immediately granted permission to observe one of their trials.

Several days later a South Korean whom I shall call Major Lo picked me up at my quarters in a Korean Army jeep. We ultimately pulled up in front of a tent on a South Korean Army base, dismounted, and entered. A field court-martial was in progress. The case involved a sergeant who was accused of stealing several truck tires from a command motor pool. There were two spectator seats, and the major and I took them. Apparently the government had rested its case, and the president of the court-martial was explaining to the defendant his right to take the stand and testify or to remain silent. Major Lo translated this procedure to me. The sergeant acknowledged his rights and bowed to the court-martial president. He bowed to the man on the left of the panel, then to the man on the right. After these formalities he announced that he elected to remain silent.

The president of the court-martial conducted a quick "off-the-record" conversation with his fellow court-martial members which Major Lo did not translate. The president then ordered the accused to take the witness stand and explain why he stole the tires. The sergeant bowed to all concerned once again, took the witness stand, and explained how he had stolen the tires. From the viewpoint of expediency, it wasn't a bad system, but no one could claim it was really American. We left the trial as the sergeant was explaining what he did with the tires. Major Lo made no pretense of the trial's being anything it wasn't. I gathered the Koreans ran their army pretty much the way they preferred—and as long as they were satisfied with it I saw no reason to complain.

In this same period Major Lo was briefing me daily on the conduct of a case that he was personally preparing for prosecution. A lieutenant colonel in the Korean Army had shot and killed an inspecting officer of his battalion, a ROK (Republic of Korea) major general who had advised the lieutenant colonel that he wished to see him on the hill behind battalion headquarters as soon as the inspection was over. This meant that the lieutenant colonel's battalion had done extremely poorly on the inspection, and that the major general was going to kill the lieutenant colonel. The lieutenant colonel, however, did not wait to get to the top of the hill to debate the point. He shot the major general squarely in the head as he left the battalion area.

Several days before the trial was scheduled to start, Major Lo, the official prosecutor, advised me confidentially that he had developed a unique trial strategy that was sure to dumfound the proceedings. I asked him what it was, and he stated that he had just been privately retained by the family of the defendant to represent the liutenant colonel. He stated that he was not going to spring his switch of roles until the day of trial. I agreed with him that his tactic would dumfound the proceedings all right, and wished him well. It was this event that convinced me that I should cease "advising" the South Koreans on the conduct of their judge advocate operation and seek a change of roles.

My boss at KMAG headquarters had recently been reassigned to the job of staff judge advocate at Eighth Army headquarters, upon the departure of the former SJA to the United States. Hence I approached the new Eighth Army staff judge advocate and told him I was no longer enchanted with advising our counterparts in the ROK Army, and asked if I could prosecute and defend American courts-martial somewhere in Korea during the remainder of my tour. He agreed to this.

One of my first cases for Eighth Army was that of the "boy in the box," as it became popularly known in the press of the day. Periodically United States troops caught "slicky boys," or girls, stealing from their compounds in South Korea. Instead of merely arresting the offenders, United States personnel at times got emotionally carried away and proceeded to torture offenders prior to turning them over to proper authorities. The degree of press interest depended generally on the degree of torture involved. The boy-in-the-box case had quite a bit of torture—and hence quite a bit of press interest, both in and out of Korea.

The facts as I learned them in my investigation of the case revealed that a small thirteen-year-old Korean orphan boy, who had been living under a bridge near one of our army aviation bases, had been caught red-handed by American troops one January night stealing an article of value from an officer's hootch. He was held until the Officer of the Day (a captain) and the compound sergeant major arrived. By then some twenty to fifty Americans were standing around watching. The Korean youth was, of course, filthy dirty. Thus it was first decided to give him a shower, a cold-water shower, clothes and all. This was quickly done. He was then taken outside in the Korean winter to cool off, and after he was sufficiently chilled, he was again taken into the shower room where he was stripped. The duty officer took out a pocketknife and, holding the blade so that only a fraction of an inch of the point was exposed, jabbed the little boy several times in the leg with the knife point.

Next it was decided to let the child think the Americans were going to cut off his penis. His penis was stretched and the Officer of the Day made several passes close to it with the open knife blade, but did not cut the youth. Portions of the boy's body were then covered with tar, and he was pushed into a corner of the room, nude, where he was kept until about 7:30 the following morning. At that time he was crammed into a small army crate. The box was nailed shut, and some thirty-nine nails were driven at random through the sides. The commander of the aviation unit, an army major, arrived on the scene soon after.

The boy in the box was carried to his helicopter and he was flown by the major to a nearby mountaintop. The box was unloaded but the major and his crew of one could not open it; they had left the necessary tools at their base. It was their intention to open the box and leave the child, cold, freezing, and naked on the mountaintop and fly away. But because they were unable to open the box, it was replaced on the aircraft and the major radioed a nearby army airfield and stated that he was flying in a box of radar parts. The plane landed and the box was removed and stored in a nearby hangar. The major and his assistant departed and returned to their home base.

The Korean Army trooper on duty with the Americans (called a KATUSA) heard whimpering from the box. He obtained tools, opened the box, and discovered the boy—and bit by bit managed to ascertain what had happened to him. The KATUSA, instead of alerting the Americans as it was his job to do, called South Korean newsmen to the scene.

Amid much fanfare the youth was hospitalized and then placed in an "orphanage." After days of investigating I found the orphanage. Already there had been a whirlwind of bad press, and it had not been easy to obtain permission from Korean authorities to interview the boy. On a freezing winter day I presented myself at the orphanage with due credentials. I was officially prosecuting the Officer of the Day (the captain) for assaulting the child. The major (the base commander) had been let off the hook by the imposition of nonjudicial punishment (a small fine and a reprimand) for his part in the affair.

I asked the director of the orphanage, through my interpreter, to see the boy. I identified him by name and age. The director corrected me on his age; he was eighteen, he stated. He produced a brand-new official Korean birth certificate to prove he was eighteen. I wanted to know, if the child was eighteen, what the hell was he doing in an orphanage for children. The question was shrugged away. Meanwhile, through a glass window I could see an official who was calling a boy from the yard, where there was a group of children. The official grabbed another child and removed a blanket from his body, leaving that child without an outer garment. He then handed the blanket to a second youth, a small, shabby individual who had no wrapping at all. The second youth wrapped the blanket about himself and was ushered inside the building. This, I was told, was the boy in the box.

His head was completely shaven. He stated this had been done to remove the tar. His head and body were covered with old and fresh scars. He quietly told me about the incident I was investigating, how he was caught, how he was tortured, and how he was placed in a box with nails driven into it and flown away. His story checked thoroughly with the account I had received from American witnesses. I asked him about his parents.

"Dead," he replied.

"How old are you?"

"Thirteen."

"Have you ever been arrested?"

"Many times."

"For what?"

"Stealing."

I was later told by my American superiors that the boy in the box was eighteen years of age. I was also told that he had a long criminal record, including robbery. I replied that I did not believe the boy was eighteen, and that I did not believe he had a criminal record for robbery. But as a prosecutor for the government, one must follow orders. So I accepted the fact that the youth was eighteen and that he had a criminal record—since that was the version that was being announced to the press by both the American and the South Korean governments.

Shortly thereafter I was advised that the captain was pleading guilty and that I was not to call witnesses for the government to the courtroom. I was advised to prepare a written stipulation of fact, and that this would suffice for the record. I prepared a detailed stipulation and the Eighth Army staff judge advocate personally edited it before the trial. The great majority of my facts were stricken. On the day of the trial the Eighth Army courtroom was packed with representatives of the press. The watered-down stipulation was read into the record. According to the edited version, it appeared as if the captain had done little more than order a cold-water shower for an eighteen-year-old thief, a criminal with a long list of convictions who had been caught red-handed burglarizing an officer's BOQ (Bachelor Officers' Quarters)—and then ordered his head covered with tar prior to turning him over to authorities. The court-martial fined the captain and ordered that he be reprimanded. And that ended the case of the boy in the box.

There was a series of other cases, although nowhere near the volume that we prosecuted in Germany in the early fifties. The Korean cases had a flavor of their own. Leading the list were large-scale black-market cases. While the Americans grew to hate the Koreans because they stole to live, we were quite tolerant of our own thieves. A nineteen-year-old private first class received six months in jail (no discharge) for stealing a two-and-a-half-ton load of army winter jackets, worth thousands of dollars, jackets that he ultimately sold to a Korean national for $600. In order to steal the jackets, the PFC forged troop issue slips that allowed him to draw the jackets from an American warehouse. On the pick-up date, he parked his truck several blocks from the warehouse and carefully painted over the bumper marking of his truck which identified his unit. On the other side of his bumper he carefully stenciled new markings on the truck, identifying it as belonging to a different unit. When apprehended, he admitted that he had gone through the operation so many times that he could not remember how many truckloads of winter clothing he had stolen. In another case, an army lieutenant colonel received a dismissal (a dishonorable discharge) by general court-martial for black marketing. He had allegedly ordered several crates of water softener for the Eighth Army Chemical Depot, but the crates sat for weeks at the warehouse, unclaimed. When opened by the CID they contained thousands of pairs of women's stockings.

An army intelligence officer who operated out of Seoul regularly infiltrated China and North Korea. He also allegedly did a large-scale side business in Japan for South Korean merchants in his privately assigned aircraft. He was double-crossed by several merchants whose money he had allegedly taken and to whom he had made no deliveries; an alerted CID waited in vain for his plane to arrive in Korea on his last flight from Japan. Instinctively cautious, the officer landed at another airport in Korea without radioing ahead his change of flight plans. When the CID arrived several hours later they found an empty aircraft. In another case, a sergeant from a long-lines signal battalion vowed he would net $300 a day from black-market activities for every day he spent in Korea. When he was arrested and investigated his Korean partner's civilian warehouse was found to be filled to the ceiling with stolen U.S. Army signal equipment. The sergeant avoided jail by incriminating his commanding officer as the brains behind the plot. His CO was tried and acquitted.

There were many sex cases. Sex mores in Korea were dictated from the top down, each new commander either outlawing it altogether, permitting it on a timely basis (say from 6:00 a.m. until the following 2:00 a.m., seven days a week), or perhaps permitting it in some locations and outlawing it in other locations. When I was in Korea, as you approached the territory of American infantry divisions a few miles north of Seoul, an imaginary line was drawn. North of the line, sex was outlawed. Only United States compounds and MSRs (main supply routes, i.e., roads) were "on limits." Everything else was "off limits." This meant that the unlucky warrant officer, lieutenant, or captain arrested in his underwear in his girl friend's hootch at midnight by door-crashing MPs in one of the many villages that surrounded our division units, was "off limits"—and this was serious (court-martial) trouble. South of division territory, however, sex was pretty much wholesale and the sky was the limit. The boundaries and ground rules were redefined from time to time as new commanders came and went, but the Korean sex scene was well entrenched and always remained much the same. With typical army humor, it was referred to as "the best kept secret in the American army." The cases were never dull.

There were also sex murders. A young, good-looking, blue-eyed, all-American youth, choked an aged toothless prostitute named "Goddamn" to death in a deserted coal yard in a creepy, off-limits area of a little town near Taegu. He drank her wine and spilled matches about her face as he checked over his work. He also spilled matches at the scene of two nearby homes that he set on fire prior to killing the prostitute. An understanding American court-martial found him guilty of accidentally choking the woman to death (involuntary manslaughter) and arson, and sentenced him to four years in jail.

As a KMAG legal officer without major advisory duties to perform, I managed to place myself as defense counsel on cases that arose in KMAG units throughout Korea. This move was ultimately to prove my undoing. The case was that of Sgt. Paul Adams, from the KMAG Detachment at a town I will call Kowon, Korea. Sergeant Adams was a middle-aged army-wise supply sergeant. He was charged in three specifications with the illegal sale of army

DDT, military property of the United States, of a value of $187.20; with the theft of the same property; and with the unauthorized use of an army truck used to haul the DDT cans to their place of sale.

The new, incoming KMAG staff judge advocate arrived as I was preparing the defense of this case for trial. When I first greeted my new boss, a full colonel, he asked why I was defending KMAG cases. I explained that the army staff judge advocate had placed me on orders to defend the cases, and that I was in the midst of preparing the Adams case for trial. Most staff judge advocates in the military can stomach an occasional defeat. Many are good lawyers, and don't handcuff their defense counsel. There are others who do not care to be proven wrong on any case, not even one. My new boss, by reputation, was of this ilk.

The Adams case, on the surface, appeared to be a routine, run-of-the-mill, black-market case. Adams, as a supply sergeant, had access to millions of dollars' worth of American equipment, and he was living in a Korean village near Kowon with his twenty-year-old Korean girl friend. It was alleged that, yielding to her urging, he stole the DDT cans to sell on the black market in order to pay a debt she owed a local Korean merchant. The sergeant was observed by a policeman informer as he unloaded the DDT from his army truck. The cans were promptly recovered by military police. They were of U.S. Army issue, each clearly marked as United States military property. The keys to the room where the cans were stored, and from which they had been stolen, were available to the sergeant. The log from the Kowon motor pool on the date involved showed a dispatch of a U.S. Army truck to the defendant. The Korean merchant from whom the cans were recovered stated he purchased them from the sergeant, and identified him as the person who delivered them to his store in an army truck. Following his arrest, the sergeant confessed. In the written statement he gave to the Kowon provost marshal he said: "I am guilty and desire to remain silent."

There was one factor in the case from the very beginning, however, that set the Adams case apart from others: it came from the Kowon detachment of KMAG. The one-star commanding general at Kowon was something of an eccentric. Contrary to informal ground rules in Korea, he prohibited all his officers and men from living with Korean women on the Kowon military post, save one—himself! It was this exception to his sex policy, of course, that made his cases stand out. The general's Korean girl friend shared his on-post quarters; she was a large, young woman who always wore red dresses. She ate her meals at his mess, and frequently was driven through the Kowon area in his army sedan. GIs and officers alike saluted her when she passed in the sedan, mostly for the hell of it. Like Sergeant Adams, if they chose permanent female companionship during their thirteen-month tour in Korea, they lived in the miserable hovels that surrounded the Kowon military reservation. Every morning scores of American officers and enlisted men emerged from their Korean "quarters" and trooped dutifully through the Kowon military gates. In view of the widespread resentment against these conditions, any court-martial case that came from Kowon was going to be carefully reviewed by the KMAG commanding general in Seoul prior to referring it to trial.

My new boss, the incoming staff judge advocate at KMAG, was, of course, well briefed on all "local" conditions, including the situation at Kowon. He was therefore doubly concerned, or doubly "uptight," about the Adams case. It was his first case which required him to confer personally with the KMAG commanding general, and it was from Kowon. If he messed it up, at least in his mind, it was going to hurt. Because I was his defense counsel and his only subordinate, he saw to it that I got the message: I was not to play games with the Adams case.

As the colonel's subordinate, I appreciated his concern. Too many acquittals do not enhance the career of either a division commander or his staff judge advocate, both of whom are struggling against great odds for their next promotion. The staff judge advocate is in an exposed position with every case tried in his command. It is he who recommends the trial of every general court-martial. It is his written and oral advice that the commanding general accepts when he orders a case tried by general court-martial. If the case is tried and lost, the commander may feel that he has been misled by an incompetent staff judge advocate. If the case is vital, or of great significance to the command, the commander may feel threatened. If he is insecure, or driven by ambition or greed for promotion, he may feel that his superiors—the men who make out his efficiency reports—will view him as a weak commander, and as a person who cannot control his men or effect discipline within his command.

If the commander is threatened in this fashion, or believes he is threatened, it is not too difficult to imagine what may happen to the staff judge advocate who recommended that he try "losers." It is the staff judge advocate who, in the eyes of the military, lets his commander down if cases are "needlessly" lost. It is he who advises the commander; it is he who supervises the administration of military justice within the command. It is his personnel who prosecute and defend every general court-martial in the command. It is his responsibility to control the conduct of his counsel, to see that they "live in peace" with each other, and do not embarrass the command. Ten acquittals in a row, for example, could wash out the best staff judge advocate in the business. Sometimes the loss of even one *important* case, or a "ridiculous" (i.e., low) sentence in an important case, can ruin the career of a staff judge advocate.

Thus if a soldier "beats" a charge, the military mind may view the case as a lessening of 'discipline" within the command. If another soldier beats a charge, and yet another, or if "inadequate" sentences are adjudged, the military hierarchy may conclude that discipline is shattered and that drastic personnel changes are necessary to regain and restore proper respect for discipline. Whether these fears are real or imaginary on the part of the military commanders and staff judge advocates, they play a part in the trial of court-martial cases.

Thus, when my new boss advised me that I was not to play games in the defense of Sergeant Adams, I read his message quite clearly. He was an uptight SJA and he considered the Adams case important, vital to his own well-being with the commanding general. Personally, he was weak and insecure and morally dishonest —and he was threatening me.

5

The Trial of Sergeant Adams:
Keeping Counsel in Line

When I undertook the defense of the Adams case, I was aware of the two-faced role assigned to military defense counsel. On one hand, it was a role designed to give the air of respectability to military justice. On the other, it was designed to furnish yet another tool for the command manipulation of the military judicial system. The assigned defense counsel, albeit a lawyer, is still a military officer. He is subject to all the pressures that can be brought upon military officers. As previously noted, the role of assigned military defense counsel has indeed been bleak. It was not until 1920 that the military defendant was given a statutory right to an assigned nonlawyer military defense counsel as a matter of right in the event of his trial by general court-martial.

The reason for the delay in providing assigned nonlawyer military defense counsel for the military defendant is not readily explained in military literature. Various explanations, of course, can be advanced that tend to reveal the low estate in which the military views the rights of the common soldier defendant. Of all the reasons advanced one of the strangest is that the military establishment perhaps felt it was an unnecessary embellishment. In 1786

Congress gave the military prosecutor an "additional" duty to perform. He was directed to "consider himself as counsel for the prisoner" as well as prosecutor for the government. While a critic of the system wrote in 1863 that the practice was "like a man playing a game of chess with himself, he can cause either the red or the white side to win," the custom lingered on until it was finally outlawed in 1921 by Congress.

When the KMAG staff judge advocate warned me not to make waves in the trial of the Adams case, I knew what the ballgame was about. I was aware that as a military officer I was subject to all the pressures that command can bring on military subordinates. I also knew what little, if any, protection I might have if I "exceeded my limits" in the defense of Sergeant Adams.

One of the first official acts my new colonel performed upon his arrival in Korea was to write a detailed pretrial advice to the KMAG commanding general, recommending that he try Sergeant Adams by general court-martial. He also advised the general that the charges were in proper form and alleged true specifications in violation of the Uniform Code of Military Justice. To my knowledge the colonel had done very little trial work in the military; as he had always worked with large legal staffs, where his staff did the work, he was unaccustomed to working himself. In KMAG at that time there were only two spots in the table of organization for legal officers, one for a full colonel and one for a captain. As I was defending the Adams case, this meant that the colonel had to do the initial pretrial himself.

One of the colonel's first steps was to direct our legal sergeant, a former airborne trooper with a bad back, to redraft the charges onto a clean piece of paper. The colonel did not wish to take a dirt-smudged, frayed-around-the-edges set of charges to the KMAG commanding general on his first case. Prior to this "redrafting," the charges had been in proper form. During the redrafting, the sergeant made a few mistakes. Accidentally, he omitted the key word "military" in the specification alleging the wrongful disposition of military property. Without this word, the sergeant was simply charged with the wrongful disposition of property, which was not an offense under the Uniform Code of Military Justice. This was a fatal omission, and the colonel missed it. Another error in the redrafting of the charges was the omission of the value of the military truck allegedly stolen by the defendant. In the original charges there had been an appropriate value listed. The colonel missed that one too. The third count, however, alleging the theft of the DDT bombs, was properly transcribed into the new charge sheet.

The colonel certified to the commanding general that the charges and specifications were in proper form and that each of them alleged an offense under the Uniform Code. He proceeded about his duties, assuming all was well with the Adams case, until I requested enlisted men to sit as members of the court-martial jury. Under the Uniform Code of Military Justice, if an accused enlisted man expressly requests in writing that enlisted men serve on his court-martial jury, the appointing authority must appoint at least one-third of the members from the enlisted ranks. When my request was brought to the attention of the colonel, he called me into his office. He patiently advised me that I undoubtedly did not know what I was doing. "Didn't I know," for example, "that counsel only request enlisted men as jurors in sex cases?" Otherwise, he frowned, enlisted men were harder on defendants than all-officer courts.

I replied that I wanted enlisted men because in my trial experience I often found they made the best jurors where cases were hotly contested. As I intended to contest the case, I would trust my own instincts and go along with enlisted jurors on the court-martial.

The colonel promptly called me a dumb son-of-a-bitch and said that I was lucky that I wouldn't have to serve any of the jail time my client was going to draw. Bending over backward, he offered me a "good deal" on a guilty plea: he offered to save me from making an ass of myself; my client had confessed and there were witnesses to the theft.

I declined his offer.

Two nights before the trial I was having a drink in the KMAG officers' club at Seoul. It was early in the evening. The colonel sat at one end of the bar and I sat at the other. His face was flushed and he had been drinking. He walked over and sat down beside me.

"So you're really going to contest this case?" he asked.

"Yes, sir." I answered.

The colonel blew up at this reply. He pounded the bar and told me how incompetent I was. Then he backed away from me, walking low and crouched over. He crossed the dance floor and stood in the entrance of the club. Flailing his arms he shouted at me from the doorway, telling me what a fool I was. I sat at the bar without responding and the colonel left the club.

The day before the trial I drove my jeep to the aviation section of Eighth Army headquarters to verify that a helicopter previously requested was still available to fly the court members (all of whom were from KMAG headquarters) to Kowon, which was about eighty-five miles due south of Seoul. This was verified, but I was advised that there would be no room on the chopper for either myself or the prosecutor, an Eighth Army judge advocate captain. I agreed to drive the prosecutor and myself to Kowon in my assigned jeep. As I walked toward the door of the aviation section I was called back.

I was told that my chopper was returning to Seoul the following night (the day of the trial) at 6:00 p.m., with or without court members. I asked if a chopper would be made available the next day to pick up the court members if we held over. I was advised that since I had not requested a chopper within the prescribed three- or four-day advance period, I'd have to make do, or take the matter up with higher authorities. I didn't have time to go through the necessary red tape, so I thanked the flight officer for his information, and told him that I would not request an additional flight in the event we held over at Kowon.

That afternoon I drove myself and the prosecutor to Kowon. The court members arrived the following morning. When the trial commenced in the Kowon courtroom, I immediately moved to dismiss the specification, alleging a wrongful disposition of "property." The prosecutor apparently had failed to note the omission of the word "military," for otherwise he could have forced an amendment prior to trial. But on the day of trial, eighty-five miles from KMAG headquarters, there could be no last-minute amendment without my consent, and I didn't consent. The military judge granted my motion and threw out the first charge. My KMAG colonel would now have the pleasure of explaining to the KMAG commanding general how he had certified a fatally defective specification for trial.

The prosecution's first witness, a master sergeant in charge of the supply room in which the defendant worked, testified to the disappearance of the DDT bombs from the warehouse where they were stored, and as to the value of the goods. Under cross-examination he testified that the Kowon supply officer was seriously short of military property at the time of the aerosol bomb theft (during the course of the trial it developed that he was short hundreds of dollars' worth of property). It appeared that the supply officer, a captain, had taken a joint inventory of the property in his account several months prior to the theft, with his intended replacement. His replacement, an incoming officer, had refused to accept the property account at Kowon (involving several million dollars) unless there was a complete inventory. The master sergeant testified that the property account had not been inventoried for several years. It was further established that the supply officer was in the process of submitting several "reports of survey" to relieve himself of financial responsibility for the missing property, and that higher headquarters had been exceedingly slow in relieving him of responsibility.

As the prosecution presented its case, the defense was able to establish that the supply officer, in an effort to make up his shortages, had requested his supply sergeant, the defendant, to "scrounge" for items of property that were in short supply. Although this is forbidden by army regulation, every enlisted man with any years in the army and most officers know that "scrounging" is part of a good supply sergeant's job. It works in this fashion: if the supply room is *short* five hundred sheets and is *over* two hundred parka jackets, the supply officer will not list the overage of jackets on his property books as "found on post," as he is required to do by regulation, but will set aside the jackets for his supply sergeant to swap with other supply rooms that might have an overage of sheets but a shortage of jackets. This is called scrounging, or moonlight requisitioning. You swap your overages for items in which you are in short supply, and if you can do it long enough and steadily enough, you'll have no problem keeping your supply account balanced. The supply officer at Kowon, however, assumed that the income supply officer would simply sign for the property in the dark, so to speak, without an inventory, the same as he had done. When his replacement demanded a complete inventory, it was fairly late to start scrounging, especially since there had been a period of years involving numerous supply officers who had not taken an inventory of the account.

But scrounging was the order of the day. A series of prosecution witnesses testified on cross-examination that the supply officer, several weeks before the theft of the aerosol disinfectant, had sent the defendant with a driver to Seoul to swap sixty wool "OG" shirts from his overage account for items in which he was in short supply (parka liner hoods, mattress covers, and sheets). It was also brought out on cross-examination of government witnesses that the aerosol bombs were excess (overage) property on the Kowon property account, and were not chargeable to the account at all. It was established that there were some 150 cases of aerosol bombs that were excess property at Kowon, and it was from this supply that the defendant allegedly stole the bombs he sold on the Korean black market. Prosecution witnesses also testified on cross-examination that the supply officer, shortly before the theft of the bombs by the defendant, had authorized the removal of the 150 cases of DDT bombs from the relative security of a well-guarded warehouse to the relative insecurity of a very poorly guarded warehouse, against the advice of his chief clerk. It was also brought out that this property was moved only days before a scheduled inspector-general inspection of the badly sagging supply account at Kowon. Had the inspecting officer found the 150 cases of aerosol bombs at Kowon, he would have officially added them to the Kowon property account and, of course, they would have no longer been a fit subject to scrounge. The inspector general inspected the secure warehouse, but he did not check the insecure warehouse (he was given to believe the insecure warehouse was a living area). He did not find the 150 cases of insecticide.

It was also established during the prosecution's case, via defense cross-examination, that shortly before the aerosol bombs were stolen, the supply officer had submitted one of his many reports of survey asking to be relieved of financial responsibility.

The supply officer himself had to testify for the government, and it was with some reluctance that he took the witness stand. On cross-examination he was nervous and misleading. He was forced to admit that he had claimed his rights against self-incrimination at the Article 32 investigation of the defendant, and that he had not answered questions at that time concerning his actions in the aerosol theft charges. He also admitted to the poor condition of his supply account, and that he had permitted the defendant to scrounge with OG wool shirts, but he hotly denied that he had ordered him to dispose of the aerosol bombs. He could not account for the $260 worth of parka liner hoods, mattress covers, and sheets that he found on post following the theft of the aerosol bombs. His only explanation for the discovery of the additional property was that the defendant told him he had found it. He stated he did not ask the defendant further questions.

The supply officer was then asked an embarrassing question: Was he the official accuser of the defendant? He stated that he was. He had sworn out court-martial charges against the defendant when the provost marshal first reported that the defendant had confessed in writing to stealing the bombs. The captain was next asked if he had used the knowledge that his supply sergeant had been charged with wrongful appropriation and unauthorized sale of government property as a basis for relieving himself "of any shortage that existed in [his] supply channel." The witness answered that he had not.

Much to the distress of the witness, I removed a theretofore unmentioned report of survey by the supply officer from my brief case that I had borrowed from the property books at KMAG headquarters. Had I not found this report while rummaging through the files it would never have come to light at all. The report of survey was for a heater, a chair, a chaplain's kit, bed sheets, and pants, and was for the sum of $252.10. The pertinent portion read as follows:

On or about 15 November 1957 I assumed the duties of Headquarters Commandant when the prior Headquarters Commandant departed on emergency leave. During the period 15 November to 15 January 1958 the Supply was operated by Master Sergeant Jones and Sergeant First Class Paul Adams. During that period a complete inventory was started because of many discrepancies discovered in 1955 vouchers in posting property books. Some shortages were found and a report of survey dated 10 February 1958 was submitted. On being assigned as Supply Officer, effective 10 January 1958 with instructions to report for duty on 20 January 1958 Captain Donald B. Williams started another complete perjoint inventory. On March 17, 1958 Captain Williams signed the property books less the items listed hereon. During the past two weeks several items have been discovered missing from Supply. Sergeant First Class Paul Adams is presently under charges for grand larceny of supplies, wrongful appropriation of government property and unauthorized sale of government property. In view of this, request I be relieved from pecuniary liability for these items.

"Did you sign that statement?" I asked the witness.

"Yes, I signed that statement," he replied.

In dating the report, the supply officer actually jumped the gun a bit on the defendant. When he submitted his report of survey on *March 27*, 1958, he noted that Sergeant Adams was "presently under charges for grand larceny of supplies." But it was not until the next day, *March 28*, 1958, that the supply officer actually signed formal court-martial charges against Sergeant Adams, accusing him of the theft of such supplies. The captain's priorities in this regard were not lost on the jury.

Following the close of the evidence in the case, the military judge refused to throw out the charge concerning the wrongful appropriation of the vehicle simply because its value had been omitted. But he did throw out the charge on another technicality: The government had failed to prove that the sergeant made a significant deviation from his prescribed route. The theft of the aerosol bombs was submitted to the jury. My argument to the jury, of course, was based on the fact that the sergeant had been ordered or directed by his superior officer to sell the DDT bombs on the Korean black market for the purpose of making up shortages for which the officer was financially responsible. The defense, technically, is known as "obedience to orders." (It was the same defense that Lieutenant Calley would advance for the My Lai massacre some thirteen years later.)

The judge in Sergeant Adams' case debated whether to grant the instruction. His reputation was as a hard-nosed, prosecution-minded judge; I had been before him several times and was personally aware of his tendency to bolster the prosecution. But the practice of law furnishes many surprises. The hard-nosed judge, this prosecution mentor, had been anything but prosecution-minded in the Adams trial. He granted my prepared instruction on the law of obedience *in toto*.

He instructed the court-martial jury on this point of law as follows:

The command of a superior officer is presumed to be a lawful command. The general rule is that the acts of a subordinate, done in good faith in compliance with his supposed duty or orders, are justifiable. It is apparent, therefore, that in the usual case a subordinate is expected to obey his superior without hesitation and to the full; and that obedience of an order may be a defense to a charge growing out of acts done in compliance with the order.

Except in a plain case of excess of authority, where at first blush it is apparent and palpable to the commonest understanding that the order is illegal, the law should excuse the military subordinate when acting in obedience to the order of his superior. Otherwise the subordinate is placed in the dangerous dilemma of being criminally responsible, if he obeys the order, or to court-martial, loss of rank and disgrace, if he disobeys the order.

The certain vexation and annoyance, together with the risk of professional disgrace and punishment which usually attend the disobedience of orders by an inferior, may safely be deemed sufficient to constrain the military subordinate's judgment and action, and to excuse him for yielding obedience to those upon whom the law has devolved both the duty and responsibility of controlling his conduct in the premises. Thus, cases can be imagined, where the order is so palpably atrocious as well as illegal, that one must instinctively feel that it ought not to be obeyed, by whomever given. But there is no rule without its exception. This one is practical and just, and the possibility of extreme cases ought not to prevent its recognition and application by the court.

Between an order plainly legal and one palpably otherwise, there is a wide middle ground, where the ultimate legality and propriety of orders depend or may depend upon circumstances and conditions of which it cannot be expected that the inferior is informed or advised. In such cases, justice to the subordinate demands, and the necessities and efficiency of the public service require, that the order of the superior should protect the inferior; leaving the responsibility to rest where it properly belongs—upon the officer who gave the command.

But while a military inferior may be justified in not obeying an order as being unlawful, he will always assume to do so on his own personal responsibility and at his own risk. Even where there may seem to be ample warrant for his act, he will, in justifying, commonly be at a very considerable disadvantage, the presumption being, as a rule, in favor of the legality of the order as an executive mandate, and the facts of the case and the reasons for the action being often unknown in part at least to himself and in the possession only of the superior. In the great majority of cases, therefore, it is found both wiser and safer for the inferior, instead of resisting an apparently arbitrary authority, to accept the alternative of obeying even to his own detriment, thus also placing himself in the most favorable position for obtaining redress in the future.

If a question arises in respect to the legality of an order, and the order is not on its face clearly and obviously in contravention of law, it is the duty of the inferior to resolve such doubt in favor of obedience, relying for justification upon the order so received and obeyed. Except in the solitary instance where the illegality of an order is glaringly apparent on the face of it, a military subordinate is compelled to a complete and undeviating obedience to the very letter of the command received.

These special instructions are given to you as requested by the defense counsel and are applicable only if you determine that the accused acted under instructions from his superior officer, Captain _____, to dispose of the items alleged in the manner in which the evidence shows they were disposed of and that all proceeds thereof did, of course, come back to the Army.

The military judge submitted the case of the theft of the aerosol bombs to the court-martial jury at 5:30 p.m. Just before the jury left to deliberate on the findings of guilt or innocence, I made an "administrative" announcement. I told the assembled court that I had neglected to tell them that the chopper was returning to Seoul that evening at 6:00 p.m., and that if the case went beyond that time we'd have to spend the night at Kowon (a very dismal prospect). A finding of guilty would have called for an additional hearing on the sentence plus a deliberation period by the court members prior to adjudging sentence. In short, anything except a very fast acquittal would require all court members to spend the night at Kowon.

The court record reveals that the court closed to vote on the findings at 5:30 p.m. and that it opened to announce findings at 5:45.

The verdict was not guilty.

The record again reveals that the court closed at 5:47 after announcing its verdict of acquittal. At 6:00 p.m. the court members boarded the chopper for the return flight to Seoul.

The trial and acquittal of Sergeant Adams by a military court-martial reflects military justice in its best light. It depicts the court-martial system in the way it was intended to operate. It brings to bear the intelligence of military jurors, and their expertise in matters of military custom. It reflects the basic honesty of an army officer and a noncommissioned-officer jury, and the forthrightness with which a court-martial jury is capable of facing complicated legal issues. Cases like the Adams case convinced me—and still do—that court-martial juries will acquit an accused soldier where the law and facts are about fifty-fifty, or evenly divided, or where there is a reasonable doubt, *where there has been no command emphasis to the contrary, or where there has been no command fix.* Sergeant Adams' trial was an honest trial. The only "fix," unfortunately, was that which was soon to be placed upon the defense counsel. The honesty of any system of justice, of course, is completely grounded if the defense counsel is castrated.

My colonel never apologized to me about the Adams case. He never admitted he was wrong. The closest to that was when he informed me shortly after the case was over that henceforth I would defend no further KMAG cases. I was told at the same time to prepare a "military affairs" opinion recommending that Sergeant Adams be reduced to the grade of private for inefficiency. At that time in military law, such "nonmilitary justice" procedures were authorized following acquittals. My first reaction was to refuse, but I realized Adams would be reduced anyway, and if I were forced to write the recommendation it would surely be a damning factor I could use against the military if I had to. I therefore told the colonel that I would write the opinion for his signature, but that I was going to protest the matter formally to the secretary of the army, pursuant to the redress-of-grievances article of the Uniform Code of Military Justice (Article 138). I prepared the inefficiency reduction recommendation, and at the same time wrote a detailed complaint of the matter to the secretary of the army, alleging maltreatment of assigned military defense counsel and a violation of professional ethics on the part of the KMAG staff judge advocate. This I mailed direct to the secretary of the army. The letter was never acknowledged

Sergeant Adams, meanwhile, was transferred to KMAG headquarters in Seoul, and ultimately assigned to the KMAG motor pool. I visited the KMAG commanding general and asked him not to reduce the sergeant at all, as the sergeant had been fairly tried and acquitted according to law, and that that should be the end of the matter. The KMAG commander was a fair man, whom I held in the highest respect. He was moved by the plight of the sergeant, but he also had to honor the loyalty system of the army. The general himself had no personal stake in the case, but he knew his staff judge advocate did. To have disregarded the SJA's recommendation to reduce Sergeant Adams would have been a disloyal act on his part to one of his key subordinates. He therefore reduced the sergeant one pay grade (one stripe) and that ended the case.

As the KMAG motor sergeant, Sergeant Adams saw to it that my jeep was running when all others were bogged down, but my major problem was not related to getting transportation in Korea. I knew my colonel would butcher me on my efficiency report and this he did. When I left Korea, I did not bother to stop by the Pentagon and read his report. The following year I was attending the advanced class for career judge advocate officers at Charlottesville, Virginia, when the executive officer from the judge advocate general's office in Washington, D.C., paid each member of the class a personal visit. In my session with the colonel, he advised me that my KMAG efficiency report was terribly low, and for that reason my requested assignment to the army foreign-language program (a seven-year program that with a little luck would have removed me completely from the Judge Advocate General's Corps for the remainder of my tour in the army) could not be granted. I was also told that I was in some danger of being passed over for promotion to the grade of major because of this efficiency report.

The news, of course, was distressing. It had taken me three years to overcome the stigma of my low efficiency reports in Germany, and after finally struggling back to the surface, I was now pushed down for the second time. I was seething inside, but I carefully took stock of my situation. I was married, with a wife and four children to support. I was thirty-six years of age and had completed about twelve years' military service, and needed only eight more for retirement. I had almost no friends within the Judge Advocate General's Corps, only acquaintances. For years I had looked down on most of my contemporaries, and senior judge advocates, as poor lawyers without integrity, but I had refrained from condemning them outright as morally corrupt. But at that moment, I resolved they were decidedly wrong in their acceptance of the status quo in military justice. I was convinced that the system was riddled with dishonesty and fraud. When I withdrew from my conference with the JAG executive officer, I made up my mind. I would stay in the service for twenty years, and obtain minimum retirement benefits, but during my remaining eight years in the army I would use whatever intelligence and expertise I had, insofar as possible, to expose every dishonest judge advocate or military commander under whom I served.

6

The First Ten Years,
a Decade of Bad Law

During the decades of the 1950s and 1960s, while I was finding the practice of military law riddled with command fraud, military appellate courts (newly created under the Uniform Code of Military Justice) were grinding out an unbelievable series of recorded cases that underlined the deeply ingrained nature of the command control of the military judicial process. *Hiatt v. Brown* (see the case of Eugene P. Brown, p. 41), handed down by the United States Supreme Court in 1950, was a strong invitation to the military to continue to march in this direction. In this decision the Supreme Court in essence ruled that service men and women were truly second-class citizens, not entitled to the protection of the Constitution, and that military convictions were not subject to federal court review on their merits, regardless of the horrendous nature of the legal process awarded to the individual military defendant.

One of the first landmark decisions of the Court of Military Appeals was in keeping with the mandate of *Hiatt* v. *Brown*. In the decision in question—*United States* v. *Clay*—the court held that constitutional due process did not protect military defendants.

However, Judge Latimer, writing for the court, announced a new ground rule for the protection of military personnel. In keeping with the long-held traditional view, he noted, "we do not bottom these rights and privileges on the Constitution," but added that they were based on the "laws as enacted by Congress." Constitutional due process was out, but "military due process" was in. Latimer, much to the dismay of the military, added that "insofar as reasonably possible," Congress and the Court of Military Appeals intended to place "military justice on the same plane as civilian justice, and to free those accused by the military from certain vices which infested the old system."

These were high-sounding words and, while they did nothing at the trial level to deter military commanders from their old "vices," military due process—even only on paper—would prove to be better than no process at all. In *United States* v. *Lee*, a 1952 decision, the Court of Military Appeals once again broke new ground. In *Lee* the court disregarded a provision written into the 1951 *Manual for Courts-Martial* by military draftsmen, which was intended to assure a most narrow interpretation of the term "reversible error." Under the *Manual* rule reversible error was defined as important, or substantial, error that was of sufficient severity to affect the verdict itself; or of such severity that had the error not occurred, a different finding (i.e., a not guilty finding) would probably have resulted. Thus, in situations where there was ample independent evidence of guilt, the existence of an error of law would not be viewed as "substantial" error. On the other hand, in such situations it would be viewed as "mere" error, more commonly known as "harmless" error, and would not require reversal.

In many command-influence situations there is in fact ample independent evidence of guilt in the record of trial. Thus, under the *Manual for Courts-Martial*'s "harmless-error" rule, it would be exceedingly difficult for an appellate court to determine that a finding of not guilty would have occurred had the alleged act of command influence *not* occurred. Take a case, for example, of barracks larceny where there was overwhelming evidence of a defendant's guilt. In this case, assume for argument that the commanding general addressed several senior members of the defendant's court-martial jury on the eve of his trial, and point-blank told them he had no use for barracks thieves, and he hoped they'd convict the defendant the following day and *hang* him. Under the *Manual's* harmless-error rule, the general's comment would be viewed as "mere" error, not requiring reversal because there was independent (ample) evidence of the defendant's guilt appearing in the record of trial. It was this comfortable buffer zone, or protected area of command fraud, that Judge Brosman, writing for himself and Chief Judge Quinn, shot down in the Lee case.

With an eye toward outlawing command influence, Judge Brosman redefined reversible error to include not only what the drafters of the *Manual* had in mind but also what he termed "general prejudice," which he defined as follows:

We have in mind here a situation in which the error consists not in a violation of a constitutional or legislative provision, but involves instead an overt departure from "some creative and indwelling principle"—some critical and basic norm operative in the area under consideration. Such a compelling criterion we find within the sphere of this Court's efforts in the sound content of opposition to command control of the military judicial process to be derived with assurance from all four corners of the Uniform Code of Military Justice. . . .

Thus the doctrine of "general prejudice" became known in the fight against command fraud.

In *United States* v. *Berry* the Court of Military Appeals bared its fangs for the first time and coupled its admonition against command influence with a reversal. In *Berry*, handed down by the court in 1952, the president of a court-martial (the senior member of the court-martial jury) had usurped the functions of the military judge, and had proceeded to make rulings of his own on the introduction of evidence and motions of defense counsel. Judge Brosman referred to the doctrine of general prejudice announced in

Lee, and then held that the duties of a military judge were to be independently performed without interference of rank or command, and that a violation of this principle constituted "an overt departure from 'some creative and indwelling principle'—some critical and basic norm operative in the area under consideration." The conviction in *Berry* was thus reversed.

The principle of law announced in *Berry* and the two cases above were not precedent-shattering in the sense that military commanders took stock of their previous illegal actions and resolved to forgo such activities in future cases. Military commanders, circa 1952, were not cut of this timber. They not only did not read decisions of the Court of Military Appeals but were not even disposed to concern themselves with such matters. While staff judge advocates may have read case-law decisions of the Court of Military Appeals, they would not have dared tell their commanders that they were bound by such decisions in the conduct of their military judicial duties. This would have smacked of heresy and disloyalty; and it would have been contemptuous of the entire military establishment. Hence, while *Clay*, *Lee*, and *Berry* were in truth precedent-setting decisions, announcing broad principles of reform, they were totally ignored at the court-martial working level for years. They would in time, however, be well understood by military commanders and staff judge advocates alike.

Appellate military boards of review, composed of senior judge advocates, were not as reticent to recognize the new principles of law which were in the offing. An air force board of review, in *Robinson*, reversed a conviction where the president of a court-martial twice recessed the court-martial to confer with the wing staff judge advocate. The air force board of review held this conduct to be "presumptively fatally prejudicial." In 1953 an air force board of review was the first judicial agency to make use of the term "command influence" in modern military law. The board cited *Lee* and *Berry* as standing for the principle that the "court must be free from command influence at all times."

An army board of review cited *Berry* as a guiding principle in 1953, although it found no evidence of "command control of the military judicial process" in the case under consideration. But in the same year an army board of review applied the doctrine of general prejudice as announced in *Lee* and *Berry*, and reversed a conviction. The case involved multiple accused who were charged with mutiny at the post stockade. Prior to the court-martial, the SJA had addressed a conference composed of at least eight members of the court-martial and the military judge that was to try the defendants. The SJA had advised the court members that the stockade housed "dissident elements" who were "unhappy." He had stated that these elements were "dangerous" and were "not responsive to discipline." The court members were advised to handle this kind of case "expeditiously and firmly." All defendants were convicted and sentences ranged from ten years' to thirty-five years' confinement. The board of review found that this case violated "that category of fundamental principles underlying the purpose and spirit of the Uniform Code . . . and must not be transgressed by the military authorities."

Unfortunately, this was not the end of such transgressions. In fact, in a sense it was a new beginning. Article 37 of the Uniform Code of Military Justice, representing the best Congress could do to outlaw command influence of court members by convening authorities, contained a loophole: It outlawed the influencing of court members only through *unauthorized* means. Hence the drafters of the *Manual for Courts-Martial*, military men to the core, drafted procedural guidelines to accompany the new law into practice that would permit convening authorities to influence courts through *authorized* means. Thus, both the 1949 and the 1951 *Manual for Courts-Martial* were written expressly to permit commanders lawfully to instruct (i.e., to influence) court personnel on the nature of their duties, to include commenting on the "state of discipline" within their respective commands, provided they did not influence the outcome of any "particular" case.

The meaning of this deviousness was that it gave a legal base for military commanders and their SJAs to influence the outcome of findings and sentences in future court-martial cases so long as they did it on a *wholesale* basis. Thus, despite the best efforts of bench and bar and the Congress of the United States to outlaw command influence at the close of World War II, military lawyers slipped a provision into the *Manual for Courts-Martial* that would permit it to continue for the next twenty years.

Instances of command influence (orientation) of court-martial members and other blatant acts of command manipulation of the military judicial process were not long in coming. In 1953, in *United States* v. *Borner*, the Court of Military Appeals affirmed a case where the SJA prior to trial had informed court members that "only real good cases will come before you as members of the court." But the court reversed similar remarks in *United States* v. *Littrice*. Here court members were advised that convicted thieves and other felons should not be permitted to remain in the army. The SJA also advised court members prior to trial not to usurp the "prerogatives of the convening authority." Judge Latimer noted that remarks of this nature meant that court members should give maximum sentences to convicted military defendants, thereby giving the "convening authority plenty of latitude in exercising his powers of clemency." Latimer was also highly critical of a provision in a command circular that warned court members that notations should be made in their efficiency reports concerning the nature of their performance of court-martial duties. Latimer termed this provision "a veiled threat" to court members to award severe sentences.

But the ink was hardly dry on *Littrice* before the Court of Military Appeals again reversed its field, and in *United States* v. *Isbell* affirmed the use of a staff judge advocate bulletin to all officers of the command wherein various "errors" of past courts-martial were discussed. The principal errors were "inadequate sentences and improper acquittals." Seventeen examples of improper acquittals were outlined, with the editorial observation that twelve of them would have sustained convictions. Chief Judge Quinn, beginning his long ride on both sides of the command-influence fence, gave his stamp of approval to this orientation of court members. Judge Latimer, a stanch defender of things military, concurred, and Judge Brosman dissented. "If we were right in *Littrice*," Brosman asserted, we "must be wrong here."

Later in 1953, in *United States* v. *Hunter*, the Court of Military Appeals reversed a conviction where the convening authority had engaged in a pretrial conference with three members of the court-martial and discussed the past derelictions of the defendant, and stated that past sentences had been "too meager." The court rendered a similar reversal the same year in *United States* v. *Guest*, where the SJA, at a recess in the trial, presented the president of the court-martial with a copy of his dissenting opinion in a previous board-of-review decision, on a question that was then pending before the court-martial. The president, in turn, directed that the dissenting opinion be read to the military judge on a motion that was before the court-martial. Judge Latimer, writing for the court, held the SJA's action as illegal, and "certainly . . . not such as to bring credit upon the administration of military justice."

In 1954 an army board of review affirmed a decision in *Lane*, where the president of a general court-martial withdrew one affidavit, asserting there was no command influence brought to bear against the court members in a particular case. He then gave a new affidavit stating that he was personally detained by the general prior to the start of the trial and was advised that the general was "very interested in the case," and that the general "would talk to the members of the court after the trial." The president stated that he had so advised each court member prior to trial. Each member of the court, including the assigned military defense counsel, gave an affidavit stating that the president did not make any statements of this nature at all.

In the same year the Court of Military Appeals held that a technical manual entitled *Psychiatry in Military Law* unnecessarily restricted the free testimony of military psychiatrists before military courts, and as such was a "coercive influence" and would "unquestionably destroy the value of the expert's opinion." Writing for the court, Chief Judge Quinn held that the manual was an "illegal and unconstitutional invasion of the judicial process."

In *United States v. Knudson* in 1954, the Court of Military Appeals reversed the conviction wherein a military judge's decision to grant a continuance during the trial of the case was subsequently reversed by the convening authority. In the same year an air force board of review affirmed a conviction where the accused testified that he was present when the convening authority addressed his assembled officers and advised them that he was dissatisfied with a finding that was made in a previous court-martial involving a flight accident, and that he would "reprimand the court or board involved in the case." The defendant testified that at least six of the members who tried him were present at this meeting. In another 1954 case, *United States v. Bourchier*, the Court of Military Appeals refused to reverse a conviction where military defense counsel, following trial, filed an affidavit that he overheard a court member state: "We were told just how we were supposed to vote in that case."

In the same year, in *United States v. Navarre*, the court affirmed a conviction where the convening authority conducted a two-hour lecture on the subject of court-martial duty for the officers of his command. At this lecture he told the parable of the "hapless lieutenant colonel and his low efficiency report." The hapless lieutenant colonel had been a member of a court-martial that acquitted too many people and rendered inadequate sentences in its convictions. Three court members in the Navarre case admitted they attended the lecture and heard the parable. Chief Judge Quinn ruled that the parable was in "no way incompatible with the requirement of an absolutely fair trial for this accused." Judge Latimer went further: "Any commander worth his salt would do the same and he should not be restrained from informing the officers of his command of his intent to downgrade those individuals who violated the spirit and intent of the law. . . . Rather than criticize him I would offer him a commendation." Judge Brosman dissented. He stated: "Regardless of the merits, what general confidence is likely to be reposed in findings of guilty returned by a court-martial three of whose five members have been subjected to threats—and with effective teeth—of reprisals unless more accused persons are convicted and severer sentences imposed?"

The Court of Military Appeals in *United States* v. *Stringer* equated a general court-martial's military judge with a civilian judge, to include mistrial authority. In this case the president of the court-martial complained on the record about the poor state of preparedness on the part of the prosecutor, and noted that unless he was better prepared "we will hang the man innocently." Judge Brosman held the remark touched on the principles "underlying the doctrine of general prejudice." Prior to trial in *United States* v. *Zagar*, a 1955 case, the staff judge advocate held a meeting with court members and informed them: (1) it was improper to consider extenuating circumstances prior to findings; (2) in military cases it was reasonably certain that a crime was committed and that the defendant committed it; and (3) guilt was "presumptive unless proven otherwise by the court." Chief Judge Quinn and Judge Brosman held that the SJA's words improperly influenced the court members, and reserved the conviction. Judge Latimer dissented.

An air force board of review in *Robinson* reversed a conviction where a military judge's ruling on a defense motion was overruled by the convening authority during a recess in the trial. The board held this was general prejudice. In *Torrente*, a 1956 case, an army board of review reversed a conviction where the military judge attempted to disqualify himself during trial because of his prior knowledge of uncharged criminal activity on the part of the defendant, but was overruled by the convening authority. The board held this was illegal command influence.

In *United States* v. *Hawthorne*, a 1956 case, the convening authority announced that two-time losers (soldiers with two or more convictions on their records) who committed subsequent offenses were to be eliminated from service via trial by general court-martial "as a general rule." The defendant was a two-time loser. The Court of Military Appeals reversed his conviction, holding that "any circumstance which gives even the appearance of improperly influencing the court-martial proceedings must be condemned." In *United States* v. *Blankenship*, a 1956 decision, the court reversed an air force case where the president of the court-martial was permitted to question defense witnesses in a sarcastic vein. In the same year the court reversed a navy conviction where a letter from the secretary of the navy to all navy commanders (a SECNAV Instruction) was read to court members following the conviction of the defendant for larceny, to the effect that it was against naval policy to retain thieves in the military service. In *Barnes*, an army board-of-review decision, the board found the military judge had abdicated his statutory duties by permitting the president of the court-martial to interrupt the proceedings and rule on a defense motion. The president informed the military judge it was not necessary for him to rule on the motion, to which the judge replied: "Very well."

Thus, more than five years after the effective date of the Uniform Code of Military Justice, the flood of recorded command-influence cases gave no hint of receding. Moreover, the cases were beginning to repeat themselves, indicating not only the low estate the military reserved for judicial reform, but also its bad faith in following the law of the land. The very existence of these cases five years after the implementation of the Uniform Code of Military Justice evidenced the failure of the Uniform Code as well as the failure of the Court of Military Appeals to rid the military court-martial system of the blight of command influence. It also evidenced an apparent constitutional inability of the American military establishment to administer a judicial system along democratic lines.

However, if overall responsibility for the debacle that was soon to follow in the area of command-influence law is to be assessed, it must lie directly with the Court of Military Appeals. Had the court taken a consistent stand against the practice of command influence in military cases, the practice could well have withered and died within the first few years. While the military hierarchy would surely have resisted the court with all its conspiratorial ability, it is doubtful if it could have withstood the repeated and consistent reversal power of the Court of Military Appeals in command influence cases. The court could have also utilized other powers, such as its injunctive and mandamus powers (powers it has to this day failed to exert), in its fight against the command control of the military judicial process. But regardless of its lost opportunity early on to curb the vice of command influence, its failure to stem the practice permitted it to grow into an acceptable risk taken by entrenched military commanders.

Judge Latimer, an ultraconservative, could be counted on to sustain the military viewpoint in all but the most outrageous situations. He could also be counted on to lend respectability to the military view with his dissents. Judge Brosman and, after Brosman's death, Judge Ferguson could be counted on to condemn the practice. Judge Ferguson's outspoken opposition to the practice would eventually become classic. He would ultimately brand SJAs as common criminals in their efforts to rig military juries to render verdicts in keeping with command viewpoints. But Chief Judge Quinn, with his inability to take a stand one way or the other on the question of command control, was perhaps the major reason for the court's ultimate failure to reform military law in this regard. His ability to side himself first with the right and then with the left added the necessary element of confusion to the law. Military commanders intent upon pushing to the furthermost limit seized upon Quinn's confusion and Latimer's conservatism. Thus the second half of the 1950s was a replay of the first, with military commanders continuing to rig military juries, and occasionally being called to account in their more callous ventures.

In *United States* v. *Deain* the Court of Military Appeals ruled that the navy improperly influenced court-martial proceedings with the appointment of Rear Admiral Ruddock, U.S. Navy Retired, as permanent president of a navy general court-martial. The evidence revealed that Ruddock indoctrinated all new members assigned to his court as to the nature of their judicial duties. Ruddock testified that he did not personally believe in the presumption of innocence as a constitutional right in the navy, because people in the navy had no constitutional rights. The admiral admitted that he believed that everyone referred to trial had probably committed "some offense." In reversing, the Court of Military Appeals noted that "disinterested observers might discern the parallel of a packed jury."

In 1957 the Court of Military Appeals reversed the convictions in *United States* v. *Estrada, United States* v. *Addye,* and *United States* v. *Walinch,* all involving the illegal introduction of SECNAV Instructions in navy courts-martial. During the same year army boards of review reversed *Connors, Best,* and *Roden* because of illegal command manipulation to secure longer sentences in those cases. In 1958 the Court of Military Appeals reversed the *McCann* decision. McCann was a ground control operator in the air force. During his trial several members of his court-martial jury attended a lecture by the local SJA where he commented specifically on the seriousness of offenses committed by air force ground control operators. Judge Latimer dissented. During the same year, the court reversed the *Hirrlinger* decision, where a navy prosecutor passed out SECNAV Instructions to court members along with their appointing orders.

That same year the Court of Military Appeals was presented with an unusual case in *United States* v. *Sheppard.* In this case a post commanding general ordered fat soldiers who failed to lose weight as ordered court-martialed. Judge Homer Ferguson, who had been appointed to the bench in the mid-fifties following the death of Judge Brosman, was emphatic in his denunciation of the case. He wrote:

When seventy-one hearings growing out of an extraordinary undertaking are ordered in a short period of time, it makes a command conscious of the creator's interest. I am certain

from all of the foregoing that the men in the Eighth Infantry
Division, and particularly those who manned the courts would
pay careful heed to the General's wishes, for they were well
aware of the fact that the project was of paramount importance to him. . . . [A] finding of not guilty would have been a
direct rebuff to the General who had ordered the accused to
stand trial for violations in connection with his specially cher-
ished project.

In 1958 an army board of review reversed *Godwin*, in which the
military judge had ruled during trial that the defendant's confession was inadmissible. At this point the SJA walked out and
slammed the door to the courtroom. At the next recess the SJA
and the trial judge conferred, and following the reopening of the
court, the judge announced he was changing his ruling, and admitting the confession into evidence. In *Cannon*, an army board of
review reversed a conviction because the president of the court-
martial interrupted the proceedings to upbraid the military judge
and counsel for their courtroom conduct. Upward of twenty cases
were reportedly reversed because of the commanding general's
comments to prospective court members at Fort Ord, California,
in May 1958. The general disclaimed any intent to "influence" the
prospective court members, but proceeded to state that he was
"horrified" at the result of some general courts-martial. He said he
had trouble controlling his temper about these cases, and that the
court members had "fallen flat on their faces." He told his audience if an accused was convicted, "the proper sentence should
include a severe sentence—a fairly severe sentence." "If the man is
found guilty, give him a punishment to suit the crime, and get that
through your heads." Every case involving court members who
attended the lecture was reversed or, in guilty pleas, the sentences
were adjusted downward.

The Court of Military Appeals has steadfastly avoided reversing
overseas convictions where the reversals would prove embarrassing to our foreign relations. Two such cases will illustrate the

point. In *United States* v. *Carter*, a 1958 case, a young German
girl of fifteen years of age was repeatedly raped by black soldiers
in Bamberg, Germany. There was an immediate outcry of anti-
Americanism from certain elements of the foreign population. To
stem this protest, the senior American commander in Germany
issued a written directive to every American officer in Europe. It
included the following comment:

> I think it is a very sad commentary on us, as commanders,
> when the reputation of the United States Army—as a matter
> of fact, when the reputation of the United States—is permit-
> ted to be jeopardized by a few "bums". . . . Again, it matters
> little that the U.S. personnel in Germany participated in about
> 700 worthwhile community events during the past three
> months when one rape case, in which seven soldiers repeat-
> edly attacked a 15-year-old girl, draws unfavorable worldwide
> publicity. . . . I don't expect people to work miracles but I do
> expect, and I am going to demand, that these criminal acts
> against the citizens of our host nation be brought to an irre-
> ducible minimum immediately. . . .

Judge Latimer, writing for the court, presumed that the comments
were read "by every member of the court," but held that the
remarks were in the "prophylactic" sense rather than intended to
"interfere in the judicial arena." The convictions were affirmed.
Whether the court members (all of whom were presumed to have
read the directive) might have paid "careful heed to the General's
wishes" in voting to convict the seven defendants was apparently
not addressed by the court at all.

The second case on the same point also was a 1958 case. It
involved a five-year-old Okinawan girl who was found brutally
murdered and raped in an abandoned quarry in Okinawa. There
had been two other recent sexual assaults against Okinawans by
American soldiers, all of which caused the commanding general of
the Ryukyu Islands to act. He called a meeting of the hastily
organized "Ryukyuan-American Community Relations Advisory

Council." The meeting was attended by the chief executive of the Ryukyu Islands, the president of Ryukyu University, the speaker of the Ryukyu Legislature, the chief justice of the Ryukyu Islands, and the presidents and the managing editors of all civilian newspapers on the islands. The commanding general was the chief speaker. He assured his assembled guests that the Americans could handle the situation, that justice would be done, and that the accused would be given a fair trial.

Five days later the general addressed a staff conference at his headquarters. At this conference he made the following comments:

> The righteous indignation [of the Okinawans] . . . has carried them away to the extent of mixing [this] up with civil rights, human liberties, reversion to Japan. . . . Get your soldiers to understand the situation. Most of them, almost all of them, will play ball with us. Let them know they have done a thing that hurts us. . . . [M]ake sure proper steps have been taken in the punishment and apprise your men of the situation. . . .

A sergeant who was poorly connected to the murder by the thinnest of circumstantial evidence was later tried, over his protest, on Okinawa by a court-martial all of whose members were picked by the general from his command. The sergeant was convicted and sentenced to death. On review an army board of review affirmed the conviction, with one member dissenting on the ground that guilt was not established beyond a reasonable doubt. On appeal to the Court of Military Appeals the conviction and sentence were affirmed. Judge Ferguson dissented. He bemoaned the scant evidence of guilt and questioned the creditability of major portions of it. He also stated that he would reverse because of command influence. "Anyone who has served in these important capacities in foreign lands," he asserted, "realizes the importance which is placed upon the attitude of the native people." The death sentence was later commuted to thirty-five years' imprisonment.

Returning to the subject of pretrial orientation of court members, in *United States* v. *Olson*, a 1960 case, the accused was charged with desertion, larceny, and six counts of bad checks. The president of Olson's court-martial supervised his command's bad-check "program." He also kept a list of individuals who had written bad checks. On the day before Olson's trial he presided at an Officers' Call which was attended by five of the court members. The president addressed the assembled officers on several subjects, including "a pointed lecture on the high incidence of bad checks within the command." Judge Ferguson, writing for himself and Chief Judge Quinn, reversed the conviction and branded the proceedings as "drumhead justice." Judge Latimer dissented and found the command conduct "perfectly proper." He continued: "I dare say that lectures of the type indicated by this record have been given daily over the entire life of our military services."

In *Pierce*, another 1960 case, an air force board of review reversed a conviction where the defendant was convicted of forty-nine bad-check offenses. On an evening recess during the trial of the case, three court members had attended an Officers' Call where the base commander announced that he didn't care how long the case lasted, just so long as the court found the accused guilty and "hanged him." In *Daminger* an air force board of review reversed a conviction where the court members had received a letter from the convening authority noting that "compassion and leniency are not prerogatives of court members," as such feelings "usurp the prerogative of the convening authority to exercise clemency."

Rounding out the first decade, *United States* v. *Danzine*, convened almost ten years to the day after the Uniform Code of Military Justice first went into effect, involved a lecture given to court members prior to the referral of cases to the court, by the convening authority and his SJA. At this lecture both officers were critical of light sentences. Court members were warned not to permit civilian standards of justice to interfere with their sentencing, or to consider the effect a sentence to confinement might have on the family of a defendant. Chief Judge Quinn and Judge Latimer affirmed the conviction. Judge Ferguson dissented. In an opinion setting forth much of the background of the Uniform Code as it related to the subject of command influence, he stated:

> I am of the view that a convening authority may not lawfully address members of a court-martial with respect to the principles of law which they are to apply or the sentences which they should impose. Such action was taken in this case, and it directly violates the mandate of Congress as laid down in Uniform Code of Military Justice, Article 37. . . . Any attempt to influence the course of justice before military courts runs afoul of that statute regardless of the commanding general's motivation, and I fear that our decision today, ignoring the pervasive influence that any commander's views have on the independence of his subordinates, simply makes the prohibition against command control depend upon the "cleverness" with which he is able to convey his meaning to them.

Thus ended the first decade under the Uniform Code of Military Justice.

7

The Powell Report,
the Second Decade

The army launched the second decade under the UCMJ with an all-out effort to effect the legislative reversal of all the reforms, however meager they were, that had been accomplished in the field of military justice during the preceding ten-year period. This effort was contained in the Powell Report, the product of a high-powered committee of army generals commissioned to make a detailed study of the Uniform Code of Military Justice and its effect upon the army.

Under the UCMJ the judges of the Court of Military Appeals and the various judge advocates general of the armed forces submit an annual report to Congress concerning the operation of military law during the preceding year, with recommendations, if any, for legislative changes. In the decade of the fifties the army had seized upon this report to "influence" Congress to return military justice to the free-wheeling days of World Wars I and II, when military command ruled supreme without the nagging guidance of civilian courts. The Powell Report, which was included in the army judge advocate general's report to Congress for 1960, was the culmination of the army's prolonged effort to sink the Court of Military Appeals.

This effort was evident as early as 1954. In the army's 1954 report to Congress, the army judge advocate general recommended to Congress that it legislatively reestablish the military judge as a voting member of the court-martial. To have done so would have neutralized the judge's responsibility to instruct the court members on the law of the case in open court, for he would have been able to contradict any instructions he might have given in closed sessions. Such an amendment to the Uniform Code would also have marked the end of the modern effort to equate the military judge with civilian judges, who do not vote with the jury on such important matters as the guilt or innocence of the defendant. It would have also furnished the military hierarchy with a direct channel of command control of the court-martial process. The recommendation was advanced to Congress in the name of military necessity, but it was not enacted into law. It appeared again in the army's 1955 report to Congress, but otherwise died without further embellishment.

The judge advocate general of the air force, not to be outdone, opined in 1955 that further changes in the Uniform Code of Military Justice should not be made at all, until more basic changes were enacted to "improve the administration of military justice." A few years later, in 1959, the same judge advocate general, speaking before a congressional committee, spelled out just what he had in mind. He warned the committee that the Uniform Code of Military Justice was grossly inefficient regarding both time and dollars, and probably would not work in time of war. He further stated: "My testimony before this subcommittee would not be complete if I did not express my recommendation as to what I think should be done to correct the inefficiencies of which I speak. I recommend the repeal of the Uniform Code of Military Justice in its entirety and the reenactment of the Elston Act. . . ." Under the

Elston Act, boards of senior judge advocates were the final arbiters of military law.

The judge advocate general of the army in his 1956 report to Congress advocated the abolition of certain "burdensome" provisions of the Uniform Code of Military Justice. One of the suggestions was to remove the United States Court of Military Appeals from the wartime administration of military law. The army judge advocate general felt the Court of Military Appeals took too long to review cases. He recommended the establishment of "decentralized" boards of review, made up entirely of military judge advocates, to administer appellate review of wartime cases, with full power to order death sentences into execution in foreign theaters. The general specified that this was necessary to effect discipline in wartime, where speedy trials and speedy execution of sentences were most vital. The recommendation was rejected by Congress.

The army's 1957 report to Congress detailed its version of what was really wrong with military justice. Specifically, the Court of Military Appeals was effecting basic changes in settled military law. This was upsetting and disturbing to the stability of law enforcement in the army. To offset the fast-changing scene of military law, and to provide military judges who were more capable of keeping pace, the army judge advocate general announced he was instituting a pilot program where only specially trained and certified judge advocates would serve as judges in future army general courts. Theretofore, captains and higher ranks were routinely certified to serve as military judges. It was hoped that with better-trained specialists sitting as military judges, the Court of Military Appeals would find it more difficult to reverse army cases.

In his 1958 report to Congress, the judge advocate general of the army listed some of the decisions of the Court of Military Appeals that were burdensome to army discipline. One such case was *Kraskouskas*, where the court ruled that in future general courts-martial, only certified lawyers could represent military defendants, despite a specific request from the defendant himself to be represented by a nonlawyer, such as his company clerk or supply sergeant. Other burdensome cases were the court's holding that the nonpayment of a gambling debt did not constitute a military offense under the "general" article (Article 134) of the Uniform Code of Military Justice; that an order to an accused to submit to a blood alcohol test, or a urine test, or a handwriting test was an illegal order, and that a defendant who refused to obey such an order could not be prosecuted. These and similar cases were defined as "sharp departures from previous military legal practice," and were cited as creating "difficult problems for military law enforcement agencies." Remedial legislation, proposed by the army, was promised to be submitted to Congress soon.

By 1959 the judge advocate general of the army reported there was growing concern among military commanders "over lack of stability in the law." The judge advocate general continued for two and a half pages listing specific cases decided by the Court of Military Appeals as disruptive of military law, and concluded that such cases reflected a "need for remedial legislation [that] is becoming more and more urgent." The army judge advocate general, of course, was laying the groundwork for his 1960 report to Congress, which was to include the famous Powell Report.

Powell, a three-star general, had been ordered in October 1959 to head a high-ranking military board, composed of no less than nine general officers of the army, to make a "searching study" of the effectiveness and operation of the Uniform Code of Military Justice and to assess its "bearing on good order and discipline within the Army." The board, whose second-ranking officer was Major General William C. Westmoreland, was directed to report by January 31, 1960, on the effectiveness of the Uniform Code, and to include proposed remedial legislation if indicated. That the board's findings might be subject to doubt was foretold at the very beginning; in its haste to study the "problem," the committee overlooked a rather important bit of evidence. In the fall of 1959, the chief of staff of the army, a four-star general, L. L. Lemnitzer, obviously unaware of his judge advocate's intent to bury the Uniform Code of Military Justice, made the following comment in an official publication concerning the administration of military justice within the Army:

> I believe that the Army and American people can take pride in the positive strides that have been made in the administration and application of military law under the Uniform Code of Military Justice. The Army today has achieved the highest state of discipline and good order in its history.

Unaware of this detail and thus undeterred, the Powell Committee, within its prescribed time-frame of four months (and less than three weeks of actual working days) dutifully found that the Uniform Code of Military Justice was ineffective to support good order and discipline in the army, and that military commanders were opposed to its "cumbersome" procedures and "uncertain" results. While the Court of Military Appeals had very much charted a cautious, middle course in the administration of military justice during its first decade, the committee was irked by its "pronounced tendency" to import "civilian rules" into military law. The committee drafted pages of detailed legislative changes to correct every defect cited, providing for the legislative reversal, among other things, of eighteen specific case holdings of the Court of Military Appeals. These cases ranged in import from a finding by the court that military commanders were bound by the stricture of probable cause in the search of military suspects, to a finding that the mere failure to account for property entrusted to one's safekeeping when an accounting was due was insufficient to sustain a larceny conviction.

The committee paid due lip-service to the rule of law in military cases, and announced at the outset that, while discipline was a function of command, the command function stopped short of the court-martial process. It announced that the rule of law and not the rule of command was to govern court-martial cases—noting that this was an area that had caused some concern to civilian critics of military justice in the past, and thus announced its avowed intention of not turning back the clock on military justice

—and then turned to its more important business. The committee recommended as a starter that legislation be enacted that would permit the president of the United States to draft Executive Orders which, unless specifically overruled by Congress within ninety days of their publication, would automatically become binding law in all military and appellate courts.

Under this provision, the president or his military adviser, if dissatisfied with a specific ruling of the Court of Military Appeals on such subjects as confessions, search and seizure, constitutional due process, etc., could effect an almost immediate change in the law without going through the bothersome process of legislative action. An Executive Order could be drafted by the military, hand-carried to the president by the chief of staff, and published as an Executive Order within a matter of days. In the unlikely event of a congressional veto, the Executive Order, and not the rule of law announced by the Court of Military Appeals, would have been the law of the land. The committee of generals, after less than three weeks of actual working days, also recommended the doctrine of general prejudice as announced in *Lee* (1952) be reversed legislatively. The committee further requested a change be enacted in the Uniform Code to provide for the enlargement of the Court of Military Appeals from three judges to five, with a provision that the two additional members be required by law to be retired military judge advocates.

The Powell Report was intended by the army to be the last word on the subject of the Uniform Code of Military Justice. Authored by nine general officers (and by a multitude of lesser lights), it represented the very best the army could produce. The Powell Report, published in book form, was 287 pages in length, and contained a multitude of charts, appendices, and tables, and a complete legislative package with which to effect a line-by-line legislative revision of offending case holdings of the Court of Military Appeals and equally offending provisions of the Uniform Code of Military Justice. The Powell Report was included in the army judge advocate general's report to Congress for 1960, with the recommendation by that official that the Powell proposals be enacted into law by Congress. Military necessity was advanced as the reason for the recommended changes. The purpose of the operation, of course, was to sink the Court of Military Appeals.

Congress, however, did not buy General Powell's recommendation to scuttle the Court of Military Appeals. Chief Judge Quinn, in writing the Court of Military Appeals' annual report to Congress for 1960, simply termed the Powell Report as "appalling." He added that the adoption of the Powell recommendations would "mark a return to the conditions that compelled the enactment of the Uniform Code." The ability of the army to stumble through a decade of war and peace since the submission of the Powell Report, without suffering a major or even a minor breakdown in discipline, points up the ease with which the military utilized the cry of "military necessity" to justify Powell's ultraconservative recommendations in the field of military law. None of the foregoing changes recommended by Powell were enacted by Congress. Thus, at best, a question raised as to the lack of real expertise by Powell and his fellow generals, who reported the state of army discipline to be on the brink of destruction in 1960, is graphically underlined.

By the time the dust had settled on the Powell Report, the navy was back into the Court of Military Appeals attempting once again to utilize SECNAV Instructions to influence its court members. In both 1960 and 1961 the use of SECNAV Instructions in navy courts-martial were affirmed by Chief Judge Quinn and Judge Kilday (who was appointed to the court to fill Judge Latimer's position after his original term of ten years expired). Judge Ferguson dissented in both SECNAV cases, ruling that the practice of permitting written instructions from the secretary of the navy to be handed to court members in criminal trials was "fraught with danger of command control." Two more army cases, where army commanders had urged their court members prior to trial to adjudge more severe sentences, were approved in the Court of Military Appeals, with Quinn and Kilday voting to affirm and Ferguson to reverse. But in 1961 *United States* v. *Kitchens*, a conviction from Fort Jackson, South Carolina, broke the chain of government victories.

Kitchens, along with several soldier buddies and a civilian ex-convict did a bit of drinking one December night in 1960. Later that night they allegedly burglarized a furniture store and were arrested. In January of 1961 Kitchens and his soldier cohorts were tried and convicted in civilian court in Columbia, South Carolina, and given suspended sentences. Kitchens' commanding officer, a captain, had been following the situation closely, and elected administratively to separate Kitchens from the army with an undesirable discharge, but not via court-martial. Kitchens' commander, however, received a telephone call from the Fort Jackson SJA, advising him that the "front office" was of the opinion that suspended sentences were not "adequate." The company commander therefore resolved that court-martial was appropriate, and in due time charges were filed against Kitchens.

About this same time an assistant SJA at Fort Jackson, a lieutenant colonel, circulated a letter on SJA letterhead to all captains and higher ranks at Fort Jackson. The letter was essentially critical of acquittals and light sentences adjudged at Fort Jackson during a particular time-frame. The letter observed that during a preceding time period, "proper" findings and "adequate" sentences had been adjudged. The writer asked his readers to advise him of the reason "for this apparent change in the approach to general court-martial cases within the command." The addressees were assured that their answers would remain anonymous.

Kitchens was brought to trial and convicted. Each of the six court members stated that he had received a copy of the letter in question. After the trial had started and after the issue of the assistant SJA's interference in the judicial process had been raised at the trial level, the officer involved handed a second letter to each member of the court. The letter was also on SJA letterhead, and was signed by the same assistant SJA. In this letter the author thanked each of the court members for the helpful comments he had received, and he further stated that while none of the addressees of the first letter had voiced any misunderstanding over its contents, defense counsel at Fort Jackson had contested the letter in every subsequent general court-martial convened at Fort Jackson as being unlawful command influence. The writer then added a comment to take the heat off his superiors at Fort Jackson. He stated that neither the commanding general nor the SJA at Fort Jackson had either "directed or approved" the first letter.

The defense counsel involved in *Kitchens* subsequently reported that he was called into the assistant SJA's office and received an official tongue-lashing for his refusal "to live in peace in the office," and that he thereafter received a substantially lower efficiency report than formerly. Chief Judge Quinn, writing for the unanimous court, reversed the conviction and observed that the "circumstances may indeed call for vigorous investigation, and if the allegation is established, may justify punitive proceedings." All in all some twenty-three convictions from this command were either reversed or, in guilty-plea situations, sentences were adjusted downward because of the letters involved.

While *Kitchens* was a jolt, the effect was short-lived. The air force, still unwilling to permit its bad-check policy to be scuttled by the Court of Military Appeals, made a comeback in 1962. The case involved reached the Court of Military Appeals, and the case was affirmed by Chief Judge Quinn and Judge Kilday. Judge Ferguson made a pointed dissent. He noted:

> only such summary action [as reversal] will serve to require observation of the Congressional mandate contained in . . . Article 37 for, though this Court has sat for *eleven years* and reversed numerous records involving the issue, *we have yet to see a single person brought to trial for violation of an accused's right to an impartial hearing*. Reversal, therefore, remains the only shield to which an accused may look for protection against arbitrary [command] interference. [Emphasis added.]

Judge Ferguson was making clear that the military establishment had not moved one inch in eleven years on its own motion to assure military defendants a fair trial, free from command influence. The military establishment, had it been willing to abide by congressional mandates, could have outlawed command influence within the first month following the enactment of the Uniform Code. First, as a command-oriented organization, it could have issued *commands* to cease the practice. Failing this, it could have court-martialed or otherwise disciplined its commanding generals for failing to obey its commands in this regard. One general stripped of rank—or better still, sentenced to military prison for jury fixing—would have ended the matter once and for all. But as Judge Ferguson pointed out in the case above, the military had for eleven years made no efforts on its own to end the practice of command influence.

In *Gordon*, a 1963 case, the accused was convicted of second-degree murder and assault with a dangerous weapon in Korea, and sentenced to ten years in jail. The facts of the case reveal that Gordon, a black soldier, was lured to a hotel room by a Korean pimp on the pretense that a prostitute would be there. Instead, Gordon was set upon by the pimp, who tried to rob him. The pimp's two male associates were in the hallway of the hotel and, in fleeing the scene, Gordon stabbed the pimp to death and slashed one of his associates. At Gordon's trial his defense counsel raised the issue of command influence. Both the commanding general of the Eighth Army and the commanding general of the accused's command (a subordinate command) had written letters to the membership of their respective commands prior to the trial of the defendant.

The Eighth Army commander in his letter to his major subordinate commanders emphasized that recent incidents involving Americans and Koreans had "brought discredit upon the United States Army and jeopardized relations with the Republic of Korea." The army commander further stated that he was "not convinced that there is full realization in this command of the damage that has been done." The commander further said that when a soldier takes the law into his own hands and punishes a local national, he "prejudices our mission here, and I will not tolerate such an act. Please make no mistake as to my intent." The army commander then directed his subordinates to place "personal emphasis on the implementation of this program."

The foregoing letter, of course, was in effect a threat to subordinate commanders, notifying them that their careers were at stake unless there was an immediate improvement in local relations. When the commanding general of the Seventh Logistical Command, the defendant's commanding general, received his superior's letter, he in turn carried out his "program." In a letter of his own, to his subordinate commanders, he prescribed certain standards, to include the following:

> All incidents in a major subordinate unit involving US military personnel and Korean nationals will be acted on immediately to the extent this is possible. *The current situation demands that guilty individuals be dealt with severely.* [Emphasis added.]

The foregoing paragraph, however, must have been read by a wary judge advocate, because a second command letter was issued a week later, officially eliminating the paragraph in question and adding the following provision in its place:

> Nothing contained in this letter shall be construed as limiting either convening authorities or court members in the free exercise of their judicial duties.

An army board of review affirmed the conviction on the basis that the army commander's letter was "aimed at the improvement of discipline and not the control of judicial processes." The board further held that the two letters from the logistical commander did not evince a "personal interest in the matter" (despite the express admonition of the army commander's letter that he would take a personal interest in the matter). On appeal to the Court of Military Appeals, the court reversed the conviction on the basis of an instructional error on the part of the military judge.

The Court of Military Appeals in 1964 ordered a rehearing on the sentence in a guilty plea case in *United States* v. *Johnson.* Although Johnson pleaded guilty at his trial, it was established on appeal that his commander had sent a pamphlet to jury members prior to trial urging the imposition of severe sentences. In *Clemens* an air force board of review reversed a conviction and forty-year sentence where the military defense counsel involved subsequently sat upon an air force rehabilitation board and voted against sending the defendant to a rehabilitation training center, where he would have had a chance to be returned to duty. In *United States* v. *Fraser*, another 1964 case, a superior air force SJA directed a subordinate SJA to recommend against giving an airman convicted of larceny a chance to be returned to duty. A unanimous Court of Military Appeals reversed the conviction, as a violation of Article 37 of the Uniform Code. The court noted:

> We are appalled to learn there may yet be extant command policies regarding action on courts-martial sentences in defiance of the Code and which we have so frequently condemned in our opinions. We are even more concerned by the allegation that a senior legal officer and member of our bar may have lent his office to the enforcement of such a patently illegal matter. Such action, if knowledgeably taken, merits the severest condemnation, and we are certain that measures will be instituted to prevent recurrence of this unfortunate situation.

In 1965 Captain Svenson drove an American army jeep across the border into East Germany and asked for political asylum, which was immediately granted. The captain unfortunately was given to drink and partying, and soon proved less than an asset to his hosts, who eventually ousted him into the waiting arms of American MPs. Svenson's defection to East Germany, however, had caused more than the average embarrassment to his American superiors. He was an *intelligence officer* and was privy to major American intelligence operations in West Germany. Therefore, upon his return to American control he was submitted to a thorough interrogation by American intelligence agents—for one full week. He was denied counsel during this interrogation, and upon its completion was ordered not to reveal anything about the questioning, even to his assigned military defense counsel. At his subsequent trial for larceny of a jeep and desertion, the prosecutor maintained that nothing Svenson said at his intelligence interrogation was used against him by the government.

Prior to Svenson's trial the chief of staff of the army, via the Department of the Army, had transmitted a message to all officers stationed in Europe. Its purpose was to emphasize to commanders the necessity of spotting possible defectors *before the fact*, especially if they were intelligence officers assigned to sensitive positions. Commanders were warned to deny access to classified information to untrustworthy individuals, and to take prompt action to remove security clearances of those personnel whose conduct might come under suspicion as unreliable. The message specifically mentioned Captain Svenson by name.

After Svenson's conviction and seven-year sentence (the maximum), his case was heard by an army board of review where the foregoing irregularities were raised on appeal. The board ruled there was no command influence involved in the Department of the Army message, nor was there error involved in denying him counsel during his interrogation by army intelligence experts. The allegation that his trial defense counsel were impeded in their defense of Svenson because he had been ordered not to discuss the matter of his intelligence interrogation with defense counsel was brushed aside. "The simple fact is," the board stated, "that this record does not disclose that this hampered the accused's defense in any way."

Whether Svenson was tortured during his interrogation by intelligence agents (as indeed he would have been had he declined to answer questions) was a subject the board of review did not raise. Had Svenson been questioned in detail about his reasons for deserting to East Germany, as indeed he must have been, we have only the prosecutor's word that nothing Svenson said was used against him by the government. While the prosecutor indeed should not be taken lightly, or his assertions held to unnecessary doubt, neither should the lips of the defendant be sealed against his own defense counsel. Unfortunately, this hear-no-evil, see-no-evil aspect of the case was avoided by the Court of Military Appeals. True to its tradition of not confronting the military on overseas cases where great embarrassment to the service or to our foreign relations might result, the court simply refused to review the case (as it has a right to do under statute) and the conviction was affirmed, thus ending one of the most shocking cases in command-influence law in modern times.

An air force board of review in *Ibbetson*, a 1965 case, affirmed a conviction where it was established that immediately prior to convening the court-martial, the members of the court were personally addressed by the convening authority on the nature of their duties as court members. In 1966 a related issue was before the Court of Military Appeals in the Albert case. Here it appeared that five of the seven court members who had tried and convicted the accused had, prior to trial, attended a lecture on military justice by the Fort Devens SJA, who lectured the court members on the desirability of including total forfeiture of pay and allowances, reduction to the lowest enlisted pay grade, confinement at hard labor, and a punitive discharge from the service in all court-martial sentences. Chief Judge Quinn and Judge Kilday affirmed the conviction. Judge Ferguson dissented. He pointed out that persons who give lectures of this nature never discussed the very real and awful consequences of a punitive discharge; nor the impact of confinement upon a youthful offender, or upon his innocent family. The only yardstick employed in these lectures, he noted, was the interests of the United States.

In 1966 in *United States* v. *Prince*, the court again condemned the introduction of a SECNAV Instruction on the disposition of homosexuals in the navy. The instruction had been furnished to court members. In *United States* v. *Wright*, 1967, the Court of Military Appeals condemned a pretrial lecture given to court members by the SJA only minutes before the court opened for the trial of the defendant. The lecture was given in the courtroom and covered many points of trial procedure, ending with the familiar admonition to adjudge "adequate" sentences. The court reversed the sentence. Judge Ferguson concurred in the reversal, noting that the SJA involved was guilty of nothing less than common "jury fixing." Ferguson restated his previous position that all pretrial lectures to court members on the nature of their duties by anyone other than the trial judge in open court constituted reversible error.

The famous Fort Leonard Wood command-influence cases were exposed in 1968. In this series of cases it appeared that the commanding general at Fort Leonard Wood was desirous of restoring the president of the court-martial to his former stature in military trials. The president of the court-martial was a line officer, and was usually senior to the military judge. Yet the judge would make rulings and run the trial while the president of the court-martial was forced to assume the role of an ordinary juror. This angered the commander at Fort Leonard Wood, and he resolved to do something about it. The commander was also incensed over speedy trial motions made by defense counsel, and especially over inadequate sentences that were meted out to war resisters. An "improper" acquittal in a manslaughter case moved him to action.

Henceforth, the commander dictated, the name of the president of the court-martial would head the list of court members in all appointing orders. Theretofore, army-wide, the military judge's name always went first. The judge's name was ordered to the bottom of the list at Fort Leonard Wood, and the judge's raised dais was ordered lowered in the courtroom. Court presidents suddenly began injecting their presence into proceedings at Fort Leonard Wood, and sentences took a sharp upturn. A defense counsel fired off a complaint to Washington, and the fat was soon in the fire. By the time the smoke settled, some ninety-three general court-martial convictions from Fort Leonard Wood were reversed, or sentences in guilty-plea cases were adjusted downward. No action at all was taken against the commanding general involved.

Senator Sam Ervin, Democrat of South Carolina, and chairman of the Senate Subcommittee on Constitutional Rights for Government Employees, had been conducting a series of prolonged Senate hearings on command influence. His hearings cataloged hundreds of pages of command-influence atrocities in much the same fashion as was done in congressional hearings following World Wars I and II. Ervin's voice for reform was indeed strong, and his recommendations for remedial legislation were always squarely on target and thus more and more difficult to ignore or to contain. In 1969 the military threw in the sponge. It abolished the *Manual for Courts-Martial* provision that permitted commanders and their SJAs to lecture court-martial members on the nature of their judicial duties and the status of military discipline within their commands.

From that day forward military commanders could not rely on a legal footing for the pretrial orientation of court-martial members. Formal lectures were hence outlawed, and could no longer be delivered in the open. Any messages there were, or any instructions that a commander wished to convey to his court members, would henceforth have to be delivered through clearly understood, nonlegal channels. Almost twenty years after the enactment of the Uniform Code of Military Justice, it was another round for justice in military trials.

But it was not the end of the battle.

8

Murder at Fort Bragg
and German-American Relations

Following my return to the United States from Korea in 1959 I
attended the army's advanced judge advocate school at the University of Virginia for nine months, and was then assigned to Third
Army headquarters in Atlanta, Georgia. In Atlanta I served primarily in military justice and reserve affairs and, following my
promotion to major in the early 1960s, I was assigned as post staff
judge advocate at Fort McPherson. I retained the job for eleven
months before I was fired.

During my tour of duty as staff judge advocate at Fort McPherson (the only time I was to serve as SJA during my army career) I
was anxious to see if most command fraud in matters of military
justice originated with staff judge advocates or with military commanders. Prior to my assignment as SJA I was morally certain that
most, but not all, of the army's legal problems stemmed from its
lawyers, and not necessarily from its commanders—and I resolved
to see if I could prove the validity of this conclusion at Fort
McPherson. I resolved to go about my task in this regard from a
reverse position. Military general court-martial sentences are not
legally effective until approved by the convening authority. I thus

resolved that in every general court-martial conviction obtained at Fort McPherson during my tour as SJA, I would furnish the commanding general a written and oral recommendation urging clemency in every conviction. It had been my past experience to see military convictions routinely approved without clemency by military commanders. I would thus be in a position at Fort McPherson to see if this harsh attitude reflected the attitude of the SJA or the commanding general.

During my tenure as SJA I put my policy into effect in almost every case. I encouraged both defense and prosecution attorneys to fight their cases to the hilt. Where convictions were obtained, I would then write up a detailed recommendation to reduce or suspend the imposition of sentence, and would personally present the recommendation to the post commander, Major General Darrell Daniel. General Daniel was an old man, a crusty combat veteran of World War II. He was a non-West-Pointer, gruff and contemptuous of military lawyers. By reputation he was hard-nosed. He was also reputed to be the most decorated combat officer ever to rise to the rank of general officer in the American army during World War II. He always spoke to me in grunts but he listened intently as I made my post-conviction pitches for clemency. And in every instance save one, he instantly followed my recommendations to the letter. I was convinced he was a man of honor, and I was morally certain that he would never overreach a military defendant on trial in a court-martial convened in his command.

But the threat to my job at Fort McPherson came from another direction. It came from the Third Army staff judge advocate who was transferred to Atlanta shortly after I was assigned duty as post SJA. He hotly contested my assignment, and almost from the day of his arrival sought to abolish my job. After some eleven months he was successful and my job was abolished. The orders came from the Pentagon. I was simply transferred to Germany—and the army SJA assumed my military-justice duties at Fort McPherson. He was not too long in getting involved after I departed.

The case concerned centered around a young lieutenant, Wayne

Loudermilch, a reserve officer from Alabama who had worked for me as a military trial attorney at Fort McPherson. Upon my transfer to Germany, Lieutenant Loudermilch remained at Fort McPherson, under the same army SJA—whom I shall call Colonel Klatt. Klatt was a no-nonsense-type JAG officer, who reputedly had high hopes of earning early promotion to brigadier general in the Judge Advocate General's Corps. He was an anti-boat-rocker, and very quickly discovered that Lieutenant Loudermilch was the opposite.

Shortly after my departure, Loudermilch was assigned temporary duty at Fort Bragg, North Carolina, for the purpose of defending a murder case. The case was controversial. It involved many witnesses and many lawyers and multiple accused. Four young black soldiers were accused of murdering a white soldier in a racial fight at Fort Bragg, and of wounding a second soldier. Racial violence was relatively new in the army at this time, and Colonel Klatt was on the spot. He wanted a speedy trial, without ragged ends, a clean conviction that he could present to the judge advocate general of the army perhaps as a model for future "problems" of this nature. But Loudermilch was a problem himself. He journeyed to Fort Bragg for the trial and, with advance notification to no one, moved for a postponement on the opening day of the trial, which the judge granted.

This was an unscheduled event on Colonel Klatt's timetable. General officers had not been notified in advance, witnesses and jurors had to be released and resummonsed. A new trial date had to be selected, all because Lieutenant Loudermilch was not ready for trial when his military superiors thought he should have been. Upon reopening, however, Loudermilch was ready and the trial proceeded. The case was hotly contested, but rocked through to a stormy conclusion. Three of the defendants were convicted of second-degree murder or lesser offenses, and received sentences ranging from three to ten years' imprisonment. Loudermilch's client, Specialist Wells, was convicted of second-degree murder and was sentenced to ten years' imprisonment.

After the trial Loudermilch and I corresponded in detail concerning certain events that occurred during and following the trial. Loudermilch thereafter presented a lengthy complaint in writing to the secretary of the army, demanding among other things that the post-trial review of the Wells case be removed from Colonel Klatt's jurisdiction. Loudermilch's complaint noted:

> Before and during the actual trial, Colonel H., the Staff Judge Advocate at Fort Bragg, communicated daily with Colonel Klatt, the Staff Judge Advocate at Third United States Army Headquarters . . . as to the progress of the trial of the cases concerned, and as to the activities of myself and Captain Smaltz, another assigned military defense counsel. Colonel H. expressed extreme displeasure with the cases, and the manner in which the defense was conducted. Colonel H. indicated to Colonel Klatt that he considered Captain Smaltz's defense tactics to be unethical, and further told him that he was particularly outraged at my having asked for a continuance, describing my request as totally unjustified and not in the best interest of the service. In the course of those conversations I was branded as a "persona non grata" at Fort Bragg, while Captain Smaltz's "persona non grata" status was extended to the entire Judge Advocate General's Corps.

Loudermilch then shifted to his reception in Atlanta following the trial. He stated he was called into Klatt's office and the following events occurred:

> [Colonel Klatt] demanded to know why I had asked for a continuance. Before I could make any comment, he stated: "You had plenty of time to prepare the case up there. It was damned stupid. I've given you opportunities to develop here— why don't you mature?" I limited my remarks to Colonel Klatt and stated that all the defense counsel did the best we could for our clients, who were charged with capital offenses, and it was beyond my comprehension how he could character-

ize my conduct and that of other defense counsel as unethical.
. . . Colonel Klatt then concluded the conference with the
statement that "I hope what I have said on these matters is
clear."

Lieutenant Loudermilch continued his account of post-trial activities in the Wells case. The second day after his return to Atlanta,
he stated that Colonel Klatt held a "critique" of the Bragg murder
cases in his office library. Every legal officer at Third Army headquarters was in attendance at the critique, including Lieutenant
Loudermilch. A reserve judge advocate officer, on active duty for
only two weeks and who had been assigned as an "observer"
during the trial, conducted the critique.

For over an hour this officer praised the finer points of the
prosecution of the case and criticized the defense. Loudermilch
was specifically accused of repeating similar requests to the military judge for instructions with only a slight change of phraseology,
and of trying to mislead the judge or trick him into misstating the
law. Captain Smaltz, another defense counsel, was accused of misstating points of law to the military trial judge in connection with
the application of certain federal statutes to military law. Loudermilch alleged in his complaint that six days after the critique he
received a telephone call from the office of the judge advocate
general of the army in the Pentagon, and was told that he was
being transferred to Fort Sheridan, Illinois, to a nonmilitary-justice
assignment. Two days later, Loudermilch asserted, he was relieved
of military-justice duties at Fort McPherson, and a week later he
was required to read and initial the *Canons of Ethics* of the American Bar Association.

Loudermilch's complaint to the secretary of the army touched
off an immediate investigation of his charges by senior judge advocate officials in the Office of the Inspector General of the Army.
Following the conclusion of this investigation, which was detailed
and lengthy, Loudermilch fired off a second complaint to the secre-

tary of the army. Loudermilch alleged that he was in fact transferred to Fort Sheridan seven weeks after the Wells trial, on July 8, 1964. He further asserted that two weeks following the trial Colonel Klatt rendered a personal efficiency report upon him which was some fifty-eight points lower than the three previous reports he had received at Third Army headquarters from other superiors.

In his second complaint Loudermilch also demanded a copy of the inspector general's report of his charges against Colonel Klatt. Loudermilch surmised that the report probably contained many verbatim statements of witnesses who substantiated his charges. He also knew that inspector general reports are secret and that their contents are generally revealed only to military superiors. Because of the devastating potential of the report in question, Loudermilch reasoned that the army would refuse to release the report to him—even if it meant it had to dismiss *murder* charges against his client. Since the report dealt with the allegation of post-trial command influence brought against a military defense counsel, Loudermilch knew that the army would have to release the report in question if he demanded it or forgo the conviction. Hence, ostensibly in order to assist him in writing an appellate brief for his client on the subject of post-trial command influence, Loudermilch formally demanded a copy of the report. Short of producing the report, the army's only option was to dismiss the charges against Specialist Wells before the case reached an appellate level.

With his options thus narrowed, rather than to attempt further appellate litigation in the case (which would have ultimately forced the release of the inspector general's report), the commanding general of the United States Continental Army, at Fort Monroe, Virginia, on January 13, 1965, after months of indecision finally dismissed the murder charge against Specialist Wells, and he was set free. The reason advanced by the general in his post-trial action on the case was "a lack of sufficient evidence to support the findings of guilty." Despite his complaints to the secretary of the army, and an extraordinary writ to the United States Court of Military Appeals, Loudermilch remained at Fort Sheridan in a nontrial job until his discharge from the army in 1966.

I have previously referred to the type of case involving an overseas situation where the actions of the American serviceman involved embarrass his commander. Many commanders faced with this situation lose their judicial objectivity and proceed with a judicial lynching to placate the local populace. I ran into a case of this nature in the spring of 1966. I was in Paris on leave when I first read of an incident that occurred in an obscure village churchyard, adjacent to the headquarters of the American Twenty-fourth Infantry Division in Augsburg, Germany, where I was assigned as executive officer of the SJA section. The article stated that at 2:00 a.m. on Easter Sunday a young enlisted man from the Twenty-fourth Division, in a highly intoxicated condition, climbed the fence surrounding the cemetery and proceeded to kick over eighty-nine tombstones, some of which were over three hundred years old. Many, quite thin and fragile, were broken. The soldier was apprehended in the act of destruction by a German policeman who heard "strange noises" coming from the cemetery. The overall effect of this soldier's actions on "German-American relations" in Augsburg was like a typhoon. In Augsburg, even under normal conditions, the press had demanded the withdrawal of American troops from Germany.

When I read the article, I was quite sure that our division commander, Major General Rowny, whose office was located in a military *Kaserne* next to the cemetery, was facing a highly indignant press and populace. By the time I returned to Augsburg the case had progressed to that of *United States* v. *Specialist 4th Class James E. Mays*, who was charged with a series of offenses carrying a maximum punishment of dishonorable discharge and fifteen years in prison. My immediate superior, the staff judge advocate, had disqualified himself in the case, and the burden of advising the commanding general on the formal charges against Specialist Mays fell to me. Upon the conclusion of the formal pretrial investigation of these charges, I prepared a written advice, an advice that was required by statute.

Portions of this advice follow:

> Command Influence. Evidence developed at the Article 32 Investigation reflects that at 1000 hours on the day following the commission of the alleged offenses the accused's entire chain of command, including his battalion commander, battalion executive officer, company commander, the first sergeant, the platoon sergeant and the platoon leader appeared before the Division Commander. The Division Commander informed the group at this time, as reflected in the Article 32 Investigation, that the offense was a very serious incident, that it reflected poorly on the chain of command and special effort should be made to know each man in the command in order to prevent future incidents of this nature. Following this meeting other events took place in regard to this case. . . .

The division personnel officer (the "G-1") had testified at the Article 32 investigation that most of the day following the incident "was spent participating in staff evaluation of the impact on the German Community and the extent of the damage." I dutifully advised General Rowny of the extent of the G-1's activity in the case. The G-1 admitted at the Article 32 investigation that he had informed all subordinate commanders in the Augsburg area of a "mass of atonement" that would be held in the German church connected with the cemetery. The message, which was sent in the name of General Rowny, provided substantially that a mass of atonement would be "celebrated at a specific time in the future at the church involved as an 'External Manifestation of our sorrow to the German people and particularly to the Holy Trinity Parish for the desecration of a local cemetery by one of our soldiers.' " The message further stated that it was hoped that the mass of atonement would convey to the German populace the "good faith" of the soldiers in the division "who share . . . the shock and grief that accompany flagrant and willful acts of destruction." The message terminated with a direction that all commanders were "urged to promote maximum attendance" of American soldiers, in uniform, at this mass.

I next advised General Rowny that he and his assistant division commander, the division chaplain, the division chief of staff, the Augsburg post commander, and the division civil affairs officer visit the priest of the Holy Trinity Church on the morning of April 13. At this time, I advised General Rowny that the record showed that he had apologized to the pastor, and personally had arranged a date for the mass of atonement (9:00 a.m., Monday, April 18). I further advised the general that on the day of the mass of atonement, he, along with some six hundred American soldiers in uniform and an equal number of German civilians, was in attendance. General Rowny was formally advised that the division chaplain delivered the sermon, which was translated into German by a local monsignor for the benefit of the Germans who attended the mass.

I further advised General Rowny that his highest noncommissioned officer in the division, the division sergeant major, had testified under oath at the Article 32 investigation that he was not aware of a meeting of Augsburg sergeants major called for the purpose of achieving maximum troop attendance at the mass of atonement. On May 16, well after the division sergeant major's Article 32 appearance, an unsolicited statement was carried to me by a soldier from his office. The statement was dated May 16 and contained the sworn statement and signature of the division sergeant major. It stated:

> I phoned the Sergeants Major of the units stationed in Augsburg on 11 April 1966, and asked them to meet me in the conference room at 2d Brigade Headquarters on Sheridan Kaserne, where upon their arrival I made the announcement of the memorial service.

I furnished General Rowny a copy of his sergeant major's statement.

In my pretrial advice to General Rowny he was further advised that he personally prepared a letter of apology to the Mayor of Augsburg concerning the incident at the cemetery, and that the letter was delivered by his assistant division commander. General Rowny was also reminded that he had forwarded a personal letter of apology to every tombstone owner, in which he referred to the cemetery incident as a "heinous incident," and further, that the German TV carried an item about the tombstone case on a video tape made in his office. I advised General Rowny that the accused's company commander had signed charges against him only after he was ordered to do so by a judge advocate officer in my office. Lastly, General Rowny was told that numerous officers within the division, including the SJA, had sworn at the Article 32 investigation that the accused could get a fair trial if he were brought to trial in the Twenty-fourth Infantry Division, but that there were other officers who swore that he could not because of General Rowny's pretrial interference in the case.

I assured General Rowny that while his actions were no doubt designed to "reduce damage to German-American relations," they had nonetheless created in my mind a "probability of prejudice if the accused were tried in this command." I therefore recommended that the general relinquish jurisdiction in the case and refer it to the next higher command for disposition. Rowny accepted my advice and the case was forwarded to a higher commander in Stuttgart for disposition. Ultimately it was referred to trial by special court-martial by that commander, where the accused received a pat-on-the-wrist sentence and was promptly returned to duty.

Thus, what appeared to be heading for a general court-martial in the Twenty-fourth Division—where the defendant would no doubt have been convicted and sentenced to a lengthy period of confinement and to a dishonorable discharge—was fortunately aborted. Had my formal recommendation been ignored by General Rowny, and had he directed that the accused soldier be tried in the Twenty-fourth Division over my objection, my finding of a "probability of prejudice" within my pretrial advice would have resulted in its reversal on appellate review. It was for this reason that I had cataloged General Rowny's injudicious actions in the pretrial stages of the case. This case, and countless others like it, illustrate a basic point in military jurisprudence—namely, that the conduct of foreign relations (i.e., German-American relations) should be left to the exclusive domain of the United States State Department, and not to military commanders. Otherwise, miscarriages of justice are almost bound to follow.

As a career judge advocate officer I knew practically nothing about commanders' conferences until relatively late in my military career. I knew they were held behind closed doors, and that the particular commander concerned would address his assembled senior commanders and his staff on any subject he desired, including military justice. Watered-down versions of these conferences were printed and distributed to all officers in the command—after careful editing by staff officers. The commanders' conference that I became involved in firsthand took place in Augsburg, Germany, on August 28, 1965. The division commander, Major General Rowny, addressed his officers on several subjects. On the subject of military justice he made the following statement:

Many of our POV [Privately Owned Vehicle] accidents occurred because soldiers drive while under the influence of alcohol. Let's save this useless loss of life. Let's protect the weak soldier from himself. Let it be known that you will crack down on anyone driving while "under the influence." This means *one* beer. Do as I am doing, deal ruthlessly with the drunken or wantonly reckless driver.

General Rowny was not an unfair commander. He was, in fact, possessed of a high degree of integrity. He was straightforward and honest. But he failed to consider that in addition to his duties as a commander, he also possessed judicial duties that required him to retain judicial objectivity in all his actions and utterances. But unfortunately military necessity was uppermost in his mind, and he thus erred in his comments at his commanders' conference. Seated in his audience, for example, were the senior officers who staffed every general court-martial convened in the Twenty-fourth Division. It would be extremely doubtful if these officers, within the next month, could erase his comments from their minds while they sat in judgment of military defendants charged with manslaughter by vehicle because of drunken driving.

Returning to the particular conference, prior to the formal publication of the general's comments, the reporter's rough notes were delivered to the staff judge advocate for his perusal (and editing). Our SJA at the time was processing to return to the United States and, because the incoming SJA was not yet well versed on division policies, the notes landed on my desk for the staff judge advocate review. I read them with considerable interest, and sent them on their way—without change. Within due time they were published and distributed to every officer in the division with the offending passage intact.

On the same day that General Rowny made the comments in question, he also signed a court-martial recommendation, referring the case of Specialist 4c James C. Rankin to trial by general court-martial. Rankin was charged with manslaughter by vehicle. The evidence adduced at the Article 32 investigation revealed that Rankin allegedly drove his POV while drinking and, in an intoxicated condition, ran off the road into a tree, killing a soldier passenger. After checking to see that the notes were indeed published in their correct form, I sought out Rankin's defense counsel, Captain Raymond K. Wicker, of the judge advocate section, and made sure that he was aware of the offending passage.

I next contacted the new SJA and advised him of the problem. He immediately shifted the burden to me. It was agreed that General Rowny would have to be told to print an immediate retraction and, to prove his "good faith" (that is, that he was not simply engaged in jury fixing), he should reduce the trial from a general court-martial (carrying a possible maximum sentence of three years in jail and dishonorable discharge) to a special court-martial (carrying a maximum sentence of only six months' confinement and no discharge).

General Rowny accepted my advice and Rankin's court-martial was dropped to a special court-martial, the review of which would be conducted entirely within the Twenty-fourth Infantry Division staff judge advocate section. A retraction was printed. But Captain Wicker raised the command-influence issue at the special court-martial anyway, and the case was publicized in the *Overseas Weekly* newspaper throughout Europe. When the smoke from the command-influence issue settled at the trial, the special court-martial, all of whose members had either attended the conference or seen the published notes, saw the wisdom of finding Rankin not guilty and he was set free. All other pending manslaughter-by-vehicle cases in the division were dropped. But there was an aftermath. Captain Wicker, a career judge advocate officer, subsequently told me tnat he was severely downgraded in his efficiency report by the division staff judge advocate for his conduct in this case.

Cover-up cases generally do not make it to trial in the military. The military may decide not to prosecute this type of case because they do not wish to hurt the individual "good" soldier involved; or for other reasons of policy, prosecution is not deemed in the "best interest of the service." The case of a soldier whom I shall refer to as Specialist Styles will illustrate one example of this type of case that was not prosecuted in the Twenty-fourth Infantry Division. Styles was a "good soldier" who was assigned to a division unit in Augsburg in the spring of 1966. But his wife was a "problem." She complained to his commanders whenever they experienced marital discord, which was about once a week. Eventually the Styleses separated. Mrs. Styles remained in their military quarters, with the intention of remaining in Germany permanently when her husband rotated to the United States in the upcoming weeks at the termination of his three-year tour of duty in Germany. Mrs. Styles also intended to keep their four-year-old son, Charles, with her in Germany.

Mrs. Styles telephoned me late in the evening of April 22, 1966, with a most strange story. Her husband had asked permission to take Charles for a walk earlier that morning. She consented and by late afternoon when neither her husband nor Charles had returned, she began frantic telephone calls to his supervisors and ultimately to the German police. Well after dark, Specialist Styles telephoned her to say that he had taken his son Charles and placed him aboard an airliner bound for San Francisco. The plane was to be met by his mother, who would care for Charles until Styles returned. Mrs. Styles also told me that two weeks earlier, her husband had stolen her passport, her Certificate of American Citizenship and other identification papers, and refused to return them to her. Despite bitter protests, his military superiors did nothing to force him to return the documents. Without these papers, Mrs. Styles, a former German national, was stranded in Europe.

I verified as much of Mrs. Styles's story as I could from Augsburg sources and then called the American consulate in Munich. When a staff member there told me she had issued a separate passport to Charles's father on April 14, I asked on whose authority she had "split" the passport (that is, removed Charles's picture and name from his mother's passport and issued a separate passport in Charles's name only). She explained that she had issued the separate passport on the assertion of Specialist Styles that his son was sick and in need of immediate air shipment home. Styles told her that he and his wife were to follow their son's return in two weeks. She then read me a letter signed by Styles's company commander (a captain), verifying the medical emergency and requesting that a separate passport be issued. It was against the law to "split" a passport without the presence and consent of its actual owner. It was also against the law to submit a false statement or document to the government for the purpose of obtaining an American passport. When I explained the facts to the consulate official she was shocked, but asserted that she could not issue Mrs. Styles a replacement passport in the absence of verification of her citizenship. I promised her that I would do the best I could to obtain the return of Mrs. Styles's passport, Certificate of American Citizenship, and other identification papers without involving the American consulate—or exposing her negligence in issuing the passport.

In Augsburg I ran into a stone wall. Specialist Styles was a "good" soldier. His company commander freely admitted he signed the letter to the American consulate, but he added that Mrs. Styles was a "troublemaker" and that he would do nothing to force her husband to return her citizenship papers. The battalion commander and the brigade commander refused to discuss the problem with me. My request to speak to the division commander, General Rowny, on the matter was unanswered. Mrs. Styles and I decided on an "unusual" approach. The next day at 6:00 a.m. she rang the doorbell of General Rowny's home and kept ringing it until it was answered. She then refused to leave until she talked not with the division commander but with his wife.

That broke the ice. The same morning at 10 o'clock, Mrs. Styles, her husband, the *brigade* commander, and I met to settle the problem once and for all. The colonel was a no-nonsense officer. For an hour he reviewed the facts of the case, and the facts of several past situations involving Mrs. Styles and her husband's command. The story of her "split" passport was not mentioned at all, but the colonel's solution to the problem was. General Rowny, it appeared, had directed that Specialist Styles's return to the United States be advanced, and that both he and Mrs. Styles be furnished *immediate* air shipment to the United States by military aircraft. The colonel's comments, directed at Mrs. Styles with hardly a nod in my direction, were laced with references to "We all want to do what is best for the division," and "None of us wants to embarrass General Rowny."

Mrs. Styles had been instructed by me, prior to the meeting, to remain silent, even though asked a question by the colonel. Thus he finally turned to me. Would I explain to her that under no circumstances was she to bother the general's wife again. I explained this fact to Mrs. Styles. I then told the colonel of the existence of the company commander's false letter to the American consulate in Munich, and of the applicable provisions of federal law that provided a maximum penalty of five years' imprisonment for the willful use of a false writing in the application for, or in the obtaining of, an American passport. The colonel was dumfounded that I would discuss this matter in front of Mrs. Styles. He directed me to cease the discussion. I replied that I had already discussed the matter with Mrs. Styles, and that no one other than I would make a decision as to what I would discuss with her or what advice I would give her.

I then pointed to my watch and told the colonel that I would give him exactly thirty minutes to have Mrs. Styles's husband lay her passport, Certificate of American Citizenship, and other documents of identification on my office desk. While a look of complete disbelief crossed his face I advised him that if the documents were not on my desk in thirty minutes, Mrs. Styles was going to board a train for Bonn that afternoon, and the next day, at 6:00 a.m., she was going to ring the doorbell of the American ambassador's home, and that she was going to ring it until she was carted off to jail or was granted an interview with the ambassador's wife. I further explained to the colonel that she would be accompanied by newsmen.

The colonel rose from his seat and in a drill-field voice told me that she would do nothing of the sort until it was cleared with General Rowny. I told the brigade commander that she would not clear anything with the division commander. The colonel then gave me an order to take no action at all until I had checked with my superior, the SJA. I responded by turning to Mrs. Styles and informing her to buy a ticket for Bonn. That ended the conference.

Fifteen minutes later I walked into my office at Flak Kaserne and discovered the brigade commander and the SJA in red-faced discussion. Both denounced me jointly and advised me that I had gone too far. The SJA volunteered that the army's legal assistance program did not extend to situations where the interests of the client conflicted with the interests of the military. I asked the SJA what possible interest the military could have in the situation except in the criminal prosecution of Styles and his company commander for the use of a false statement in the obtaining of an American passport. I volunteered that Mrs. Styles would cooperate fully with the government in that prosecution. The officers left my office and huddled in the hallway. Two minutes later Specialist Styles stalked into my office and laid his wife's passport, Certificate of Citizenship, and other identification papers on my desk and walked out.

That closed the case.

9

The Claymore Mine Case:
Investigating Accidental Deaths

In the fall of 1965 I was assigned to defend a first lieutenant involved in a fatal Claymore mine accident in West Germany. Lieutenant Samuel A. Bloch was a young reserver officer, a college graduate from Alabama. He was one of the first of many antimilitarists I was to encounter in the army. He was facing almost insurmountable odds when we met: he stood charged with dereliction of duty arising out of his alleged failure as right-flank safety officer "to observe" the emplacement of a Claymore mine to ensure that it was facing downrange during a recent live firing demonstration at Grafenwoehr, Germany, on September 24.

The mine was allegedly emplaced backward, and its seven hundred steel pellets fired to the rear into the spectators, killing one young soldier and wounding eighteen others (including the defendant). At the time of the accident many senior German, French, British, and American officers were in the spectator stands, including the commanding general of the United States Army's VII Corps, a lieutenant general who was also in overall command of the organizations responsible for the firing demonstration. Also present were several American major generals, one of whom was the commanding general of the Twenty-fourth Infantry Division, General Rowny, who commanded one of the two divisions that comprised VII Corps.

The organization of the various units conducting the firing demonstration was complex. The corps commander delegated the responsibility for the conduct of the firing demonstrations to General Rowny. Long prior to the firing demonstration, both corps and division units had been "on the ground" at Grafenwoehr, painstakingly organizing and practicing endless hours to get ready for the event, which was to be a major demonstration of most of the weapons utilized by ground soldiers in an infantry division. In mid-August it was decided to split the safety function of the demonstration from the firing function. A separate safety organization was established and placed under the command of the VII Corps artillery commander, a brigadier general who hereafter will be referred to as General Fox. In turn, General Fox passed his responsibility to his deputy safety officer, another VII Corps artillery officer and a full colonel who will be referred to as Colonel Diamond. The firing organization remained under the command of the commanding general of the Twenty-fourth Division, General Rowny, but he delegated this function to his assistant division commander, who redelegated it to the commanding officer of the Twenty-fourth Division's Third Brigade, a full colonel, whose three battalions were to conduct the actual firing demonstration. After this game of pass-the-eight-ball certain minor adjustments were to follow.

The deputy safety director, Colonel Diamond, split his safety organization into two parts. A lieutenant colonel was placed in charge of safety of all weapons that were to be fired on one range, and an officer who will be referred to as Major Williams was placed in charge of the safety of all weapons that were to be fired from a second range. Lieutenant Bloch reported to Grafenwoehr in mid-September, and was immediately assigned to Major Williams' safety organization. Several days before the firing demonstration Bloch was handed a set of written orders by Major Williams. At the same time he was advised that he was appointed as right-flank safety officer. The written orders received by Lieutenant Bloch read, in part, as follows:

> Claymore Firing. Right flank safety officer will observe the emplacement of the Claymore to insure that it is facing in the proper direction. He will insure that an area 50 meters to the rear of the Claymore is clear prior to the firing.

A Claymore mine is deceptively easy to emplace in the ground. Colored army green, it blends with green foliage. It is about six or seven inches long, three inches high, and perhaps an inch thick. It sits on twin scissor legs, about two and a half inches long, that are placed into the earth to give directional stability to the mine prior to firing. It is crescent-shaped, bent in the middle along its vertical axis as it sits on the ground, with the outside of the curve, or convex side, facing the enemy. The hull of the mine is constructed of plastic, and opens as you would open a clam, into two equal halves. During its manufacturing process, the hull is opened and seven hundred small steel pellets imprinted in a tinfoil sheet are placed flat against the interior of the convex, or outside, face. The mine is then sealed shut, and plastic explosive is poured into the vacant space immediately to the rear of the steel pellets. A firing device is connected to the top of the mine, which is connected to a coil of wire that is electrically activated by a plunger operated by a soldier who is under cover well to the rear of the mine. When the mine explodes, the force of the explosion, which is to the rear of the pellet sheet, blows the ordnance forward and outward, into a 60-degree fan-shaped pattern of deadly steel pellets, ranging in height from one to six feet from the ground, and reaching a maximum effective range of about three hundred feet. The Claymore mine is almost impossible to detect if placed in grass or foliage. But it does have a flaw. The flaw lies in the human error of emplacing the weapon. In an alarming number of instances the mine has been emplaced *backward*. When the outside of the curved face is pointed to the rear, dire consequences may follow.

Human error is also found in the manufacturing process of the Claymore mine. For example, it is possible for the pellet sheet to be inserted against the *rear* face of the mine, instead of the forward face. If this should occur the plastic explosive that is poured into the mine will be inserted *forward* of the pellet sheet, and when the mine is exploded, if it has been properly emplaced, its pellets will fire to the rear. There are other manufacturing possibilities for error. If the tinfoil sheet of steel pellets should crumple in the process of placing it in the forward section of the mine, some of the explosive can seep forward of the crumpled section, and the detonation could send pellets in almost any direction. Another possibility for error exists where some of the pellets are dislodged or broken from the tinfoil sheet prior to placing the sheet in the forward section of the mine. Explosive material can thus seep through these holes and find its way to the front of the pellets.

Thus the Claymore mine is an exceedingly dangerous instrument. There is, unfortunately, no method by which infantrymen can take the mine apart prior to firing it to verify it against manufacturing error. The American soldier is taught simply to stick the mine into the ground with its curved, outward face toward the "enemy," to take cover and fire. Most of the time it works.

During my initial interview with Lieutenant Bloch, he explained the basic organization of the Grafenwoehr firing and safety organizations. He also explained an unorthodox "safety" concept that was utilized during the firing demonstration at Grafenwoehr—the "inconspicuous-safety-officer" concept—one that was nowhere discussed in the voluminous written instructions that were published by the officials in charge. It was a concept that all participants, save one, ultimately acknowledged as fully operable at Grafenwoehr. The only individual who professed no knowledge at all of this concept was Brigadier General Fox, the officer in charge of the safety organzation.

Shortly after World War II the army took a lesson from Hollywood, and decided to put on big-time, professionally staged firing demonstrations for the special viewing of prominent politicians

and rich taxpayers. In order to get the most out of these demonstrations, the army realized they had to be made interesting with
bits of comedy injected along with the serious gunplay. They had
to be fast-moving, with clocklike precision, and with no hurry-up-
and-wait routine. Foremost, the firing demonstration was to be a
show. These shows were to entertain as well as teach; they were to
leave the politicians and rich taxpayers in awe of army fire power
and at the same time impress them with the fact that the army
could put together a first-rate show.

For openers, a company of concealed infantrymen in front of
the spectator stands might open fire on several hundred balloons
and completely destroy them in less than a minute. Then a voice
might announce: "Ladies and gentlemen, there is a volley of 100
millimeter artillery fire coming in over your left shoulder at twenty-
five hundred yards which in three seconds will burst fifteen hundred yards to your right front in the vicinity of that disabled tank."
Three seconds later in comes the artillery and the tank is blown to
bits. The spectators are awed. Another announcer slices in with an
announcement that a ground trooper will fire a guided missile into
another disabled tank some fifteen hundred yards to the front of
the stands. The missile is fired and the audience watches as it
twists on and off course to its destination. Immediately in front of
the stands expert small-arms shooters are called upon to show how
well they can shoot. Trick shooters and clowns and more balloons
join the routine. An "intoxicated" member of the audience insists
on showing up the sharpshooters and is obligingly handed a machine gun. He shoots it from the hip, and pops all the balloons.
Next: "A soldier will emplace and fire a Claymore mine fifty yards
to your right. . . ."

Inherent in this type of demonstration is much practice. The
firing organization is responsible for writing the scenario and firing
the weapons. The safety organization, subject to the overall command of the firing organization, is responsible for the safety of all
weapons fired. An individual safety officer, in fact, is responsible
for each individual weapon fired. If a safety officer yells, "Cease-

fire!" the entire show halts while the unsafe condition is corrected. To eliminate "cease-fire" embarrassments, the army takes months of practice to perfect a major firing demonstration. Every flaw is ironed out in advance. There are dry runs and wet runs, and there are script changes and rechanges, and there are daily meetings between representatives of the firing and safety organizations to check and recheck every detail, and every change.

It was this big-show aspect of firing demonstrations that gave birth to the "inconspicuous-safety-officer" concept. To add realism to the show, years ago someone suggested keeping the safety officer inconspicuous, to keep him out of the view of the spectators in the stands. He would spoil the fun, ruin the timing, and leave the wrong impression with the audience. Hence the safety officer was ordered to ensure the safe firing of all weapons under his jurisdiction, but to do so *without coming into view of the spectators in the stands*. The orders to ensure the safe firing of weapons were delivered in writing; the orders to stay out of sight of the spectators were delivered orally.

Individual safety officers who receive these orders are usually first or second lieutenants. They do not refuse orders or question them. If the show proceeds without a hitch, and the spectators are awed and properly entertained, their superiors are most pleased to receive the credit for a marvelous show. But if something goes wrong and the spectators are ripped with seven hundred steel pellets from a Claymore mine while the air is filled with cries of "Medic! Medic!" heads are going to roll and someone is going to be court-martialed. The most likely candidate is the hapless safety officer who was given written orders to ensure that the Claymore mine was properly faced downrange prior to firing.

In the firing demonstration at Grafenwoehr on the date of the accident, Lieutenant Bloch was standing 152 feet directly to the rear of the Claymore mine moments before it was fired. He witnessed the emplacement. He saw the soldier take cover, he heard the announcer give the firing cue, and he saw the weapon fired. He was in telephonic communication with his immediate superior,

Major Williams, who was in an abandoned church tower 150 feet to his rear. Bloch, however, was not in telephonic communication with any member of the firing organization—but he was out of the view of the spectators in the stands. He was not in possession of fieldglasses and had been issued none. He was expected to "eyeball" the emplacement of the mine from 152 feet, an absolutely impossible task at that distance. Nothing was questioned by Major Williams, who did have fieldglasses. No member of the safety organization gave a positive all-clear or go-ahead sign to any member of the firing organization prior to the Claymore firing. The firing signal was given by the announcer: "Ladies and gentlemen, to your right flank, a Claymore mine will now be fired."

Had Bloch detected an unsafe condition he would have been expected to drop his telephone and run forward into the very teeth of the mine's most deadly range of fire, yelling "Cease-fire!" This was another safety concept in use at the firing demonstration that was not discussed in the written directives—the "cease-fire safety system" as opposed to the "positive safety system." The cease-fire safety concept permits the announcer to proceed full tilt with his firing cues, unless he is shouted down by a safety officer; the positive safety system requires the person giving the cue to receive a positive all-clear signal from a safety officer before giving the signal to fire each weapon fired during the demonstration.

While Major Williams did not originate the inconspicuous-safety-officer concept or the cease-fire safety system, both of which were in use at Grafenwoehr prior to the Claymore mine accident, he did not object to either of them, nor did he point out their dangerous potential to his subordinate safety officers. While Williams denied it, there was direct evidence from his control sergeant that Williams had given Bloch orders to stand by his telephone at all times and to keep it to his ear at all times. ("When I yell right flank I want you to answer, Right Flank!") When measured from its farthermost extension point toward the mine emplacement site, Bloch's telephone line permitted him to stand 152 feet from the mine, the exact spot where he was standing at the time of the blast.

Williams admitted that he passed on the inconspicuous-safety-officer concept to Bloch, and expected him to honor it, but he emphatically insisted that he expected him to do his job, even if it meant walking into the view of the spectators in the stands. This was also the stated belief of the safety director, General Fox, but Fox insisted that he did not know his safety officers were expected to stay out of the sight of the spectators in the stands in the first place.

Some of Fox's officers, however, swore that the inconspicuous-safety-officer concept was discussed in his presence, and that he was briefed on it in detail prior to the commencement of the firing demonstration. General Fox's chief assistant, Colonel Diamond, was also questioned on this point. During Diamond's long cross-examination at the Article 32 investigation he freely admitted that Lieutenant Bloch was standing in his proper place at the time of the Claymore blast. He testified that he himself had checked out his position before the signal to fire was given and that he was satisfied Bloch was standing where he was supposed to stand. He also admitted that Lieutenant Bloch had been in this position at all prior rehearsals, and that the position was satisfactory to both Williams and himself. To have stated otherwise, Colonel Diamond would have had to admit that he himself was not attending to his job at the demonstration. But Colonel Diamond was unsure whether his superior, General Fox, was aware of the inconspicuous-safety-officer concept prior to the Claymore mine blast. He stated that in his opinion he was aware of it, but added: "I cannot be sure."

Colonel Diamond also admitted that immediately following the Claymore mine accident, both the inconspicuous-safety-officer concept and the cease-fire safety system were junked and proper safety concepts were followed throughout the remainder of the firing program.

During the lengthy formal Article 32 investigative stage of the case, the defense was able to establish high-level negligence and buckpassing on the part of both the safety and the firing organizations. The soldier whom the firing organization had selected to fire the Claymore mine on the day of the demonstration had never fired one before. Two days before the accident this soldier was permitted to emplace several mines, but he did not fire any of them. The firing organization also changed the model of the Claymore mine from an M18 to an M18A1 without informing the safety organization of the change. The M18A1 model that was fired at the demonstration was a far more powerful weapon than the M18. It had *twice* the range of the former and *twice* the backblast danger area. Bloch had been instructed in writing to clear an area of only 150 feet to the rear of the M18 mine. The model that was fired at the demonstration, the M18A1, had a backblast danger area of 300 feet. Had Bloch been advised of the change in weapons, and had he cleared an area of 300 feet to the rear of the weapon, there is every likelihood that no one would have been hurt, as every person who was struck with a pellet was standing between 150 and 300 feet to the rear of the mine. The failure of communication between the firing and the safety organizations in regard to this change was almost unbelievable—but it was an established fact.

The most startling testimony of the entire Article 32 investigation, however, came from another direction. The *left-flank* safety officer, Second Lieutenant Joe W. Hammonds, who had nothing to do with the Claymore mine accident, stated that he received written orders to safety a self-propelled 155 mm howitzer that was located on the left flank in front of the spectator stands. Since the weapon was in front of the stands, he too was instructed by Major Williams to safety the weapon from a distance of forty-five to sixty feet—without exposing himself to the view of the spectators. The lieutenant furnished the investigating officer a written list of the reasons why this was impossible. He stated that without entering the cabin of the gun he could not check the seating of the projectile or check the fuse. He could not check the powder charge to ensure the correctness of the charge, nor could he check to see that the igniter pad faced to the rear. He could not ensure that a proper and safe deflection and quadrant elevation were placed on the sight, or that the bubbles on the sight were level and that the crosshairs of the sight were properly placed on the aiming stakes. The lieutenant had also been given written safety orders "to insure firing is conducted on the proper target." He testified that it was impossible for him to perform the latter requirement since he was not permitted to enter the cabin of the gun, and because the targets were fourteen hundred meters away and very close together and he was without binoculars. The lieutenant stated that from his position forty-five to sixty feet away from the gun, he could not tell if the weapon was aimed at any target.

Thus the defense investigation during the Article 32 stage of the case produced powerful facts in favor of Lieutenant Bloch. But the real clincher was to come from yet another direction—command influence. Experienced military defense counsel know that in any case involving a great deal of high-level command embarrassment there is going to be enormous pressure to prove that the command is clean. Thus, it was quite predictable that the army was not going to sit idly by on the side lines while a thorough and impartial investigation was conducted that pointed the finger of responsibility squarely at the artillery commander, General Fox. Nor would it relish an equal portion of the guilt being aimed at Colonel Diamond and Major Williams. On the other hand, it was predictable that it would be preferable to have a major portion of the guilt placed upon the shoulders of Lieutenant Bloch, a junior officer from the Twenty-fourth Infantry Division, and this is exactly what happened.

The corps commander ordered an immediate investigation of the accident, to commence on the very day of the incident. Three days later the VII Corps investigation was completed. The report placed the entire blame upon Lieutenant Bloch, who allegedly had failed to carry out the plain-language provision of his written orders, "to insure that the mine was facing downrange." There was nothing more. The report did not bring out any facts favorable to Lieutenant Bloch, nor did it bring out detrimental factors on the part of any other person involved in the firing demonstration. It was this report which convinced the corps SJA that charges should be placed against Bloch, and it was this report that he forwarded to General Rowny, the commanding general of the Twenty-fourth Infantry Division for "appropriate action." General Rowny, however, was made of sterner stuff. He did not accept the compliment. He administered a written reprimand to Lieutenant Bloch, but refused to prefer court-martial charges against him.

This action did not smooth the feathers of the corps commander. Rather than have it appear that no one was court-martialed for such an obvious act of negligence involving a Claymore mine, he directed his SJA and inspector general to visit the Twenty-fourth Division and to convince General Rowny of the virtue of bringing court-martial charges against Lieutenant Bloch. The meeting was conducted. The corps SJA opined that charges should be brought against Bloch, but General Rowny, very much laying his own military career on the line, refused.

As a result of the second refusal, the corps SJA gave the VII Corps report to the VII Corps chief of military justice, a major, and told him the corps commander wanted him to make an "inquiry" into the facts of the case. He was also told to determine if it was appropriate to bring court-martial charges against Lieutenant Bloch of the Twenty-fourth Infantry Division.

The VII Corps chief of military justice made his "inquiry" and arrived at the conclusion that court-martial charges were in order against Lieutenant Bloch. He drafted and signed charges. These charges were in turn handed to the corps SJA, who took them to the corps commander, who directed that they be forwarded to Lieutenant Bloch's battalion commander in the Twenty-fourth Division. Pursuant to the direction of the corps commander, Bloch's battalion commander was ordered to conduct an Article 32 investigation of the charges, and to return the completed report and recommendation directly to VII Corps.

Following the completion of the Article 32 investigation, which took three weeks to conduct, I, as Bloch's attorney, prepared a detailed brief setting forth the complete chain of circumstances surrounding the Claymore mine accident, including the action or lack of action on the part of VII Corps officers, particularly Brigadier General Fox, Colonel Diamond, and Major Williams. Pages 23 through 31 of the brief, however, were devoted to the subject of command influence. My brief in this regard began as follows:

> While it is with extreme displeasure that I make these allegations against a Corps Commander and a senior Judge Advocate, whose friendship and esteem I value, my duty as a lawyer, my oath as a military defense counsel, my responsibility to my client, and military case law require that these errors be alleged, and be alleged with appropriate vigor. . . .

It was with perverse pleasure that I omitted the phrase "my duty as an Army officer" from the above introduction. I followed the introduction with a detailed account of the corps commander's efforts and those of his SJA to persuade the Twenty-fourth Division commander to prefer charges against Lieutenant Bloch.

In military law an accuser cannot serve as the convening authority in the same case. An accuser is defined as anyone who signs charges or who directs anyone else to sign them. Also a convening authority who has any interest except an official interest in any case is automatically barred from acting as convening authority in the case. If it can be shown that a convening authority has a personal interest in a particular case he will be disqualified. The personal interests of the corps commander in the Claymore mine case were obvious. The accident happened within his command. It was highly publicized and he personally witnessed it. His subsequent actions in the case could be argued as reflecting a fear that he himself might be officially blamed for the accident, and that he sought the court-martial of a Twenty-fourth Infantry Division officer to divert blame from himself and his command.

Under the circumstances, I submitted that the corps commander and his SJA were the real accusers in the charges against Lieutenant Bloch, and that the use of the chief of military justice as the formal accuser was sham. I argued that the actions of the corps commander and his SJA in securing court-martial charges against Lieutenant Bloch after the Twenty-fourth Division commander, a general court-martial convening authority in his own right, had twice considered the matter and had twice refused to prefer charges against Lieutenant Bloch struck at the very heart of an independent military judicial process. Lastly, I submitted that the corps commander's directive, that the Article 32 investigation be returned directly to VII Corps headquarters for disposition, illegally precluded two major intermediate commanders from exercising their independent statutory authority to dismiss court-martial charges—namely, Bloch's battalion commander and General Rowny, the Twenty-fourth Infantry Division commander.

In preparing the brief I stenciled each page, something I had never done before in the military. Upon completion of the brief I printed 250 copies. Ten of these copies I mailed directly to the commanding general of VII Corps. I gave a stack of them to my immediate boss, the SJA at the Twenty-fourth Division, and I gave a large sampling of them to Lieutenant Bloch. Others I mailed to friends in the United States. The remainder I stacked neatly on a bookshelf next to my office desk in the division judge advocate office. During the conduct of the Article 32 investigation as it became more and more evident that the investigation was proceeding in Bloch's favor I began to receive unsolicited advice not to attack the corps commander personally in my pretrial brief. But in criminal cases it is never wise to withhold evidence favorable to your side—if you expect to win. I therefore included the attack against both the corps commander and his SJA in my brief. My reason for printing so many copies, and making such a generous distribution of them, was to convey the message that it was impossible to cover up this case, and that if any reprisal actions were taken against me an even further distribution of the briefs would be made.

But no reprisal action was made directly against me. My promotional prospects in the army were over. I purposely delayed signing the brief until the day I was promoted to lieutenant colonel, the last rank I would attempt to make in the army prior to my retirement. Thus I no longer cared about efficiency reports. No one said, "Well done," however, except Lieutenant Bloch and his wife. And there was an absolute silence from VII Corps.

Three weeks later there arrived a two-sentence directive. It simply stated that the charges against Lieutenant Samuel A. Bloch, Company C, Second Battalion, Nineteenth Infantry, Twenty-fourth Division, were dismissed. That was the end of the case.

10

The Cooks-McGuire Case:
Injustice and Extraordinary Writs

My final assignment in the army was as chief of military justice at an army headquarters, on the east coast of the United States, which I will leave unnamed. Upon leaving Germany I had requested a terminal assignment at Monterey, California. Thus when orders came through sending me to the east coast, I was not totally surprised. I had long since given up hope of receiving a gift horse from the military.

At this post, a year before I planned to retire from the military with twenty years' service, I ran into a colonel who was most intent on earning promotion to brigadier general. According to local gossipmongers, the colonel concerned was already "near knighted" by the secretary of defense, who had handpicked him for promotion. But the promotion was apparently delayed until the colonel underwent a dry run in the United States. He was first to command a newly activated Armored Cavalry Regiment at the post I had been assigned to. After a successful period of state-side command the colonel would move on to Vietnam, and promotion to brigadier general hopefully would follow in due course.

Once in command the colonel was a take-charge type. He left

nothing to chance. To prove himself worthy of promotion, he quickly established an iron discipline within his regiment; he also made it clear that all personnel under his command were to perform at top effectiveness. Whenever and however tested, his regiment was to perform second to none, with maximum accuracy, whether on the firing range or the tank gunnery course, or any other course or test the army could devise to sort out one commander's performance over another's. To better ensure maximum efficiency in unit tests, a system was developed whereby known inept soldiers—the poorly motivated, the below average, the general misfit—were "weeded out" of his regiment and eliminated from the army.

The "weeding out," at least in major part, was accomplished through the court-martial process. As the regimental commander, the colonel personally appointed special courts-martial that were to try all soldier defendants in his regiment for military or civilian offenses. The colonel's courts (at that time) could impose a maximum sentence of six months in jail and partial forfeiture of pay for a six-month period. The colonel himself chose what offenses to prosecute. As a regimental court-martial convening authority, he chose the prosecutors and defense counsel from his regiment (all of whom were nonlawyers). Also, he selected the court members (the jury) from his regiment. Every person involved was subject directly to his orders. Everyone concerned was also subject to his efficiency reports. One bad word from the colonel on an officer's efficiency report, and the officer's career in the army was almost ruined.

Defendants from the Armored Cavalry Regiment quickly flooded the local stockade on a variety of charges, ranging in severity from a few days AWOL to possession of marijuana. Once convicted, we found that a confined soldier from the cavalry regiment was soon visited by his troop commander, who would offer him an administrative discharge. If the soldier accepted the offer, the remaining portion of his confinement was remitted at once and he was released with a general discharge. Most soldiers accepted the offer, waived their rights to a hearing, and were thus quickly and quietly discharged from the army.

The first official complaint about the "weeding-out" process came from the post mental health office. Psychologists and other professional workers in that office who were charged with monitoring discharges of this nature were concerned that the regiment involved was grossly overworking its discharge prerogatives. Mental health officials fired complaints to my office, the military justice section, army headquarters. Other early complaints came from army chaplains and from stockade personnel themselves. I assigned these complaints to subordinate legal officers for investigation within my office. Their reports were made directly to me and they were shocking. The conviction rate in the colonel's regiment was approaching 100 percent, and the sentences imposed by his courts were almost invariably maximum or near-maximum sentences. Later we discovered that soldiers who were convicted in the colonel's court-martial jurisdiction and who declined the offer of a general discharge were marked men. After serving their sentences in the stockade, they would be returned to his regiment, where they quickly found themselves facing follow-up court-martial charges. An unbuttoned shirt pocket would bring a charge of being out of uniform, and if a soldier objected to this indignity, a charge of insubordination was added. Once again there would be a threat of a special court-martial, a conviction, and a maximum sentence. Most soldiers broke at this point. This time around, even the most stubborn would accept the offered administrative discharge and be drummed out of service. The regiment thus rid itself of another "misfit," another nonproducer, another soldier upon whom the regiment could not count to produce 100 percent efficiency in regimental tests.

This was the system. Along with Saturday afternoon drills and Sunday parades, it broke the will of most of the personnel—and it separated the regimental commander from the rest of his high-ranking competitors in the race for promotion to general-officer status. It was a calculated system that probably offered no real improvement whatever in the quality of the colonel's regiment. But it gave the commander the degree of notoriety that was desired, it separated him from the common herd, it afforded him a high profile. The colonel was court-martialing his enlisted men in wholesale fashion. And we received numerous allegations that the findings and sentences of courts-martial in the Armored Cavalry Regiment were dictated in advance of trial.

Despite the number of complaints received in the military justice section which I dutifully passed on to my superior, the army staff judge advocate (who was stationed at the same post), and despite the widespread allegations of illegal command influence that were raging throughout the regiment, no command action was taken by the army commander or by the army SJA to investigate these complaints. My own efforts to obtain hard evidence of the legal fraud in this regiment proved exceedingly difficult. While junior officers and enlisted men made oral complaints to me and to others in my office, none would put his complaints in writing. The Armored Cavalry Regiment was an individual replacement and small-unit pipeline to Vietnam. The personnel of the regiment feared Vietnam; and they feared shipment to Vietnam. The handful of Vietnam veterans within the regiment feared being placed on orders to return to Vietnam for a second tour. And all of the complainants feared the senior officers of the regiment, the true "lifers" who would support the command in the event of a showdown.

Thus the pot boiled and no one would step forward and make a formal accusation.

My reaction, as chief of military justice, was to direct every judge advocate officer who worked for me, about a dozen or so, to encourage complaints from the regiment. I also directed my counsel to assign themselves as defense counsel for any defendant from the cavalry regiment who requested legal counsel, without formal authorization or approval by higher authority. These counsel, in turn, successfully blocked several convictions in cases in which they served—but they were not able to gather the necessary elements of command conspiracy to prove illegal command influence within the regiment.

In November 1967 Captain Charles Bell, who was then chief defense counsel within my office, formally served written notice that he would refuse to review further convictions from the Armored Cavalry Regiment because he was morally certain that the cases were rigged. Thus he would not continue to approve a conviction merely because no legal error was reflected as such in the record of trial. At about the same time, the assistant post judge advocate (a captain) began keeping a diary in which he noted what he felt were excessive nonjudicial punishments that were approved in the regiment. Other judge advocates within my office angrily awaited the right case, hoping to get a clean shot at the Armored Cavalry Regiment.

Three weeks before I was to retire from the army, I got my chance to nail the Armored Cavalry Regiment. I received a telephone call at home from First Lieutenant Thomas McGuire. He had heard that I was seeking proof of the illegal control of the judicial processes within the cavalry regiment and said he was ready to give information of this nature. I told McGuire he was wasting his time unless he was willing to put his complaint in writing and swear to it. He said that was no problem.

McGuire then went into detail. He stated that he was serving two years' active duty in the Armored Cavalry Regiment as a tank platoon commander. Because he was a lawyer in civilian life, licensed to practice in Michigan, his commanders had selected him to prosecute special courts-martial in the regiment in addition to his regular duty. Recently out of law school, and only two months in the army, McGuire set about to prepare a particular case for trial, the case of *United States* v. *Cooks*. Cooks was an armored cavalry soldier charged with the possession of marijuana. As McGuire reviewed the evidence he discovered what he conceived to be an error fatal to the prosecution. Specifically, he believed that the seizure of marijuana from Cooks, which served as the basis of the charge against him, was gained by an illegal search. McGuire told me that he reported this fact to his regimental commander, and recommended that either the charges be dropped or that the case be postponed for a few days to permit him time to write a memorandum supporting the admissibility of the marijuana into evidence. According to McGuire, the colonel informed him that Cooks was guilty, that he would be tried on schedule as were all defendants within his regiment, that he would be convicted, and that legal technicalities did not concern him or his courts. When McGuire argued that Cooks could be convicted only upon the basis of legally admissible evidence, McGuire said the colonel reprimanded him and fired him on the spot as prosecutor.

I told McGuire that if what he told me was true, it was my opinion that the colonel had not only barred himself from acting as the convening authority in the case, but that he had violated Article 37 of the Uniform Code of Military Justice, which, in part, specifically provides that no court-martial convening authority "shall censure, reprimand, or admonish . . . any . . . counsel thereof . . . with respect to any . . . exercise of . . . his functions in the conduct of the proceedings."

I told the lieutenant that if he still desired to make the complaint I would assign him a full-time judge advocate defense counsel, and that I would direct counsel on my own authority to start an immediate investigation of illegal command-control activity in the regiment. I also explained that I could give him no assurance that the investigation would continue five minutes after its existence was reported to post officials, but that if he were willing to proceed on that basis I would be most happy to take his statement.

McGuire came to my office, and I assigned Captain Juan Keller, a legal officer on my staff, as defense counsel. No sooner had McGuire given his sworn statement than a second military defense counsel, Captain William Bish, a former member of the *Notre Dame Law Review* staff, entered triumphant. Working on his own, Bish had taken a statement from another officer in the Armored Cavalry Regiment, a Lieutenant William McKay, describing command manipulation of assigned (nonlawyer) defense counsel who were harassed and coerced into rapid trials within the regiment without time for preparation of their cases. McKay, who was due to be discharged from the army within a matter of days, had sought out Captain Bish to make a formal complaint. I assigned Bish to be defense counsel for McKay, and told him to work with Captain Keller in obtaining further proof of command influence within the regiment.

Then, only a few minutes later, a third judge advocate entered my office. He was Captain Larry Bird, who earlier had assigned himself to defend Specialist Cooks, upon Cooks's request. Bird asked me why Lieutenant McGuire was no longer prosecuting Cooks, and I told him. I then suggested to Captain Bird that if his client, Specialist Cooks, were to request the services of Judge Advocate Captains Keller and Bish, as additional counsel, I would appoint them. In the military, once a defense counsel is assigned to represent a defendant, nothing short of real military necessity can remove him without the consent of the client himself. I knew that once three lawyers were assigned to represent Specialist Cooks, no command official at our post or anywhere else possessed the authority to disengage the lawyers so assigned. Lieutenants McGuire and McKay officially were not defendants, and hence their "defense" counsel had no real official standing, but once I tied their defense counsel to the Cooks case, which was an ongoing criminal case, there could be no stopping the investigation of the Armored Cavalry Regiment.

Captain Bird left my office and returned a few minutes later to tell me that he and his client, Specialist Cooks, were officially requesting the services of Captains Keller and Bish as additional defense lawyers. As chief of military justice, it was a routine matter for me to assign judge advocate officers as defense counsel in military cases—one per case. This was certainly no routine case, and I immediately granted Captain Bird's request and assigned all three judge advocates to proceed with the defense of Specialist Cooks. I urged all three lawyers to use the two written statements of McGuire and McKay as wedges, and to question every officer and enlisted man in the regiment. I was convinced that once we could show personnel of the regiment written statements incriminating the command, others would be inclined to follow suit. Essentially I hoped to make McGuire's and McKay's two statements snowball into an avalanche.

I had another hunch. Knowing the character of the regimental commander, I did not feel he would long tolerate the presence of three military lawyers in his unit, actively interrogating the personnel of his command in an avowed effort to nail him. I believed we could "spook" the colonel into taking retaliatory action against the three defense counsel or myself. If we succeeded in this endeavor we would at least have maneuvered him into an untenable position as convening authority in the Cooks case, and possibly in future cases. The law requires that convening authorities must be impartial, and that those who appoint courts-martial and refer cases to them for trial must act with judicial restraint, the same as civilian judicial agencies. If we could prove that the colonel was not acting judicially or fairly in the conduct of a specific case, it might be possible to use that action to bar him from acting in all cases.

There was one additional detail needed to set the stage. I had to establish my own role in the Cooks case in a way calculated to infuriate command authorities to the point that they would conceivably react against me. I relied on the dual nature of the role of the chief of military justice to accomplish this. The duties of chief of military justice in every trial office in the army, at least on paper, include the supervision of *both* the prosecution and the defense sections of his office. In actual practice, however, it would be heresy for the chief of military justice in any office to align himself aggressively with the interests of the defense. Except in the most routine cases, no chief of military justice to my knowledge ever gave meaningful assistance to defense counsel. His supervisory role was always that of alter ego to the prosecution. I decided, therefore, to add further fuel to the flames by officially announcing to the army SJA that I was serving "as counsel" to the three defense lawyers defending Specialist Cooks.

After I explained my strategy to the three defense counsel, I reported the situation for the first time to my immediate superior, the army SJA. I gave him copies of the statements we had taken from McGuire and McKay, and I told him about the "arrangements" I had made. In an effort to bolster the case, I pointed out to my superior that the defense counsel in the Cooks case felt that judicial action in the regiment concerned was dead, that search-and-seizure authority could not be obtained from an "objective magistrate" within the regiment, because there was no one in the regiment capable of objective judgment. I asserted that I believed that command interference in the judicial process had voided every court-martial conviction from the unit involved since its activation. I told the staff judge advocate that in my opinion the command was guilty of "jury fixing," and that I was going to prove it. I told my superior that I had no intention at all of withdrawing from the case, in my role of counsel to the defense counsel, or of withdrawing my charges. The army SJA received these charges in silence. No questions were asked to firm up the charges, nor were suggestions made as how best to proceed to gather additional evidence. I was simply attacking the command, and the army would be on the other side, without question.

One of our first breaks in the case came when the regimental commander called McGuire into his office for a "report" on what McGuire had told the staff judge advocate office. During this session, McGuire was forced to stand at attention while he was interrogated. The same tactic was used against Lieutenant McKay. Both men promptly gave second statements to their assigned defense counsel, asserting they had been insulted and threatened. The next break came when we obtained written statements from better than twenty additional witnesses from the Armored Cavalry Regiment, including an eyewitness account of McGuire's initial confrontation with his regimental commander.

From past experience I knew the Armored Cavalry Regiment (and army headquarters) would react in several predictable ways. First, the command would attempt to defuse the threat. It would see that no witnesses gave further statements. Second, it would attempt to cover up any illegality involved in the Cooks case, and failing that, stop the investigation. Last, if all else failed, it would simply drop the charges against Specialist Cooks, and thereby moot the entire investigation. There could be a multitude of scenarios at each stage, but the plot would always be the same— and that was to protect the command at all times.

The cover-up stage was the first command reaction, and it moved into high gear. The case was immediately transferred from the Armored Cavalry Regiment to the post commander for trial. A judge advocate prosecutor was assigned to prosecute the case. New court members were selected by the post commander to sit on the jury. Most important, a very senior colonel was appointed to "investigate" the complaints of Lieutenants McGuire and McKay. The investigator was a full colonel, assigned to the inspector general's office from army headquarters, an office that was designed by the army to investigate complaints of wrongs by soldiers. The "IG's" investigation, of course, was to be a command-oriented, secret investigation, with the results going only to the army commander.

Local judge advocates advised me urgently that we were skidding on thin ice and playing a very dangerous game. I was asked, specifically, where was my "loyalty" to the staff judge advocate, and to the army commander. I declined comment to these individuals, but I was worried about the progress of our investigation. After the first bloom of success our efforts were dwindling. Personnel from the regiment were becoming more and more reluctant to give statements to defense counsel. After several days of very slow progress, I knew that the morale of defense counsel had sagged, and that we had to force a breakthrough.

I decided to raise the stakes. In the past I had been very cautious in discussing the progress of the defense investigation with the army SJA. Now I began to feed him glowing reports of progress. At the same time I directed defense counsel to redouble their efforts in the regiment. We knew that the regimental commander held daily meetings to keep pace with our investigation. We knew that command authorities in the regiment interrogated and intimidated many of our witnesses. Thus I asked defense counsel to be highly visible in the regiment, with notebooks in hand, and to give the appearance that they were taking many, many statements from Armored Cavalry personnel.

Our first major success came a day or so later. Defense counsel Captain Bird reported to the regimental adjutant that he was going to be in the regiment taking statements for the next several hours. The adjutant conferred with the sergeant major, and Bird was asked to see the regimental executive officer. He reportedly told Bird he couldn't permit him to take statements in the regimental area. Bird balked, and was called into the regimental commander's office. According to Bird, he was thereupon told by the regimental commander that he would not take statements in the regiment. This was backed up by a telephone call to none other than the army staff judge advocate, who told Bird if he wished to interview witnesses he should request them by name from the regimental adjutant, and the witnesses would be sent to his office for interview.

This procedure was in violation of the *Canons of Professional Ethics* of the American Bar Association, which provide that counsel in civil and criminal cases (which include military cases) shall have uninhibited access to all witnesses and, specifically, that they shall not have to resort to intermediaries to interrogate potential witnesses. We felt we were making progress.

The next day was Saturday, and of the ten witnesses from the regiment requested by Bird, only one showed up. On Saturday afternoon we decided on another confrontation with the regimental commander. I asked Captain Bish to report to the regiment and proceed to interview anyone who would talk to him. His reluctance was understandable, but Bish agreed to go. That afternoon he reported to the regimental adjutant and advised him that he was going to interview witnesses from the Second Squadron. Later that afternoon a very discouraged Captain Bish called me at home. He said it was difficult to find anyone to talk to, that virtually nothing was being accomplished, and that he did not believe anyone was going to order him out of the regiment. He asked if he could leave. I asked him please to remain for the rest of the day, and to interview the telephone poles if necessary. Bish stayed in the area.

That evening, after Captain Bish had returned to his quarters, the army staff judge advocate called him on the telephone and gave him an order. He was told that henceforth all defense counsel on the Cooks case were to stay out of the Armored Cavalry area, period. The following Monday morning, the staff judge advocate repeated this order to all defense counsel and to myself. We were told to request witnesses by name, and the witnesses would report to our office for interview. Of course we objected to this approach. We stated that we did not wish to name our witnesses because the command would intimidate them before they got to our office and thereby thwart our investigation. But we accepted the order, and that morning submitted a list of witnesses to the regimental adjutant. It was arranged that the witnesses would report to the defense counsel for interview at fifteen-minute intervals throughout the day.

At 4:00 p.m. the same day I called Captain Bish and asked him how many of the scheduled witnesses from the Armored Cavalry Regiment had reported for defense interview that day, and he replied that none had shown up. I asked him to meet me in the staff judge advocate's office with a list of the witnesses who had failed to appear. Bish and I reported there, and told the SJA that no witnesses had reported for interview. I asked the staff judge advocate to pick up the telephone and direct the regimental adjutant to get the witnesses to our office. The colonel shook his head and refused to make the telephone call. Bish then announced that he would personally deliver the list to the adjutant, and departed.

When Bish arrived at the regiment he was met by the adjutant, the regimental executive officer, and the regimental commander. The regimental commander told Bish that he had been assured by the army commander that "you people" would be kept out of "my area." The colonel refused to accept Bish's list of witnesses. Instead, he called the army staff judge advocate and told him to order Bish out of the regiment. The staff judge advocate did as he was told, and Bish picked up his list of witnesses and left. The following morning the staff judge advocate ordered defense counsel, in my presence, immediately to cease interviewing *all* witnesses from the Armored Cavalry Regiment concerning the issue of command influence, either in or out of the regimental area. He added that typed statements ready for signature were not to be signed.

The colonel attempted to justify his actions on the basis that the Cooks case was in abeyance while the IG investigated the issue of command influence in the cavalry regiment. When the SJA and I were alone, I advised the colonel that no one could lawfully order defense counsel to cease and desist while they were investigating pending court-martial charges. I also told the colonel that the Cooks case had just jumped from the cover-up stage to the dead stage, as there could never be a successful prosecution of the case in view of his order to defense counsel.

While the defense counsel and I knew for practical purposes we had won the Cooks case, we had one more detail to accomplish. We were racing against time preparing a writ to the United States Court of Military Appeals, documenting everything that had occurred in the Cooks case. Our biggest problem, as we saw it, was to complete the writ and file it at the court *before* the army mooted the entire issue by dismissing the court-martial charges against Specialist Cooks. In our writ we requested the Court of Military Appeals to order the secretary of the army, the army commander, the army staff judge advocate, and the commanding officer of the Armored Cavalry Regiment to permit defense counsel to investigate the issue of command influence in or out of the regimental area. To substantiate our request we attached to the writ every statement taken in the case. Our purpose was simply to publicly document the case.

The writ was filed on July 26, 1968, and, as we expected, the court denied the writ, but denied it without prejudice to return to the court following the completion of the trial. This gave the kiss of death to the army's case, because it meant that if a conviction was had in the case, counsel could then litigate the issue before the Court of Military Appeals. We also knew from past experience that the army seldom litigated its own alleged dishonesty in an open, public court-martial. But the pot continued to boil. The IG attempted to interview the three defense counsel several days later, and this prompted a second writ to the Court of Military Appeals. Once again the entire matter was detailed for public-record purposes by defense counsel, but before the court could act on the second writ, the army dismissed the court-martial charges against Specialist Cooks, and mooted the entire issue of command influence in the Armored Cavalry Regiment. At the same time the army administratively withdrew the colonel's authority to convene subsequent trials by court-martial (thereby preventing the issue from being litigated in future cases from the cavalry regiment), and shortly thereafter the colonel was transferred to Vietnam.

Ordinarily the case should have ended at this point. But there was a sequel. I had extended my stay in the army some thirty days to complete the Cooks case, but about two months after I retired I received an emergency telephone call from Lieutenant Thomas McGuire, the young army officer who had initiated the complaint against his regimental commander. McGuire told me that he had just received a rotten efficiency report from the Armored Cavalry Regiment, which recommended that he not be promoted to captain along with his peers. It was signed by personnel loyal to the departed commander. They depicted McGuire as disloyal, deficient in character, integrity, and judgment, and as possessed of a "quixotic urge to serve his idea of justice." He was also accused in his efficiency report of making a *false* complaint of command influence against his regimental commander. Along with this adverse report, he was ordered to Vietnam.

My first reaction to this violation of Article 37 of the Uniform Code of Military Justice, which prohibits command reprisal against court-martial counsel, was to file a writ with the Court of Military Appeals, asking either that McGuire's shipment to Vietnam be enjoined, or that the offending efficiency report be removed from his files. Once again we prepared a writ to include every detail from the Cooks case, and once again asked the Court of Military Appeals to use its power to stop the practice of command influence in the court-martial process. But the court denied the writ.

We also released the story to the public press. *The Washington Post* ran the story under an inch-high headline. It was headlined across page one of Lieutenant McGuire's hometown newspapers, together with photographs. The comments of McGuire's commanders from his efficiency report, stating that he was "disloyal, undependable, impulsive, immature [and] of doubtful loyalty, integrity or stability under stress" were quoted. Then McGuire's acid comment was quoted: "How would you like someone like that to lead your son in combat?"

The press rehashed the details of the Cooks case, and McGuire's return blast: "Either I'm as bad as they say I am, or the efficiency report is a phony, rendered in spite against me." The army threw in the sponge at this point. It could not be made to appear publicly that it was shipping misfits to Vietnam to lead American soldiers in combat. Thus the army administratively withdrew McGuire's offending efficiency report. He was shipped to Vietnam on schedule and ultimately was promoted to captain along with his contemporaries. He is currently practicing law in Detroit, Michigan.

11

The My Lai Trials:
Red and Green Lights

An analysis of military court-martial practice would hardly be complete without a discussion of the My Lai cases. I was not professionally involved in these cases, other than as a writer on military law; but I attended most of the Calley court-martial trial and interviewed counsel and court personnel in several other trials, and closely followed all of them in the press. My treatment of these cases will be related solely to the question of command influence, and the command manipulation of the Calley trial, and the trial of Calley's two superiors, Captain Ernest Medina and Colonel Oran Henderson.

In June of 1969 Lieutenant Calley had been returned to Fort Benning, Georgia, for the purpose of standing trial by United States Army general court-martial for the premeditated murder of over a hundred unarmed and unresisting Vietnamese civilians on March 16, 1968, in the subhamlet of My Lai 4, in the Quang Ngai province of South Vietnam. On September 5, 1969, Calley was officially charged with the wholesale murder of the citizens of My Lai, but the story was slow to break in the press. Finally, on November 12, Seymour Hersh, an independent journalist generally credited with breaking the My Lai massacre in the American press, published an account of the massacre that was carried in thirty newspapers.

The story picked up momentum. On November 20, several days before the first scheduled pretrial hearing in the case against Lieutenant Calley, and over the objection of the army, the *Cleveland Plain Dealer* published former army photographer Ronald L. Haeberle's photographs of the massacre. Although army efforts to block the spreading publicity of the massacre were failing, the My Lai incident was yet to stun America. Several days later, however, Seymour Hersh uncovered Paul Meadlo, a former soldier from Calley's Charlie Company, and within a matter of hours Meadlo told the story of the My Lai massacre on nationwide TV.

Meadlo told a startled America that after his group of soldiers rounded up men, women, and children at My Lai, Lieutenant Calley, his platoon commander, said "You know what to do with them, don't you?" Meadlo replied that he did, thinking that Calley meant only for his men to guard the people, but when Calley returned ten minutes later he asked, "How come you ain't killed them yet? I want them dead." According to *Time* magazine, Meadlo said that Calley started shooting the people, and told him to do likewise. "I poured four clips [sixty-eight shots] into them. I might have killed 10 to 15 of them." Meadlo then described a second execution at a drainage ditch east of the village of My Lai. "And then they had about 70–75 people all gathered up by a ravine, so we threw ours [seven or eight additional Vietnamese] in with them and Lieut. Calley told me, 'Meadlo, we got another job to do.' And so he walked over to the people, and he started shooting. We just pushed them off and started using automatics on them."

America was stunned. Then in rapid succession came more interviews with veterans of My Lai and even more shocking accounts of the tragedy. The number of victims soared to over five hundred —even the infants were not spared. *Life* magazine quoted Private Jay Roberts: "Just outside the village there was this big pile of

bodies. This really tiny kid—he only had a shirt on, nothing else—
he came over to the pile and held the hand of one of the dead. One
of the G.I.s behind me dropped into a kneeling position thirty
meters from the kid and killed him with a single shot." Secretary
of the Army Stanley Resor showed Haeberle's color photographs
of the massacre to the Senate and House Armed Services committees.

"A simplistic, deliberate act of inhumanity. . . . One of the
darkest days in American history," responded Pennsylvania's
Richard Schweiker. Ohio's Stephen Young said he had seen a
picture of a young woman begging not to be shot, while a child
clung to her neck. He called the massacre "an abominable atrocity." A White House statement called the massacre "abhorrent to
the conscience of all the American people." Defense Secretary
Melvin Laird said he was "horrified." Secretary of the Army Stanley Resor termed the story "appalling." Mississippi Senator Stennis, chairman of the Senate Armed Services Committee, said he
was "shocked."

President Richard Nixon, who had known of the My Lai massacre since April 1969, and who probably had directed Calley's
court-martial in August and again in September of 1969, publicly
announced on December 8 that My Lai "certainly" appeared to be a
massacre, and "under no circumstances was it justified." *Life*
magazine went further. It purchased the grisly pictures of My Lai
from photographer Haeberle and published them, the single most
damning indictment of America ever printed. Women, children,
old men, and babies lay slaughtered before the eyes of a startled
world, a horrible massacre that could not be denied by the
American government. In its own eyes America lost its innocence
with the publication of these pictures, and First Lieutenant William Laws Calley, Jr., a college dropout and OCS graduate, red-
faced and slight in stature, only 5 feet three inches in height and
weighing but 130 pounds, was selected by officialdom to answer
for America's shattered image.

The first major issue to be resolved in Calley's pretrial hearing

at Fort Benning, Georgia, concerned itself with the mountain of
pretrial publicity that the case had generated in the American
press. If a defendant in a criminal trial is convicted in the press
prior to trial, and if the press "conviction" prejudices his court
trial, the entire process of justice is a sham. The right of the public
to know the facts cannot, legally, extend this far. Military Judge
(Colonel) Reid Kennedy handled this portion of the pretrial issues
with dispatch. With an overflow demand for press seats at the trial,
he ordered a reporter whose newspaper had most frequently violated his ban against interviewing prospective witnesses to leave
the courtroom and not return. The press got the message, and the
interviewing of prospective witnesses all but stopped.

The second major issue to be resolved at the pretrial hearing,
and by far the more important, was that of command influence.
Unfortunately, it was not as easily resolved as the first. The
command-influence issue dealt with the actions of the president of
the United States, the secretary of state, the secretary of defense,
the secretary of the army, and numerous congressmen and senators, where these individuals branded the My Lai massacre as an
atrocity shocking to the conscience of all Americans. Specifically,
did this condemnation of the incident affect the decision of subordinate army officers in resolving to court-martial Lieutenant
Calley? Did the words of the president of the United States, in
which he donounced the tragedy, directly or even indirectly,
amount to an order to army subordinates to court-martial Calley
for mass murder? To the military mind, which is a product of a
tightly controlled military system, callous remarks of the president
or other high officials relating to a specific case could be translated
to mean hang the defendant, evidentiary problems to the contrary
notwithstanding. Thus defense counsel in Calley's pretrial hearing
at Fort Benning were to address themselves to whether the decision to court-martial Calley was independently made by subordinate commanders at Fort Benning, as our law requires, or whether
it was a decision dictated from the top down, a command-controlled
decision—an illegal decision.

Under military law, if a higher commander directs a subordinate commander to sign charges against an individual or to court-martial someone already accused, he violates Article 37 of the Uniform Code of Military Justice in that he has illegally "influenced the action of a convening authority." In such a situation, under the provisions of Articles 1 (11), 22, and 23 of the Uniform Code, the charges would have to be referred to a still higher authority for disposition, as both intermediate commanders concerned are technical "accusers" in the case, and are precluded by law from referring such charges to trial themselves. The purpose of these safeguards is to assure a serviceman a fair trial before a court-martial none of whose members might have been selected by a convening authority who was personally involved in the case, or who had directed a subordinate to prefer charges, or by a convening authority who was bent upon pleasing a superior officer in referring a case to trial. In the Calley pretrial hearing the major thrust of the defense was that the president of the United States ordered the army to prefer charges against Calley and to try him by general court-martial. If this allegation were true the net effect of the president's order would preclude Calley's trial by military court-martial, as the president would in essence be the "accuser" in the case, and there is, of course, no "superior competent authority" above the president of the United States to act on court-martial charges. This issue thus reached the ultimate in command-influence impropriety.

George Latimer, former judge on the Court of Military Appeals and chief civilian defense counsel for Lieutenant William Laws Calley, made his first appearance in Calley's defense at a pretrial hearing on December 16, 1969, at Fort Benning, Georgia. Soft-spoken and timid in appearance, "Judge" Latimer was a white-haired gentleman of the bar. He did not engage in the rough-and-tumble tactics frequently used by common practitioners of criminal law. From the very beginning it was necessary to provide him with a microphone for the press corps even to hear his voice while addressing the court and witnesses.

Kicking off the command-influence issue at the pretrial hearing, Latimer observed that *Time* magazine of December 12, 1969, reported that Secretary of Defense Melvin Laird, following a full-scale investigation of the My Lai incident in the spring of 1969, reported to the president in August that "we would have to court-martial Calley for murder," and that the president told him "to go right ahead." Latimer also objected to the comments of the president and other officials to the effect that a "massacre" had in fact occurred, and that the tragedy was "in direct violation not only of the United States policy but also abhorrent to the conscience of all military people."

At this point military defense counsel, Major Kenneth Raby, asked about the "strange looking machine" in the office of the Fort Benning staff judge advocate. Judge Kennedy shared the office of the Fort Benning SJA, and the strange-looking machine was a Xerox Telecopier, set up especially for the Calley court-martial. Major Raby asked Kennedy point-blank if copies of the Calley pretrial hearing record were being sent to Washington daily on this machine, and Kennedy answered, "Yes." Judge Kennedy had permitted this, despite the illegal-command-influence allegations that the president of the United States, acting through his secretary of defense and the army's chain of command, had illegally directed Fort Benning officials to prefer mass murder charges against Lieutenant Calley. Kennedy surely knew that prospective witnesses in command-influence allegations are not usually afforded access to the trial record prior to their testimony, nor to a daily briefing from the judge advocate general of the army on the developments of the trial. Briefings of this nature add nothing to the appearance of justice. At worst they lead to perjured testimony.

On January 20, 1970, Mr. Latimer formally demanded that Judge Kennedy subpoena necessary witnesses to prove the president's command influence in the case. Specifically, he asked that Secretary of Defense Laird, Secretary of the Army Resor, and Army Chief of Staff General Westmoreland be subpoenaed and required to give sworn testimony as to their actions after receiving

President Nixon's direction to court-martial Calley for murder in August 1969. Kennedy refused to issue the summons at that time, but instead directed the prosecutor to "rebut any possible influence upon Fort Benning officials." He said that after all the evidence was submitted he would then determine whether to call the witnesses requested by Mr. Latimer.

Prosecutor Captain Aubrey Daniel called his first witness on this issue, Colonel Robert M. Lathrop, staff judge advocate at Fort Benning. Lathrop, testifying in the pretrial hearing, stated that knowledge of the massacre first came to his attention in early August 1969. At that time he read a statement of Paul Meadlo's, and several days later a Colonel Wilson from the inspector general's office in Washington, D.C., came down and briefed several officials at Fort Benning. Lathrop subsequently sent a member of his office to interview Mr. Meadlo, and additional data began to filter into Benning. Colonel Lathrop said that "we were drafting specifications [charges] about this time," and that he went to Washington to get assistance from the office of the judge advocate general of the army in this regard. He denied, however, that he received "other instructions" in Washington. It was after he returned to Fort Benning that he received what was later described as a "red light" in the Calley case. The call came from Colonel William Chilcoat, chief of military justice, Department of the Army, who ordered: "Do nothing until you hear from us."

Lathrop testified that Chilcoat gave no reason for setting up a "red light" in the Calley court-martial process. He stated that this was in late August or early September. On September 4 he received a "green light" from Colonel Chilcoat stating in effect, "It's all yours." Lathrop again swore that Chilcoat gave no reason. Lathrop passed the information to Colonel Lon Marlowe, the commanding officer of the student brigade at Fort Benning, where Calley was assigned. "I had called Colonel Marlowe when I first got the [stop-order] call from Colonel Chilcoat, and had passed on that message to him. Then when I got the green light, as we refer to it—that is, 'OK Fort Benning, the case is yours to do with as you wish,'—I passed that on to Colonel Marlowe."

The witness was asked to recite the next event in the Calley case. He replied: "The charges were preferred on the fifth of September."

Major General Orwin Clark Talbott, commanding general, Fort Benning, Georgia, was called to the witness stand by Captain Daniel. He testified that he assumed command at Fort Benning on September 10, several days after charges were preferred against Lieutenant Calley. His major interest in the case was to see that Calley was fairly treated, and given meaningful work prior to his trial. He stated that he received no instructions on the disposition of the charges, and that he referred the charges to trial by general court-martial solely on the basis of the information that was presented at the Article 32 investigation.

On cross-examination, Talbott speculated that President Nixon might have been consulted on the case. The case was sent to "San Clemente," but General Talbott testified he did not know this as a matter of fact. He again affirmed that he had not talked to anyone in Washington on the case, that he did not lecture the court members (the prospective jurors) on the nature of their duties, but that he did personally select each member of the panel from the membership of his command. Talbott also testified that he read Secretary of Defense Laird's comments to the president ("We'll have to refer this case to trial"), but that he read it long after he had in fact referred the charges against Lieutenant Calley to trial by general court-martial. Asked if he was aware of the copying machine that had been set up in the staff judge advocate's office, Talbott replied that it was installed to enable the SJA and his counterpart in Washington, D.C., to communicate "conveniently" on the case.

Brigadier General Oscar E. Davis, acting commanding general of Fort Benning, Georgia, at the time charges were preferred against Lieutenant Calley, testified he did not receive any instruction from higher headquarters in the Calley case, and that he did not pass any instructions to a subordinate headquarters. He did not direct anyone to prefer charges against Lieutenant Calley, nor did he discuss the case with the accuser, Lieutenant Colonel Henry E. Vincent.

General Davis was asked if he knew the president of the United States had been consulted on the case. The general replied that he did, but added: "I don't recall if that was just before I took action or not, but I recall that the President was quoted on TV as having made some statement . . . regarding this particular case." He added, however, that he was not aware of any action by General Westmoreland.

Colonel Lathrop, the Fort Benning staff judge advocate, was recalled to the stand on February 10, 1970, and stated that he received no instructions from the president of the United States on the Calley case prior to September 5, the date charges were preferred. He admitted that he was told the president had been briefed on the case in San Clemente, California, and that he was advised of this fact by either Colonel Chilcoat or Colonel O'Donald, of the judge advocate general's office. He stated that he had talked to Chilcoat from the very beginning. He admitted that Chilcoat's order not to proceed any further in the processing of the Calley case (the "red light") was an unusual order—but he insisted that Chilcoat gave no reason for the order. It was Chilcoat who ordered the installation of the electronic equipment—a Xerox Tele-copier—in his office. Lathrop said he had never heard of such equipment being installed anywhere in the Judge Advocate General's Corps prior to the Calley trial. The machine, Lathrop testified, could transmit entire documents to Washington, and was used to transmit the Calley record of trial to Washington daily—before the record was authenticated.

Colonel Lathrop testified that at first he refused to install the machine. "I was told they wanted it. I said, 'I'm not going to send that transcript up unless I get a written directive to do so.' I got the written directive and I sent the transcript."

"You thought it was wrong, didn't you?" Latimer asked.

"I did," Lathrop replied.

Lieutenant Colonel Henry E. Vincent, executive officer of the school brigade, Calley's formal accuser, testified that on September 5, 1969, he preferred charges against Lieutenant Calley for murdering 107 Vietnamese. Vincent swore he received no outside influence of any kind, and that he preferred charges against Lieutenant Calley because "there was sufficient evidence to warrant trial by court-martial." His only instruction was "just to review the evidence, and if appropriate, prefer charges or determine if they should be preferred."

On cross-examination he swore that he had made up his mind to prefer charges against Calley on September 4 or 5, and that he had *not* been told of President Nixon's interest in the case at any time—or of General Westmoreland's.

Captain William R. Hill, who had signed additional charges against Calley alleging the murder of two Vietnamese (approximately a week after Vincent's original charges were signed on September 5), testified that he was made aware of presidential interest in the case on September 3 or 4. He also contradicted Lieutenant Colonel Vincent's assertion that he (Vincent) was not told of President Nixon's interest in the case.

Captain Hill testified there was talk about flipping a coin to see who would sign charges against Lieutenant Calley if the president vetoed the project. "Well, I think that all of us were a little frustrated that the incident had become politically oriented. We felt and we were in fear that it would not be charged because of the political repercussions which could result. . . . We talked about this more or less as a rebellion against any decision they might make not to prefer charges."

Latimer asked Hill if he discussed the president's involvement with Colonel Marlowe.

Hill answered: "Yes, sir. I think it was on 5 September, the day we charged him. I am not sure. Colonel Marlowe found out independently from another source that this matter had gone to the

President. The way it came up, . . . Colonel Marlowe said: 'You know this thing has gone to the President?' I said 'Yes.' I wanted to advise him that regardless—regardless of the President's action, we had the right to prefer charges."

Hill said that Marlowe (who was the immediate superior of Lieutenant Colonel Vincent) replied that "he knew he was free to do what the President wanted or not and if he didn't do what the President said, he would be either a fool or a jackass, and he was inclined to believe the latter." Captain Hill was asked if Colonel Vincent (the accuser in the original charges against Calley) was present at this conversation. Hill replied that he was.

"At the time the comment was made?" Latimer asked.

"That's correct," Hill answered.

Shortly after Colonel Marlowe made this comment about doing what the president wanted (and after the "green light" had been received at Fort Benning), Colonel Vincent made his decision to formally accuse Lieutenant Calley of over a hundred counts of first-degree murder.

It will be recalled that Vincent had sworn in his testimony at the pretrial hearing that he did not know of the president's interest in the Calley case at *any* time, and that he received no outside influence of any kind in preferring charges against Lieutenant Calley. But Captain Hill's testimony placed him in Marlowe's office while the subject of presidential influence was being discussed, on the very day that he signed charges against Lieutenant Calley. Yet neither counsel for the government nor the defense nor the trial judge thought it expedient to return Vincent to the witness stand and question him further on this contradiction in testimony—i.e., whether he had been influenced by the views of the president of the United States in preferring court-martial charges against Lieutenant Calley.

The final pretrial hearing on this aspect of the case took place a few days later, on February 12, 1970. Judge Kennedy announced: "I went over the record in considerable detail last night and reread the motions filed by the defense for the requested statements of

Secretary Laird, Resor and General Westmoreland. At this time, I am going to deny those requests for subpoenas on procedural grounds that they don't comply with the law in setting out with specificity what the defense wants." (Kennedy was resorting to legalism on this point. The *Manual for Courts-Martial* requires defense counsel to set forth what desired witnesses will testify to if called. If he has not interviewed the witnesses, it is most difficult for him to set forth with "specificity" what such witnesses will testify to if they are called as witnesses.) Kennedy continued with the basis of his ruling: "I also say that I am satisfied [on the issue of command influence] that the government has met the burden of going forward with the evidence."

Judge Kennedy either missed the point or dodged the issue. In command-influence law the very appearance of command control is as much outlawed as the proven fact. It is almost beyond reasonable argument that the appearance of command control in the preferring of court-martial charges against Lieutenant Calley, and the referring of those charges to trial by general court-martial, were established by the evidence at the pretrial hearing in Calley's court-martial. Presidential direction to a secretary of defense to charge a military defendant with wholesale mass murder of men, women, children, and babies adds up to the strongest example of command influence possible. The appearance of evil is indeed substantial when (1) this direction is followed by various statements of high-level government officials condemning the My Lai massacre as an atrocity shocking to all Americans, (2) "stop" and "go" orders are relayed up and down an obedient military chain of command, and the accuser puts his pen to charges almost immediately after receiving the "go" order, (3) the immediate military superior to the accuser, shortly before charges were signed, engaged in a discussion in the presence of the accuser concerning the virtue of obeying the president's wishes relative to the signing of charges in the case, and (4) it is followed by the installation of a Xerox Telecopier at Fort Benning over the objection of the local staff judge advocate, for the purpose of relaying copies of the pretrial hearing record to Washington, D.C., where the record could be read by potential command-influence witnesses.

For Judge Kennedy to have ruled that the government had dispelled the appearance of evil under these circumstances by calling the military subordinates involved and having them disclaim any undue influence upon themselves comes close to judicial nonsense. Under the circumstances, Kennedy's failure to summons the principals involved—the secretary of defense, the secretary of the army, and General Westmoreland—and subject them to defense cross-examination makes it impossible to determine what role they played in bringing Calley to trial.

But there were other violations of Calley's rights of even greater significance—in both his own trial and the follow-up trials of his superiors.

12

The Calley Conviction:
The Cover-Up

On Monday, March 16, 1971, following the completion of testimony in the Calley court-martial, counsel for both sides addressed the military jury in final argument. Three years to the day subsequent to the My Lai massacre and after the longest court-martial in American history, Captain Aubrey Daniel, boyish, handsome, pure in heart, and two years senior to Lieutenant Calley, stood almost immobile in front of a military jury at Fort Benning, Georgia, and in dull but rapid-fire language hammered out his case against the hapless lieutenant from Miami, Florida.

"There was a village named My Lai 4, and it was there on March 16, 1968, when Lieutenant Calley landed there. . . . They received no fire at all. None. They found no armed Viet Cong. They found only unarmed men, women, children and babies. . . ."

Only four years out of law school, Daniel in final summation was lacking in color. As a trial practitioner, he was thorough, detailed, complete. But as a speaker he had not yet found himself. He could not entertain—he could not keep his audience spellbound. He could not re-create the momentum or the drama of his witnesses' testimony. But he hit obvious points. He emphasized that there was no combat at My Lai; that there were no Viet Cong units in the village at all; and that there was absolutely no armed resistance to the American attack. References to babies and unarmed women and children were sprinkled through his delivery. The fact that Calley in his own testimony did not deny he was at the ditch where many of the victims were massacred was stressed: "There is no dispute between the prosecution and the defense that the accused came to the irrigation ditch . . . and that a group of Vietnamese was placed in the ditch and was shot by the accused's platoon and by the accused himself."

Daniel recounted his statistics against Calley. He recalled names like Sledge, Dursi, Conti, Grzesik, Turner, Olsen, Hall, Maples. . . . They were men who testified against Calley. They were from all parts of the country. They had no motive for lying. Eleven former GIs testified as to how victims were rounded up and delivered to Calley for execution. Twenty witnesses testified they saw the bodies of the Vietnamese victims along the north-south trail south of My Lai. Thirteen witnesses identified prosecution exhibit 12, a large color picture of these victims. Twenty-five bodies appear in that picture—men, women, children, and babies. Twelve members of Calley's platoon put him at the ditch, where upward of seventy Vietnamese were slain. "That's half of Calley's platoon. He can't refute he was at the ditch. Do you think he could get on the stand and deny he was there?"

Daniel scored Calley's defense of obedience to superior orders. Calley in his courtroom testimony had attempted to justify all his actions at My Lai, Daniel asserted, on the theory "that he was doing his duty, that he was following *orders*, orders received from his company commander, Captain Ernest Medina."

But there is a law of war, Daniel stated, that protects those who are noncombatants. "These persons have the right to be treated as prisoners of war until they are released or tried." But summary execution is forbidden, Daniel insisted. And then, touching very close to the heart of Calley's defense, he added that even if Calley *did* receive an order to execute his prisoners, the order would have been illegal, and that Calley, as a reasonable man, would have known it was illegal and that he had no right to obey it.

"The obedience of a soldier is not the obedience of an automaton," Daniel asserted, paraphrasing Judge Kennedy's anticipated instructions to the court-martial jury which had been furnished to both counsel in advance of their delivery. "If a soldier puts on the American uniform, he is still under an obligation to think, to respond not as a machine but as a reasonable person, to respect life, to make moral decisions. . . ."

"A reasonable man," Daniel stated, speaking precisely, "should know that any order to gather up 30 people at that trail intersection, some of them women, children and babies, and summarily execute them is an unlawful order and should not be obeyed." The same was true, he asserted, of placing over seventy unresisting people in an irrigation ditch "like a bunch of cattle" and killing them. Such an order cannot be justified, he said. "A reasonable man knows an order of that nature is illegal."

Then Daniel came to Medina's personal defense. He insisted that Calley received no orders to wipe out "unarmed and unresisting noncombatants." Calley had been told only that he was and should expect to meet "a fierce, determined and armed enemy." Calley was running that show, Daniel stated, "on his own initiative and under his own direction." His platoon members did not kill until they received his orders—not Medina's. Meadlo, crying as he shot Vietnamese children, did not shoot them because Captain Medina ordered him to shoot them—but because *Lieutenant Calley* ordered him to shoot them.

Daniel made mocking reference to Latimer's defense psychiatrists. These witnesses, he stated, would have you believe that Calley was suffering from a "transitory mental impairment" at My Lai, an impairment that would preclude Calley from having the capacity to premeditate. But, Daniel asserted, those same psychiatrists admitted that Calley was mentally alert enough to know that when he pointed his M-16 at someone and pulled the trigger, the victim would die. All you have to have for premeditated murder,

Daniel emphasized, was intent to kill. And one of Calley's psychiatrists stated that Calley was capable of forming an intent to kill at My Lai. "You don't have to be a genius, a college graduate . . . you don't have to have even higher than average intelligence to commit premeditated murder. All you have to have is intent. . . ."

Calley sat throughout Daniel's two-and-a-half-hour summation without flinching. He crossed and recrossed his legs several times. He blushed at the mention of certain events by Daniel, but he held his own throughout. At the conclusion, Daniel turned to him for the first time during his summation and pointed his finger at him. Calley, he stated, "did not do his duty. He failed in his duty to his troops, to his country and to mankind." Harsh words by the young prosecutor, so fresh upon the American moral scene. "You," he turned to the six-man military court-martial jury, "are the conscience of the United States Army, the conscience of the nation." Daniel asked the jury, as such, to convict Calley of first-degree murder of all 102 persons charged against him.

George Latimer pleaded with the jurors not to make Calley "the pigeon" for the entire massacre. Calley, the "lowest officer on the totem pole in this whole business," he asserted, was merely "following orders. Don't make him the scapegoat for the actions of his superiors simply because he followed orders, just because he did as he was told."

Latimer cautioned the military jurors that Calley's conviction would tarnish the "army's image beyond all recognition." He reminded the jurors that "this was not a one man carnage" and he urged them not to turn it into a two-man race to death between Captain Medina and Lieutenant Calley. Hippies and bearded, long-haired youths would turn our courts into barrooms, spoke the seventy-year-old Latimer, and would destroy our country and the things we hold dear. *They* get defended right up to the Supreme Court, but Lieutenant Calley, whose only crime was committed in *defense* of his country, would be sacrificed, would be scapegoated by those elements that would destroy our army, and our country.

Not the heart of logic, but Latimer continued his complaint

against his times in this vein. The long-haired, bearded *civilian* witnesses, witnesses who had chosen to leave the military and who testified against Calley, were also involved in the massacre—and they were biased. They pointed the finger of guilt "at those who remained loyal and wanted to remain in the service." Latimer ignored the fact that many of the government's witnesses against Lieutenant Calley were still in the service. He also ignored the fact that Calley had testified that the only reason he was still in the service was that he had been involuntarily extended to stand trial. Otherwise, he too might have been a long-haired civilian. But Latimer was seventy years of age and he was speaking in clichés, and he meant well. He did not have to stick to facts this late in the trial.

It's all right for the air force to bomb cities, Latimer continued. It's all right for artillerymen to bomb cities. But for an *infantry-man* to destroy a village, using modern weapons provided him for that purpose, is condemned. Latimer continued his infantryman's pitch for sympathy from the jury composed entirely of infantry officers. You mix the stark horror of a battlefield with raw troops and you court disaster, Latimer asserted, drawing on his World War II infantry background. This was the lesson of My Lai. Charlie Company was understrength, it was inexperienced. It had no business going into combat. Add a pre-assault briefing like Medina's (wherein he allegedly ordered his men to kill every living thing in My Lai) and you can well see that "something might go wrong!" My Lai was a tragedy, Latimer finally conceded. Signals went wrong, and now officer is pitted against officer. Everyone else was given an honorable discharge, all except poor Calley and Medina, who were selected to fight it out to see who'd get a death certificate.

Latimer plugged his own pride in the United States Army. His record as a full colonel in the army reserve and his World War II record caused him to cry out against those who encourage the army to destroy itself from within. "This case is a vehicle," he stated, "to further destroy the Army." He urged the jury to "make a difference between an honest error of judgment and criminality." Calley should not have followed his orders, Latimer admitted. He should have told Medina to go to hell . . . but are you going to hang him by the neck until he is dead just "because he was trying to do his job?" Latimer stated that he felt close to Lieutenant Calley, as though he were an adopted son, and "I wouldn't adopt a murderer." He pleaded with the court-martial jurors to free Calley. "I ask your serious consideration, and I ask that you let this boy go free. . . ."

As noted previously, Judge Kennedy's instructions had been furnished to both counsel before their final arguments—and their arguments were within the tenor of these instructions. Latimer's acquiescence and acceptance of these instructions was tragic to Calley's defense—for Kennedy's instructions blew Calley right out of the water.

Kennedy's instructions to the jury were detailed, covering almost forty pages in the record of trial. They dealt with four specifications alleging 102 murders. At issue legally were findings of first-degree murder, second-degree murder, voluntary manslaughter, or acquittal. Kennedy spelled out to the jury the legal definitions of the various offenses involved. First-degree murder is the intentional killing of another, without justification or excuse, planned or brought about pursuant to a predesigned scheme. Second-degree murder is the intentional killing of another without premeditation or predesigned scheme. An example would be a barroom fight, where the murderer did not know his victim, or an individual who on the spur of the moment might toss a live hand grenade at another. And voluntary manslaughter is an intentional killing, done without justification or excuse, while in the heat of a sudden rage, passion, or fear, brought on by adequate provocation, before the mind has had time to cool. The jury might thus resolve Calley's guilt as either first- or second-degree murder, or manslaughter, or in keeping with Kennedy's instructions acquit him of guilt.

In regard to the defense of partial insanity raised by defense counsel, wherein the defense presented evidence to the effect that

Calley lacked mental capacity to premeditate at My Lai, Kennedy instructed the jury, in view of this evidence, that the burden of proof was placed upon the government to prove beyond a reasonable doubt that Calley could premeditate at My Lai. Otherwise the defendant could not be convicted of first-degree murder, but could only be convicted of second-degree murder or manslaughter, or be acquitted, as the jury might view the evidence. Kennedy advised the jury that the testimony of the defense psychiatrists, the rebuttal evidence of the government psychiatrists, and the testimony relating to Lieutenant Calley's killing a woman who attempted to surrender to him, and to his killing an old man in a well four weeks prior to My Lai, were relevant facts to be considered on the issue of whether Calley would premeditate at My Lai. It was up to the jury to weigh the evidence concerned, Kennedy stated, and make a determination of the contested sanity issue.

The subject of superior orders was given considerable attention by Kennedy. He informed the jurors that if Calley were found to be responsible for any deaths at My Lai, the jury must then determine whether Calley had acted "pursuant to orders received by him." Kennedy reviewed Medina's testimony where Medina denied ordering Calley or anyone else to "waste" prisoners at My Lai—or to kill women and children indiscriminately. Next he reviewed Calley's testimony on this point. Twice Calley stated that he was briefed by Medina on March 15, that no one was to be allowed to "get behind" his troops, "and that nothing was to be left standing in the village of My Lai 4." Then, on March 16, during the assault, Calley stated he twice received orders from Captain Medina to get rid of his prisoners—or to waste them.

Kennedy did not summarize for the jury the testimony of other witnesses on this point, but he quickly got to the heart of the law of obedience to superior orders. He noted, in part:

Summary execution of detainees or prisoners is forbidden by law. Further, it is clear under the evidence presented in this case, that hostile acts in support of the enemy . . . forces by inhabitants of My Lai 4, at some time prior to 16 March 1968, would not justify the summary execution of all or a part of the occupants of My Lai 4 on 16 March, nor would hostile acts committed that day, if, following the hostility, the belligerents surrendered or were captured by our forces. I therefore instruct you as a matter of law, that if unresisting human beings were killed at My Lai 4 while within the effective custody and control of our military forces, their deaths cannot be considered justified, and any order to kill such people would be, as a matter of law, an illegal order. Thus, if you find that Lieutenant Calley received an order directing him to kill unresisting Vietnamese within his control or within the control of his troops, that order would be an illegal order.

But Kennedy cautioned the jury that the inquiry did not end there.

Soldiers are taught to obey orders, he stated, but the obedience of a soldier is not the obedience of an automaton. "A soldier is a reasoning agent, obliged to respond, not as a machine but as a person." The legal test of the defense of superior orders was then defined by Kennedy as follows:

The acts of a subordinate done in compliance with an unlawful order given him by his superior are excused and impose no criminal liability upon him unless the superior's order is one which a man of ordinary sense and understanding would, under the circumstances, know to be unlawful, or if the order in question is actually known to the accused to be unlawful.

In determining whether Lieutenant Calley knew the order was an illegal order (assuming the jury found that he received one), Kennedy instructed the jury that it should consider *all the circumstances* introduced during the trial relative to this factor. He summarized some of the relevant evidence in this regard to include Lieutenant Calley's rank, his educational background, his OCS and other army training, his combat experience, his age, "and any other evidence tending to prove or disprove that on March 16, 1968, Lieutenant Calley knew the order was unlawful." In determining whether a man of ordinary sense and understanding should have known the order was illegal, Kennedy instructed the jurors "to think back to the events of 15 and 16 March 1968." He informed the jurors to consider all the information "which you find to have been given Lieutenant Calley at the company briefing, at the platoon leaders' briefing, and during his conversation with Captain Medina prior to lift off," and to consider the gunship "prep" and "any artillery he may have observed." Kennedy then summarized his instruction on this point:

> Consider all the evidence which you find indicated what he could have heard and observed as he entered and made his way through the village to the point where you find him to have first acted causing the death of occupants, if you find him to have so acted. Consider the situation which you find facing him at that point. Then determine in light of all the surrounding circumstances, whether the order . . . is one which a man of ordinary sense and understanding would know to be unlawful. Unless you are satisfied from the evidence, beyond a reasonable doubt, that a man of ordinary sense and understanding would have known the order to be unlawful, you must acquit Lieutenant Calley for committing acts done in accordance with the order.

After Kennedy gave the above instruction, he had covered the heart of Calley's defense. He quickly passed on to lesser points, routine instructions given in all military cases. Kennedy instructed the court-martial that "it takes the concurrence of two-thirds of you to find Lieutenant Calley guilty of any offense charged." As there were six officers on the jury, Kennedy instructed that "four of you would have to vote guilty" before a guilty verdict could be returned, and if less than four vote to convict, a finding of not guilty results. Lastly, he instructed the jury that it could adjust the number of victims downward, "to reflect the number of persons which two-thirds of you . . . are agreed beyond a reasonable doubt were killed by Lieutenant Calley."

Overall, the tone of Kennedy's instructions was fair, as indeed
the overall tone of his conduct had been throughout the entire
trial. Kennedy at times during the trial approached greatness. His
rulings permitted both prosecution and defense to prove every
grisly fact of My Lai, rulings that could not have endeared Kennedy to the hearts of his military chieftains in Washington, D.C.,
who beyond question would have appreciated a much more ab-
breviated trial. But Kennedy kept the trial an open trial. Whatever
speculations there had been before trial that the military might put
the wraps on the trial through the agency of the military judge was
proven dead wrong by Kennedy. He knocked the heart out of any
move, by the prosecution or defense, to restrict the evidence in this
regard. As a result of Kennedy's decision to play it down the
middle, history has a detailed, recorded version of the My Lai
massacre, and Kennedy deserves a place in the military judicial
hall of fame for this fact. But yet with all his easygoing manner,
his charm, his Irish wit that so won over the press, and his honesty, Kennedy seriously undercut Calley in his instructions to the
jurors.

The crucial portion of Calley's defense was, of course, the con-
tention that he acted at My Lai in obedience to superiors' orders to
waste, or kill, his prisoners. In this regard, as already noted, Kennedy instructed the court-martial that the order concerned, if the
jury believed the order was given, was an *illegal* order, and as
such, Calley had no legal right to obey the order, unless the jury
believed that *under all the circumstances involved*, a man of
"ordinary sense and understanding" could have viewed his order
as legal. Or, as Kennedy put it, and in his words, unless the jury
was satisfied beyond a reasonable doubt "that a man of ordinary
sense and understanding would have known the order to be unlawful, you must acquit Lieutenant Calley for committing acts done in
accordance with the order."

Kennedy further instructed the jury to consider the "situation
which you find facing" Calley at the time of My Lai, and to
consider *all the surrounding circumstances* in determining whether

Lieutenant Calley should have known that the order which he allegedly received from Captain Medina was lawful. While Kennedy was careful to list many circumstances for the court-martial jury to consider, he *omitted* two circumstances that would have borne quite heavily upon the jury's determination in this regard— and might well have even changed the nature of Medina's alleged order to wipe out the inhabitants of My Lai from a clearly illegal order, as Kennedy instructed it was, to a clearly *legal* order. The omitted circumstances, circumstances that were proven in the Calley trial and circumstances that were undisputed by the government, were (1) that the village of My Lai 4 at the time of the massacre was located in a *free fire zone*, and (2) that the mission on which My Lai was destroyed was a *search and destroy mission* (terms conjured up by the American government to sanction wholesale, indiscriminate killing of Vietnamese people in total contradiction to the rules of land warfare).

In short, while Lieutenant Calley and his men might as reasonable men know that a specific order to kill women and children and babies in Trenton, New Jersey, was an illegal order, and that if they obeyed it they did so at their peril, transplant the scene to Vietnam in the year 1968, into a village located in the midst of a *free fire zone* during a *search and destroy mission*, and the legality of the order becomes less clear.

Add other "practices" of the American government in Vietnam and the plot thickens even more. In 1968 American personnel in Vietnam had employed other "tactics" designed by the American government to thwart its obligation to obey the rules of land warfare designed to protect noncombatants. Under the concept of "harassment and interdiction fire," for example, American field commanders in Vietnam had reasoned that it was perfectly legal to fire artillery rounds at night into any radius vector of a "free fire zone," on the theory that the artillery fire would "harass and interdict" Viet Cong troops operating in the area. The fact that the "H and I" fire also killed countless noncombatants (villagers) who lived in villages located within the free fire zone did not deter the practice. The fact that the practice was and is a vicious violation of the rules of land warfare, i.e., a war crime, has yet to register with the American government. And there were more "practices" in contradiction to the rules of land warfare and in existence at the time of My Lai wherein thousands of Vietnamese noncombatants were killed, and their deaths routinely accepted by the American government: "saturation bombing," "pacification," "defoliation," and the "resettlement" of civilian populations into American-constructed concentration camps. Another one, of course, was the acceptability of the ground combat slaughter of noncombatants by American personnel—the slaughter of *gooks, slants, dopes*, and *dinks*—a slaughter that did not seriously concern American field commanders, as most such slaughters were not investigated or even reported to higher authorities (as indeed, even the My Lai slaughter itself was not reported). Thus, had Kennedy asked the jury to consider some of these factors in determining whether Calley met the test of an "ordinary reasonable person" in accepting Medina's alleged order to kill the citizens of My Lai 4, the jury would have had a closer issue to determine.

Unfortunately, it was this type of evidence (genocide) which Latimer did not introduce in Calley's defense—despite the fact that throughout the year 1970 various commissions of inquiry had held public hearings across America wherein scores of young Vietnam veterans had given testimony of this nature, and despite the fact that during the Calley trial Todd Ensign of the Citizens Commission of Inquiry personally offered to bring 150 such witnesses to Fort Benning, Georgia, to testify in Lieutenant Calley's behalf. (The offer was turned down by George Latimer.) Kennedy cannot, therefore, be faulted for failing to list these circumstances, for Latimer (despite the availability of this evidence) did not see fit to offer it in Calley's behalf.

But Latimer did prove beyond a doubt that My Lai was within a *free fire zone* at the time of the massacre, and that the mission involved was a *search and destroy mission*. Latimer went further. His witnesses testified as to the nature of a free fire zone (a zone within which all living things were subject to execution by American troops without further inquiry), and they testified that they were trained how to execute search and destroy missions at installations located within the United States.

Latimer could have called scores of witnesses to prove the criminal nature of search and destroy missions and free fire zones. He could have proven the long-standing acceptance of these concepts by the American government through the direct evidence of former GIs who were willing to testify. He could have proven long-standing command involvement in these practices. Moreover, he could have proven that the My Lai slaughter was in direct conformity with the free fire zone concept (where all living things are subject to execution). But while Latimer can be faulted for not meeting these issues head-on in defense of Lieutenant Calley, his evidence did prove that the concepts of free fire zones and search and destroy missions were in contradiction to the laws of land warfare.

Yet, when it came time for Judge Kennedy to instruct the jury on the circumstances it could consider in determining whether Calley, as a man of ordinary sense and understanding, was reasonable in accepting Medina's orders to slaughter his prisoners, *Kennedy made no mention of the free fire zone and search and destroy concepts.* He did not instruct the jury where these concepts originated. He did not instruct the jury whether these concepts were in fact originated by the American government. He did not advise the jury whether these concepts *changed* the responsibility of American soldiers to safeguard the lives of noncombatants in Vietnam. He did not instruct the jury what *effect* these concepts had upon the laws of land warfare itself.

Furthermore, Kennedy's instruction to the jury that the "summary execution of detainees is forbidden by law" was a statement of law that existed *prior* to the creation and implementation of the free fire zone and search and destroy concepts by the United States. Therefore, one of the major issues of the Vietnam war to be raised in the Calley court-martial was avoided by Kennedy's failure to clarify these matters in his instructions to the jury. Had

Lieutenant Calley been tried by a nation other than the United States, that is, by a nation that was not guilty of inventing the concepts in question or condoning their continued use in Vietnam, the existence of the illegal concepts could not have affected his guilt at all. Where Calley was tried, however, by his own nation, the creator of the murderous concepts in question, it is less clear whether *this nation* with its dirty hands should be permitted to ignore the legal effect of these concepts upon the guilt of the defendant.

By ignoring the effect of these concepts in his instructions to the jury, Judge Kennedy completely grounded the legal effect of the concepts in question and did not explain to the jury whether they had any role at all in determining Calley's guilt. Only once did Kennedy mention either concept. In instructing the court-martial jury on the issue of whether Medina had or had not given an order to kill prisoners, Kennedy listed several items of evidence that were relevant to this issue. In this listing he included the statement: "There is evidence that this was labeled a search and destroy operation." That was all. There was no further mention of either term in his instructions.

The fact that Americans had been slaughtering Vietnamese noncombatants for years in free fire zones and in search and destroy missions exactly similar to My Lai, except perhaps in size, might have reasonably affected Calley's decision to obey Medina's orders (assuming he received such an order) to commit genocide at My Lai. It is also probable that such genocidal practices greatly affected all American combat soldiers in Vietnam—before and after the My Lai tragedy. In fairness to Lieutenant Calley, the legal relevance of these issues should not have been ignored. If Kennedy resolved that they played no part in the rule of law applicable to the case, he should have spelled it out in his instructions, for the factual issue as to whether or not these concepts affected Calley's determination to obey or not to obey Medina's alleged orders, was, under American law, susceptible to determination by the triers of fact (i.e., the jury) alone.

The failure of Judge Kennedy to pass upon these issues tended to relieve the United States government of its responsibility for the My Lai massacre—and shifted it entirely to Calley, Medina, and Charlie Company. Whatever Kennedy's reasoning or justification for not submitting this issue to the jury, the failure in this regard choked the breath of life from Calley's defense.

After some thirteen days of deliberation, Calley's military jury returned with a verdict: guilty of premeditated murder of twenty-two people at My Lai. Calley's long ordeal at the bar of American justice was soon to be over. The following day he was sentenced to life imprisonment. The "wretched" officer who "failed" his country, the "aberrant murderer" who faced his accusers (the American government) with so little real knowledge of his crime was finally brought to heel by a military jury composed of fellow combat officers.

And Captain Daniel, the relentless advocate, the young American prosecutor with the soft Southern accent who proved the facts of My Lai so well at Fort Benning, waxed indignant when the president of the United States ordered Calley removed from the stockade and confined to his quarters at Fort Benning following his sentence and pending final appeal of his conviction. It hurt the image of "military justice," Daniel complained, to free Calley of the rigors of imprisonment so lightly.

13

The Acquittal of Captain Medina:
The Ground Commander

Captain Ernest Medina, thirty-four years of age, of Mexican ancestry, pinched-faced, worried, and beautifully resplendent in military uniform, folded his hands and listened to prosecutor Major William G. Eckhardt deliver his opening address to the five-member military jury at Fort McPherson, Georgia. The date was August 17, 1971, some four months after Lieutenant Calley had been sentenced to life imprisonment.

"The government does not intend to prove that Captain Medina intentionally instructed his men to destroy men, women and children," Eckhardt intoned, in startling contradiction to the testimony produced by George Latimer at Calley's court-martial on this aspect of the case.

Eckhardt continued with his opening statement: "Captain Medina knew his orders were being misconstrued and that his troops were murdering noncombatants. When he did not intervene, he chose calculatingly not to intervene and thereby offered comfort and encouragement to his men in carrying out the carnage."

These short sentences constituted the theory of the government's case against Captain Medina. Gone was the thrust of Calley's recent defense, where Latimer called some fourteen witnesses to testify that Captain Medina briefed his company on the eve of the My Lai assault to kill every human being in My Lai, including old men, women, and children. Apparently the government had resolved to ignore this direct evidence of murder and was going to rely upon circumstantial evidence only (specifically, that Medina was present in or on the outskirts of the village for four hours while the assault and destruction of the village was taking place, that he either saw or, through the exercise of his senses, should have seen what was going on, and failed to halt it, thereby constituting tacit approval of the slaughter). Eckhardt's theory was plausible, but his assertion that he did not intend to prove Medina "intentionally instructed" his troops to murder noncombatants at My Lai, in view of the Calley court-martial evidence to the contrary, is difficult to understand.

The most immediate justification for the government's failure to utilize direct and available evidence to prove Medina's murderous instructions to his troops on the eve of the My Lai assault possibly lies in the fact that the military hierarchy was playing it safe in this regard. It would reflect badly on the military if planned *genocide* of the village by *anyone* was proven. Calley had raised the issue at his trial, and defended on the basis that he was ordered by Medina to destroy the inhabitants of the village. He called many witnesses to verify this fact. On the other hand, Medina testified at Calley's trial that he did not order the slaughter, and furthermore, did not know the massacre was taking place until after it was over. Thus Medina did not pass the massacre up the line, so to speak, to involve higher military officers. From the command viewpoint Medina put a lid on the massacre in his testimony at the Calley trial. Hence, if the prosecution at Medina's trial attempted to prove that Medina ordered a massacre, it could blow the "lid" right off again. The inference could easily be drawn that Medina also received orders to destroy everyone in the village, and that because of this order he in turn ordered his men to do it. In an effort to end the incrimination, and to pass the entire *active* guilt to

Lieutenant Calley, and to contain the intentional, planned genocide at the lowest command level possible, it appears that the
United States declined to use its available evidence that Medina
ordered his troops to destroy the inhabitants of My Lai. This was,
of course, a highly questionable course of action for the government to follow.

F. Lee Bailey, Medina's chief counsel, was terse and to the
point in his opening statement to the jury. He asserted that Captain
Medina remained on the outskirts of My Lai while his men made
the assault, and that when he discovered what was going on later
in the day, ordered the massacre terminated. "When it was brought
to his attention, he immediately issued the appropriate order: 'Cut
it out! Knock it off!' " Bailey asserted that Medina did not order,
observe, or encourage the massacre and that he did not observe
any dead bodies until after he ordered the cease-fire. "Then he saw
the bodies," Bailey stated.

Bailey did not deny a massacre took place, but blamed it on the
company's lack of "combat experience," false intelligence reports
on the presence of a strong VC force (the Forty-eighth Viet Cong
Battalion), and upon an assurance from intelligence that all civilians would be out of the village by 7:30 a.m., the time of the
assault.

Unlike Calley, Medina had an additional assist from the start.
The government declared his case noncapital. Although charged
with the murder of 102 villagers, a woman and a young boy, and
assault by shooting at a prisoner, Medina faced, if convicted, a
maximum sentence of only life imprisonment. Also unlike Calley,
Medina was represented by one of the foremost criminal defense
attorneys in the United States, F. Lee Bailey.

The prosecution's first three witnesses, Ronald Haeberle, James
Dursi, and Gregory Olsen, did not contradict Medina's defense.
Photographer Haeberle, who sold his action photographs of the
My Lai massacre to *Life* magazine for upward of $19,000, de-
scribed the massacre scene and his photography of the slaughter.
There were scenes of American soldiers setting fire to Vietnamese

straw homes with cigarette lighters (the "Zippo" squads); there were scenes of murdered women and children, of a mother clutching a daughter to her bosom, and a "group of dead bodies along the trail." These were horrible, shocking pictures, but they were not shown to the jury at this time. Bailey's objection that the government had not shown a connection between the photographs and Captain Medina was sustained by the military judge, Colonel Kenneth Howard of the army's Judge Advocate General's Corps. Olsen and Dursi, both damaging witnesses against Lieutenant Calley at his trial, proved less a threat to Captain Medina. Like Haeberle, they merely described the slaughter, the carnage. But similar to Haeberle, they did not identify Medina as present in the burning village while the massacre was in progress.

Dursi, a rifleman at My Lai in Calley's First Platoon, was asked to describe Medina's pre-assault briefing that took place the day prior to the My Lai Massacre. Dursi answered, "I remember one statement, that if we saw men, women and children they probably would be with the enemy and we should use common sense in dealing with them."

An overconfident Bailey did little cross-examining. "It's the first case I've ever seen where the defense witnesses go first," he quipped to newsmen.

After three days of testimony and after some fifteen witnesses had testified, Captain Medina was finally placed at the scene of a killing. But the witness obligingly hedged his way out. "Captain Medina was talking with his head down [at the time of the shooting of a small wounded boy] and I don't even know whether he saw the incident." Bailey mildly objected to the "overkill" tendency on the part of the prosecution, i.e., to its repeated evidence of My Lai deaths with no attempt to link them with Captain Medina, "directly or indirectly." The objection was overruled.

Bailey was concerned, however, with a possible prosecution theory that could convict his client despite the failure of the government to link him personally to the killings that took place at My Lai. The theory feared most by Bailey was the *Yamashita* ruling of the United States Supreme Court in 1946, wherein the Supreme Court affirmed Japanese General Yamashita's death sentence on the basis that he *failed to prevent* troops under his command from killing innocent Filipino civilians toward the close of World War II. Yamashita's defense was identical to Medina's (namely, "I didn't know my troops were killing civilians"). Yamashita's defense, however, was more plausible than Medina's. Yamashita, at the time his troops committed atrocities in the Philippines (1945), was at one end of the islands, and his offending troops were on the other end. Sandwiched between was a hostile American army that was doing its best to smash both ends of General Yamashita's army. Yamashita furthermore was not in communication with his troops, he did not know what they were doing, and he had no way to control them even if he had desired to do so. Yet General Yamashita was *hanged* because he had in fact "failed to control his troops." As General Douglas MacArthur stated, "responsibility lies with command."

But Bailey was outraged with the notion that the *Yamashita* ruling might be applied in Medina's case. "I don't think that what is done to a Jap hanged in the heat of vengeance after World War II can be done to an American on an imputed theory of responsibility," he asserted.

Colonel Howard was quick to soothe Mr. Bailey's fears. He assured him that Captain Medina could be held criminally responsible for the My Lai massacre only if it was proven that he personally participated in the massacre, or that he had knowledge of it and did nothing to stop it. (Otherwise, the *Yamashita* ruling might be applied against any number of Americans, including no less than the sacrosanct chief of staff of the United States Army, General Westmoreland himself. Bailey's fears were perhaps more pretended than real. Judge Howard would hardly have remained on the "bench" throughout the close of the day had he ruled that the *Yamashita* principle applied to American officers who were on trial for genocide.)

Third Army commander Lieutenant General Albert O. Connor

stole the headlines from the Medina trial temporarily. On August 20, 1971, he announced that upon official review of the Calley court-martial conviction, he had reduced Calley's sentence from life in prison to twenty years' confinement at hard labor. Connor stated that he deemed the reduced sentence "was appropriate" after reviewing the record of conviction. Connor's review was the first of three statutory reviews under the military judicial system. Additional reductions in Calley's sentence could come at any level of review. F. Lee Bailey's comment upon the reduced sentence was identical to Connor's. Bailey stated the reduction was "appropriate" and that he would submit a motion to drop the mass murder charge against Captain Medina on the basis of Connor's action in the Calley case. Meanwhile, Major Eckhardt called former First Lieutenant Jeffrey LaCross, of Grand Rapids, Michigan, as a witness for the government against Captain Medina.

But LaCross, who had been the platoon leader of Charlie Company's Third Platoon at My Lai, and who had willingly testified against Calley at his court-martial, managed to say a good word for his old boss, Captain Medina, before he got off the witness stand. On cross-examination, he was asked by Bailey if Medina gave his men a "license to slaughter civilians."

"No, sir," La Cross answered briskly.

Bailey's next question was more involved. "If something had happened to Captain Medina and you had become the company commander, did you see anything at My Lai that would have caused you to stop misconduct by American troops?"

"Not a thing, sir," LaCross shot back.

Other prosecution witnesses were equally pleased to say nice things for Mr. Bailey. Abel Flores, Jr., a mortician from San Antonio, Texas, stated he overheard Medina ask Calley on the radiophone, "What's happening in your area?" When Calley made no reply, Medina sent a soldier to look for Calley. It was shortly after this that Medina gave his cease-fire order.

"In angry tones?" Bailey asked.

"He shouted it out, yes, sir."

Captain Hugh Thompson (former helicopter pilot at My Lai), the twenty-third prosecution witness against Captain Medina, testified he saw an army captain shoot a wounded Vietnamese woman at My Lai. Thompson stated he had just "dropped smoke" to mark the location   the woman for medical aid when a captain and several other soldiers arrived on the scene. The captain shot her. "I couldn't understand why the Captain shot her. And I couldn't understand why all the bodies were in the ditch."

Lawrence Colburn, Thompson's door gunner, testified Thompson's aircraft hovered over the scene momentarily. "As I remember he [the captain] turned her over with his foot and shot her," Colburn stated.

Neither Colburn nor Thompson could identify Medina as the person who shot the woman. On cross-examination, both witnesses stated that had they been on the ground and seen the woman make a sudden movement and thought she had a weapon, they might have shot the woman too.

Louis B. Martin, a former radioman in Charlie Company, and at the time of the trial a policeman in San Jose, California, proved to be the only witness to connect Captain Medina directly with the massacre. The government's twenty-sixth witness, Mr. Martin testified the captain was within ninety feet of the execution of eight to twelve women and children, shortly after he entered the village and long before he ordered a cease-fire. Martin stated he was with Captain Medina's command group, and that they passed several American soldiers who were guarding eight to twelve Vietnamese women and children. The command group had "just passed" the group when the Americans mowed them down.

Bailey asked Martin why he didn't report the shooting to Medina, "to insure that the Captain didn't miss it?"

Martin fired back: "I was with my commander. I felt the people around me were seeing the same thing."

The case for the government was entering its final stages. Frederick Widmer, described as a vital prosecution witness, refused to testify, despite the offer of immunity and despite the threat of prosecution if he didn't. Next, two Vietnamese soldiers testified via deposition from Vietnam. The witnesses, two army interpreters at My Lai, testified they questioned an American captain of Spanish ancestry at My Lai during the massacre as to "why he let soldiers kill the people," and the captain replied: "That is the order. You don't ask questions." On cross-examination the two Vietnamese soldiers admitted they did not speak or understand English "very well" at the time of the My Lai slaughter.

The thirty-first and last witness for the government was army polygraph examiner Robert A. Brisentine, of Fort Holabird, Maryland. Brisentine testified that Medina told him during the course of a lie-detector examination that he had lost control over his unit during the My Lai assault and that he first became aware of this fact during the early morning hours of the assault. This, of course, contradicted Bailey's opening-statement assertion that Medina did not realize that he had lost control over his unit until several hours *after* the assault was over.

Following the conclusion of the government's case, Mr. Bailey asked for a finding of not guilty.

"Nobody testified that he was encouraged by Medina to shoot anybody," Bailey declared. "There must be a criminal intent and purpose shown. The mere relationship of subordinate and superior is insufficient," Bailey declared (overlooking the *Yamashita* principle).

Eckhardt did not argue the *Yamashita* principle either, but recited his evidence instead. He concluded his argument by asserting that direct and circumstantial evidence showed that Medina's troops were murdering people at My Lai, that Medina knew about it while the slaughter was in progress, and "afraid for his career," "calculatingly did nothing to stop them," thereby encouraging his troops to continue the slaughter.

Judge Howard denied Bailey's motion and directed the defense to move forward with its case.

Bailey was up to the task. With an eye for news coverage, his first witness was none other than Lieutenant Calley, whom Bailey billed as having undergone a change of heart since his trial, at least insofar as Medina's role was concerned. Calley appeared, flanked by soft-spoken George Latimer. The only noticeable change however, was in the length of Calley's hair, which was considerably longer than it had been during his trial. Otherwise, in a hearing outside the presence of the jury, Calley quickly made his decision not to testify and was promptly excused from giving further testimony on the grounds of claimed self-incrimination.

Bailey's next witness was more down-to-earth. Gene Oliver, a former rifleman at My Lai, and a star witness against Lieutenant Calley, testified for Medina. He admitted for the first time in the My Lai investigation and trials that he himself had shot and killed the small boy Medina was formally charged with murdering. Oliver stated he saw a movement in a rice paddy, a human form. "I raised my rifle and fired. Medina, who was nearby, shouted, 'Goddammit, cease-fire!' "

Oliver said the boy fell near the group of civilians shot down on the trail intersection south of the village of My Lai. He stated that Medina had given him no orders to shoot the boy. He also stated he had never "specifically" described "this event" to army investigators. He said he stepped forward at the moment because he did not wish to see Captain Medina blamed for something that he (Oliver) had done.

When asked by Bailey why he did not volunteer this information earlier, Oliver replied, "It was just something that I tried to bury." Asked why he refused to discuss the nature of his testimony with the prosecutor before taking the witness stand, Oliver came back with a roundhouse: "I think this whole proceeding is unfair. The Army knows it's unfair the same as I do."

Bailey continued his sandbagging of the government's case. Captain Robert Hicks of Fort Benning was permitted to testify, over vigorous prosecution objections, that when he questioned Calley shortly after the massacre, Calley told him that Captain Medina was "certainly surprised" when he first learned of the massacre of civilians following the conclusion of the operation.

If Bailey had managed to bring his witnesses in from left field, his next witness came from clear out of the ballpark. Leonard H. Haralson, a lie-detector operator from Niles, Illinois, testified that he examined the prosecution's star witness, Lewis Martin (the only witness who placed Medina at the scene of a massacre). Under standard American rules of evidence, lie-detector examiners cannot give their opinion as to whether a suspect who has taken their test was truthful in his answers, but examiners are permitted to relate the content of their answers. Haralson thus testified that Martin admitted to him that he'd had "delusions" throughout his life, and that it was possible that the execution and group of bodies that he thought he and Medina saw at My Lai might have in fact "never really existed at all."

If there was any credibility left in Martin's trial testimony connecting Medina to the massacre, the next witness for the defense demolished it completely. Bailey called upon an assistant defense counsel for this assignment, John A. Johnson. Mr. Johnson took the witness stand and related a conversation he had with Mr. Martin following his testimony against Captain Medina, wherein Martin conveniently labeled his trial testimony as "inaccurate and misleading." Johnson further quoted Martin, a San Jose policeman, as saying, "I cannot say if anyone was shot at all. . . . I don't know where Captain Medina was. Possibly I didn't see a group of people shot." That Judge Howard and prosecutor Eckhardt submitted to this type of impeachment without recalling Martin, citing him for perjury or having him explain or deny the contradictory statements involved, is most perplexing.

Captain Medina was the last defense witness. He stated that he ordered his troops not to kill innocent civilians at My Lai and that Lieutenant Calley was inept and could not follow or understand orders.

Medina stated his troops were inexperienced and had received heavy casualties in the My Lai area. Additionally, American intelligence had passed faulty information to him, Medina asserted. He stated that intelligence had advised him that the crack Forty-eighth

Viet Cong Battalion was entrenched in My Lai and had further assured him that no civilians at all would be in the village on the morning of the attack, as all civilians on the day in question would have departed the village en route to market some miles away. Medina advanced the foregoing reasons as justification for the My Lai slaughter. Personally, he stated, he did not know noncombatants were slaughtered at My Lai until his troops took night defensive positions on the day of the assault, hours after the My Lai operation had terminated.

It was at this time that Lieutenant Calley after much hemming and hawing finally gave him a direct answer and told him he "guessed" he had killed fifty noncombatants. Medina stated it wasn't until then that he was first made aware of the fact that he, Medina, had lost control of his troops at My Lai and that a massacre had occurred. He admitted that he shot the woman as alleged, but it was instinctive. "I thought she had a grenade."

Medina testified that the small boy was shot in his presence. He stated that he yelled, "Stop him, get him, shoot him, or don't shoot him," but after realizing it was only a small child, he lowered his own rifle. At this time an M16 rang out. Someone else had shot the boy and he fell. Medina said he didn't inspect the boy to see if he was dead or wounded.

It was after this testimony, and at the close of the defense case, that Colonel Howard partially granted Bailey's motion for a directed verdict of not guilty. Howard first threw out the murder charge relating to the small boy. Next he reduced the murder charges relating to the murder of 102 Vietnamese villagers to involuntary manslaughter, an offense carrying a maximum sentence of three years. He refused the motion completely, however, in regard to the alleged murder of the Vietnamese woman. Howard stated his reasons for the reductions were simply that in his opinion there had been no proof that Medina "intended for these people to be killed." "In my mind," he stated, "I don't feel it is fair to expose Captain Medina to a murder conviction where there is insufficient evidence of guilt." Howard stated there was evidence that Medina "negligently and unintentionally" permitted the members of his unit to kill unresisting, unarmed men, women, and children at My Lai. For this reason, Howard stated, he would permit the jury to decide if Medina was guilty of involuntary manslaughter of the villagers, with the exception of the woman. The jury, in regard to the death of the woman, would decide whether Medina was guilty of murder.

One hour after the case was submitted to the jury, the jury of two full colonels, two lieutenant colonels, and a major returned with its verdict.

Captain Medina was acquitted of all charges and specifications.

The court-martial jury that found Captain Medina innocent of murder at My Lai did not hear testimony concerning the murderous content of Captain Medina's pre-assault briefing for the My Lai operation. This testimony, which was produced at Calley's trial, concerned the instructions Medina allegedly gave his company of infantrymen on the eve of the My Lai massacre. Medina's briefing was described as follows:

Elmer Glen Haywood: "It was a search and destroy mission. . . . Every one in the village was to be destroyed. All living things. . . . To me, his order meant to destroy everyone in the village. . . . [He] said it was a free fire zone."

Staff Sergeant L. A. Bacon: "We were to kill all the Viet Cong and Viet Cong sympathizers in the village, to destroy all food stuff, to kill all animals and to burn the village."

Steven R. Glimpse: "My impression was that we were to kill the inhabitants of the village . . . including the women and children."

Staff Sergeant Martin Fagan: "Kill everyone. The livestock was to be destroyed, the village burned. Everything was to be destroyed."

Sergeant Charles A. West: "It was a search and destroy mission . . . completely level the village . . . we were to kill everything . . . put them out of their misery . . ."

Michael Bernhardt: "To destroy the village and all its inhabitants."

Salvador Lamartina: "To kill everything alive . . . to kill every-thing that breathed."

Leonard Gonzales: "To wipe out the village, and to kill every-thing and everyone you saw."

Sergeant Isaac Cowan: "To kill everything that was in the vil-lage . . . to destroy it."

Thomas H. Paetch: "To wipe out the whole village . . . to kill everything."

Thomas J. Kinch: "My impression was that everyone would be dead when we left there."

Tommy Lee Moss: "Medina ordered his troops to kill everyone in the village including the women and children."

James H. Flynn: "Medina said to kill everything in the village that moves. . . . Someone asked, 'Are we supposed to kill women and children?' and Medina replied, 'Kill everything that moves.' "

The prosecution's failure to produce incriminating evidence of this nature in the trial of Captain Ernest Medina cannot help but leave a distinctly acid taste in the mouths of those who would espouse the integrity of "military justice"—or the fairness of Lieu-tenant Calley's trial and conviction. Calley, at his trial, had at-tempted to pass responsibility for the massacre to only one mili-tary superior, Captain Medina, and Medina and the army successfully crammed this defense down Calley's throat. Sergeant Hutto was able to win an acquittal for the murder of fifteen non-combatants at My Lai on this same defense—namely, that he killed because Captain Medina ordered his troops to kill every man, woman, and child at My Lai. But Calley's case was too big, and the army could not readily afford Calley the same right to pass the ball to Medina in this fashion, and Calley's bid was rejected.

Had Calley's jury accepted this defense, it would have translated to the world that the My Lai massacre was not the aberrant act of a murderous lieutenant but that it had been planned and ordered, albeit by only a captain, but even this command involvement was too much for those who wished to keep responsibility for the mas-sacre at the lowest command level possible. It is also true that the army permitted the Calley trial to stir its top-secret bag of worms relating to genocide. But the information that was released to the public through the medium of the trial was, in the final analysis, as pro-army as possible under the circumstances. It must be remembered that the public was already in possession of most of the My Lai massacre story. What it wanted to know most of all was the army's responsibility for the massacre. This was *not* public information, and unfortunately, after a four-and-a-half-month showcase trial, the public was as much as ever in the dark on this part of the story.

From the army viewpoint Calley's conviction no doubt proved only that a first lieutenant was responsible for the massacre. But the conviction also raised the possibility that a captain might be involved, with the further possibility that the entire massacre was hidden from the eyes of the public by senior military commanders. These were "loose ends" and they demanded further court-martial action by the army. Following the acquittal of Captain Medina a command "lid" was placed over the massacre. There would be no further incrimination of army commanders for ordering the massacre to occur. But there was still one loose end to be attended to. Following Medina's acquittal the final act of Calley's tragedy was already under way: Colonel Oran Henderson was undergoing trial by court-martial at Fort Meade, Maryland, for "covering up" the My Lai massacre.

14

The Trial of Colonel Henderson:
The Superior Commander

Colonel Oran Henderson, decorated wartime veteran of three wars, was the highest American officer to stand trial for complicity in the My Lai massacre. Of all the officers originally charged with responsibility for the cover-up, non-West-Pointer Henderson was the *only* officer to answer before the bar of justice. His attorney, Henry B. Rothblatt of New York City, was a successful criminal lawyer and had co-authored several legal books with Boston's famed F. Lee Bailey.

As brigade commander of the Eleventh Brigade of the Americal Division, Henderson had a box-office seat for the massacre. His command helicopter flew him over the scene of the slaughter for some three hours at altitudes varying from ground level to fifteen hundred feet. Having arrived in Vietnam only one day before the massacre, the bespectacled colonel, soft-spoken and timid in appearance, was thus almost from the very beginning put in a front seat at My Lai. But Henderson was not the commander of the operation. Immediately superior to Henderson and the senior officer at My Lai was the Americal Division commander, Major General Koster, who flew as a passenger in a second command helicopter over My Lai; and immediately junior to Henderson at My Lai, also airborne in a third command helicopter, was Lieutenant Colonel Frank Barker, the actual commander of the operation, who had planned it and whose name the Task Force adopted —Task Force Barker. Barker probably called more shots at My Lai from the command position than his seniors, Koster and Henderson, combined. Unfortunately for Henderson, Barker was killed several weeks after the My Lai assault, and Henderson fitted nicely into the vacuum occasioned by his death.

Henderson, as charged by the prosecution, was ordered by the assistant division commander, Brigadier General George H. Young, to conduct an informal investigation of the massacre only two days after the slaughter. While Barker was still alive, Henderson conducted an investigation of the massacre and orally reported to General Young and to General Koster that only twenty noncombatants had been killed at My Lai, and that they had been killed by artillery and infantry cross-fire. He also reported there had been no general massacre of the villagers by American troops. It was a result of this report, which was followed up by a two-page written report several weeks later to the same effect, and by a more formal report sometime thereafter, that Henderson found himself in hot water with My Lai investigators. Called before the General Peers Investigating Committee in December 1969, and again early in 1970, Colonel Henderson freely answered questions about his role in the My Lai investigation.

As a result of his testimony before the Peers Committee, Henderson was formally charged with dereliction of duty in failing to investigate the massacre as ordered to do and with failing to report to General Koster that American troops committed war crimes at My Lai. He was also charged with making a false statement to the Peers Committee to the effect that during his investigation of the massacre he ordered Major Glenn D. Gibson, a helicopter commander, to survey all pilots from his unit who participated at My Lai, and that Major Gibson in turn reported that he had made such a survey and no pilot had witnessed "wild shooting" at My

Lai. Last, Henderson was charged with falsely informing the Peers Committee that he had not interviewed Warrant Officer Jerry R. Culverhouse or Specialist Lawrence M. Colburn, pilot and door gunner respectively of different helicopters at the My Lai massacre. The charges carried a maximum confinement of six years in prison.

In April 1971, prior to his trial, Henderson was asked by the press why he had failed in his investigation to uncover the atrocities that had been revealed in the Calley court-martial. Unlike Calley, Henderson had no press agent to conduct his relations with the news media. "I was told that nothing happened at My Lai during my inquiry," he asserted. Then his voice broke: "I was told that . . . I wasn't asked to look into atrocities . . . I was looking into "wild firing" . . . and one individual who fired on what appeared to be a wounded female. . . . These were the incidents I investigated . . . that I absolved and said did not happen."

The immediate effect of this statement was that Henderson was shooting from the cuff, that he would really do much better at his trial, which was still several months away. It was almost impossible to believe that Henderson would actually base his defense, or the major portion of it, on the fact that he was not investigating a massacre at My Lai at all, and that when he conducted his inquiry of the "wild shooting," people "simply informed me that [the massacre] did not happen." But this *was* Henderson's defense— that and his service in three wars, his five silver stars, his five bronze stars, and his four purple hearts.

The trial proper got under way in early August 1971.

The prosecutor, Major Carroll J. Tichenor, a thirty-one-year-old regular army Judge Advocate General's Corps officer, asserted in his opening statement to the jury that he would prove Henderson was guilty of "neglect and wilful deceit" in his reports to General Koster and to the Peers Committee. Tichenor informed the jury that he would call sixty-five witnesses to prove his case against Colonel Henderson. Henderson, he alleged, could not have been ignorant of what happened at My Lai. He was briefed on the assault one day prior to the operation, the same day that he took command of the brigade. He knew artillery fire was planned as a pre-assault "preparation" of the village, to soften the enemy before Medina and his company landed. Yet Henderson, Tichenor stated, was later to say that he did not know artillery fire struck the village. On March 16, 1968, the day of the My Lai massacre, Henderson in his command helicopter orbited the village during most of the massacre. He monitored Medina's command radio net. He knew Medina and his company landed without opposition— because this is a matter that any brigade commander, whose troops are engaged in combat fifteen hundred feet below his circling helicopter, takes it upon himself to ascertain immediately and not four hours later, or one year later. By the same token, Tichenor stated, he knew that by day's end only three enemy weapons were recovered—and that the astounding body count of enemy dead was reported to higher headquarters as 128 Viet Cong killed in action. He also knew by day's end that only twenty civilian noncombatants were reported as killed, and that they were reportedly killed by artillery or ground cross-fire. He also knew or should have known by day's end that there was no real combat at My Lai, that the entire U.S. effort was completely unopposed by an armed enemy; and that the Viet Cong had withdrawn from the village *before* the operation began.

Tichenor stated that the burning village was sending up so much smoke that it interfered with the navigation of United States helicopters in the area, but yet Tichenor quoted Henderson as subsequently stating under questioning that he saw no smoke over the village. Two days after the slaughter at My Lai, and after American helicopter pilots had refused to fly further support of the mission, Tichenor stated that Henderson attended a meeting called by the assistant division commander of the Americal Division, Brigadier General H. Young. The purpose of the meeting was to initiate an inquiry into the massacre reports that Koster and Young received concerning the My Lai operation. Tichenor stated that at this meeting, attended by Henderson, command pilots

Watke and Holladay, the late Lieutenant Colonel Frank Barker, and General Young, Henderson was given a direct order by General Young to investigate the massacre reports and to report back to Young in seventy-two hours. On March 18, the same day of his meeting with General Young, Tichenor asserted Henderson interrogated Warrant Officer Hugh Thompson, whose complaint of the massacre initially set off the furor of the pilots. Tichenor claimed that Henderson, at the same time, interviewed Thompson's door gunner, Specialist Colburn. Tichenor further asserted that Henderson questioned a dozen of Medina's men about "atrocities" at My Lai. He also questioned Medina about a woman whom Medina allegedly shot at My Lai. Yet, Tichenor asserted, after Henderson's participation at My Lai, after his knowledge of massacre rumors, after his receipt of orders from his commanding general to investigate the massacre, and after his investigation and in contradiction to the genocide, death, and destruction of the village, Henderson officially reported no *unusual happenings* to his commanding generals, Young and Koster. He reported no "improper" conduct on the part of American troops at My Lai. It was this report, Tichenor asserted, that constituted the heart of the government's case against Colonel Henderson. Tichenor stated that Henderson failed to perform his duty in this regard, that he was *derelict* in failing to investigate the massacre as ordered, to uncover its existence, and to report upon it to his superiors. Tichenor further asserted that over a year later when Henderson was questioned by the Peers Committee, Henderson engaged in "wilful deceit."

In his opening statement, defense attorney Rothblatt took pains to make the jury hang on his every word, and at times spoke in a near whisper. Yet at other times he shouted his points across to the jury. He asked the jury not "to Monday Morning quarterback" Henderson's combat behavior on March 16, 1968. Henderson was a "busy commander" that morning, he asserted, who did everything that "could reasonably be expected of a battlefield commander." Tichenor's account was based on "innuendo and suspicion," Rothblatt announced. While conceding that 100 to 150 My Lai villagers died at My Lai on March 16, 1968, Rothblatt dealt mostly with clichés. He flatly refused to address himself to the basic issues—nor did he, for a moment, indicate that Colonel Henderson was to point a finger of guilt at anyone higher up the chain of army command. He did not allege that Henderson's superiors knew about the massacre anyway, before they ordered him to "investigate" it, and that they did not need Henderson's report to know the extent of it. He did not allege that they ordered Henderson to "report" upon the massacre only to protect themselves, knowing and fully expecting him to *whitewash* the atrocity. Rothblatt did not assert he would prove that genocide and cover-up were long-accepted American combat practices in Vietnam, reaching all the way from private soldier to General Westmoreland —and to the president of the United States. He did not assert that Henderson was only following this practice when he reported that no atrocities were committed by American soldiers at My Lai.

In presenting his case, Tichenor set about his task in a lawyer-like fashion. He laid the foundation for the massacre. Combat photographs depicting the murdered villagers were introduced into evidence. Henderson's command role was established. His presence at My Lai was proven. Barker's radio operator was called to the witness stand and testified that while circling My Lai in Lieutenant Colonel Barker's command helicopter, he overheard Barker comment that he received a "report from 'higher' that some innocent civilians were being killed down there," and to put a stop to it. Barker reportedly ordered an immediate cease-fire, and asked his company commanders to check the reports of civilian slaughter and report back to him. The radio operator testified that two company commanders, including Captain Medina, reported that their men "were not involved."

The much heralded combat tapes of the My Lai massacre were unveiled in Henderson's trial by the prosecution. Transcribed by an officer at a nearby fire base, the tapes, spliced into one thirty-minute tape, purported to be a transcript of conversation among the helicopter pilots supporting the My Lai assault. Interlaced with background noises, static, and whirling helicopter engines, human voices could be heard on the business of war:

"We just killed two dinks that got weapons out here in this rice paddy. . . ."

"It's a good idea to get their gear before someone else comes up and uses it."

"The majority of them look like women and children. . . ."

"There could be some military age males mixed in with them. . . ."

Thus the tapes moved in and out of the spotlight without adding any clarity as to what happened on the ground—nor did they necessarily incriminate Henderson. Tichenor shifted to other subjects. He called eight former enlisted men of Charlie Company who swore that they were part of about fifteen to twenty men that Henderson questioned superficially two days after the massacre, and *after* Henderson had been directed to investigate the massacre by General Young. Their testimony was, essentially:

"He asked us if we had seen anything out of the ordinary, and if so to speak up. No one spoke up. Then he pointed to several soldiers and asked them 'Did you see anything?' The soldiers he pointed to said, 'No sir.' "

Master Sergeant Jay A. Buchanon, who witnessed atrocities at My Lai, testified that Colonel Henderson questioned another group of soldiers as they returned to Landing Zone Dottie following the My Lai assault. They were collectively asked: "Men, do you believe you have conducted yourself in a manner so that the Vietnamese would say here come our friends the next time they see you?" Buchanon testified no one answered this question, and Henderson turned to him and asked him if he had anything to say, and he told the colonel, "No comment, sir."

Tichenor was attempting to prove that Henderson was not making a good-faith effort to investigate the My Lai massacre. After speaking to the two groups of enlisted men in the foregoing summary fashion, Henderson dismissed them, thus constituting the sum total of his interrogation of ground combat enlisted men who participated in the My Lai assault. Tichenor was making use of the unwritten rules of the military. Had Henderson really wanted knowledge of the slaughter he would not have appeared as a stranger to troops disembarking from helicopters following a combat operation with questions designed to secure brush-off answers. High-ranking officers who want real information from enlisted men go through the chain of command to ask questions. And if direct questioning is in order, the enlisted man is brought to the officer, stood at attention, and ordered to answer questions. Thus, the inference Tichenor was laying in the minds of the jurors was that Henderson was conducting a halfhearted investigation, designed more to cover up facts of the massacre than to expose it—or that he was extremely derelict or dolt-like in the conduct of his investigation.

Somewhat contrary to Henderson's pretrial theory of defense, he included a statement in his written report to General Koster to the effect that Major Charles Calhoun (Barker's executive officer) had been formally interviewed by Henderson and had reported to him that "at no time were civilians gathered together [at My Lai] and killed by Charlie Company."

Calhoun was called as a prosecution witness and testified that Henderson did not question him about allegations of misconduct by Charlie Company at My Lai. Calhoun stated that he could "have been queried by Colonel Henderson concerning the conduct of the operation . . . [but] I don't recall any questions about misconduct."

Tichenor was again hitting Henderson with military custom, or the rules of the game. Henderson would now have to call his former subordinate a liar, a disagreeable task for any commander, or tacitly admit his own dereliction in failing to question him in depth concerning the massacre. Additionally, if Henderson admitted that he did not question Calhoun (because he was not conducting an inquiry into a *massacre*), then he would be admitting that he lied to General Koster when he asserted that he did. If he insisted that he did question him along the lines of his written statement to Koster, Henderson would appear to admit that he was in fact conducting an investigation of a massacre (a factor which Henderson would consistently deny throughout his trial).

Also touching the issue of whether Henderson was conducting an investigation of a *massacre* (and not an inquiry into some "wild shooting" as alleged by Henderson) was the testimony of Calhoun and Captain Eugene Kotouc, a former intelligence officer at My Lai who was acquitted by general court-martial of maiming a prisoner at My Lai. Both officers swore that Colonel Henderson ordered Captain Medina's company to "resweep" My Lai a few hours after the operation terminated on the afternoon of March 16, 1968. Kotouc stated that the purpose of the resweep was to ascertain how many Viet Cong had been killed at My Lai. But Calhoun swore the purpose of the resweep order was to determine the number of civilians who had been killed, and what had caused their wounds.

Calhoun swore he relayed the message to Captain Medina over his helicopter radio, that Medina rogered the message and objected to returning his company to My Lai. The hour was late. Night was approaching and the danger of land mines in the area was critical. These were Medina's reasons, but they were not sufficient for Henderson. He ordered Calhoun to insist upon the resweep. At this moment, Calhoun testified, General Koster personally came on the radio net and rescinded Henderson's order without explanation. Both Calhoun and Kotouc testified there could have been a "re-sweep" of My Lai the next day by Charlie Company, without danger, but that there was no order of any description given and Charlie Company did not return to My Lai to count its victims.

Tichenor attended to details. He called witness after witness to testify to the openness of the atrocity, that the bodies were lying in the open, that helicopter pilots were complaining over the radio that "civilians were getting killed down there . . ." that "there was wild firing . . ." that a "massacre was taking place." Other witnesses testified to Warrant Officer Hugh Thompson's bitter denunciation of the mission, and to the fact that for several days after the completion of the mission the massacre was a matter of common discussion by the helicopter pilots involved. A helicopter pilot who flew over My Lai the day after the assault testified that the bodies were still visible, that he saw as many as fifty bodies in My Lai from the air, and that he observed fifteen bodies of women and children scattered along the ditch east of My Lai. "It was not running red with blood, as I expected," he testified. "It was a kind of brown."

Several witnesses for Tichenor appeared to balk when called to the stand, some with obvious motivations and others without apparent cause. Foremost, perhaps, in the motivated department was Brigadier General Samuel W. Koster, former major general and former commander of the American Division at My Lai. Koster had been demoted for "dereliction of duty" at My Lai. In testifying for the prosecution the general played it close to his vest—namely, he did not know that a massacre had been committed on the ground at My Lai, only "wild shooting" and a confrontation between ground troops and helicopter pilots had been reported to him, and he, of course, took Colonel Henderson's report that there had been no massacre at all at face value. "I accepted his report as truth," Koster stated. "I thought that he brought me all the facts. . . ."

Koster admitted that he countermanded Henderson's order to Medina to "re-sweep the hamlet" to determine "what had caused civilian casualties." Several weeks later, after he learned of Viet Cong allegations of a massacre, he asked Henderson to submit a written report, which he received sometime thereafter. It was conducted by Lieutenant Colonel Frank Barker, and endorsed by Henderson, and contained some ten to twenty statements of American witnesses who had been present at My Lai. The report reaffirmed Henderson's report that nothing was amiss at My Lai. It was filed in division files and, despite an exhaustive search and interviews of witnesses, it was never found.

Captain (former Warrant Officer) Hugh Thompson was a disappointment to the prosecution. Thompson was central to the exposure of the massacre. He had heroically rescued several women and children from certain execution by Lieutenant Calley at My Lai, but Thompson in his courtroom testimony refused to point the finger of guilt at any of the My Lai defendants. Thompson, at Henderson's trial, recited the facts of the massacre. He testified that he saw between 50 and 125 dead Vietnamese in the village, and that at one point he landed his helicopter and told his door gunner, Specialist Colburn, to train his 50-caliber machine gun on Calley's troops and to shoot them if they interfered with his rescue of Vietnamese women and children from a nearby bunker. Thompson testified that he first reported these atrocities to Major Watke at Landing Zone Dottie on the morning of the massacre, and that two days later he was called before a "full colonel" whose name he could not recall, and that he repeated his accusations to him. Months before the trial, when Thompson testified before the Peers Committee, Thompson named Henderson as the "full colonel" who interviewed him two days after the massacre. His refusal to name Henderson as the interrogation officer at the court-martial probably had little effect on the verdict, other than perhaps psychological, as Henderson himself would ultimately admit in his own testimony that he in fact interviewed Thompson—as indeed his written report to General Koster, which was introduced in evidence, also revealed. But for better or worse, Thompson refused to identify Henderson at his trial.

Two more key witnesses would refuse to name Henderson as the officer who interrogated them some two days after the massacre: Captain Jerry Culverhouse, a helicopter pilot at My Lai, and Specialist Lawrence Colburn, Thompson's door gunner at My Lai, both of whom had given previous testimony to the Peers Committee that Henderson in fact had interviewed them. Their refusal to identify Henderson at the trial, however, knocked out a formal charge pending against Henderson that he lied to the Peers Committee when he stated under oath that he did not interview either of these individuals. But Tichenor had evidence to spare. Even with the Culverhouse and Colburn specifications eliminated, there were still three years of offenses remaining against Henderson, and the witnesses involved in these charges would prove to be damaging witnesses.

The first of these witnesses was Lieutenant Colonel Frederick W. Watke, a highly decorated army pilot, and possibly the central witness of the trial. Watke, a major at My Lai, testified that during the massacre many of his pilots told him that they were disturbed by the happenings at My Lai. He testified that later that morning he contacted Lieutenant Colonel Barker and told him he had to stop this "unnecessary killing." Barker, according to Watke, immediately ordered his executive officer, Major Calhoun, who was over My Lai at the time in a command helicopter, to stop the operation, to hold positions, and to report. But by that time, noon on March 16, 1968, the My Lai massacre was over.

On March 17, the day after the massacre, Watke testified that he and his superior, Lieutenant Colonel John Holladay, officially reported the massacre to Brigadier General George Young, the assistant division commander of the Americal Division, at Landing Zone Dottie. Young, who was not present at My Lai, in turn reported the matter to the division commander, Major General Koster, and a formal meeting was called for the next day among key personnel involved at My Lai.

According to Watke, this meeting took place in Lieutenant Colonel Barker's crowded operational van at Landing Zone Dottie. Present at the meeting were Brigadier General Young, Colonel Henderson, Lieutenant Colonel Frank Barker, Lieutenant Colonel John Holladay, and Major Watke. Watke testified that at this meeting Henderson was told officially of the alleged massacre and ordered to investigate it by Brigadier General Young.

Watke testified that Young directed him (Watke) to repeat his story to Henderson. Watke stated that he told Henderson "of the observations made by my pilots on the 16th and I told him that there were noncombatants killed at My Lai . . . and that Warrant

Officer Thompson threatened to shoot the ground troops if they interfered with his evacuation of noncombatants."

"Did you tell Colonel Henderson of the number of civilian casualties involved?" Tichenor asked.

"I'm sure I did. I imparted to him the large number of noncombatants who were killed." Watke further testified that he told Henderson that one of his pilots, Jerry R. Culverhouse, refused to continue flight operations at My Lai because of the indiscriminate slaughter of Vietnamese civilians by American ground troops.

Henderson listened to his report, Watke stated, and then asked him to make his pilots available for his interrogation. Watke testified that he informed Henderson that his pilots were available, and he subsequently contacted his pilots himself and told them not to worry, but to tell it to Henderson as it really was. Watke testified that he saw Warrant Officer Thompson later that day walk toward Henderson's operational van.

The net was drawn closer around Colonel Henderson. Colonel William Wilson, the officer who had conducted the initial pretrial investigation of the My Lai massacre for the Department of the Army, was called as a prosecution witness by Major Tichenor. Wilson produced Henderson's formal report to Major General Koster, wherein Henderson reported to Koster that a Viet Cong allegation that between four hundred and five hundred civilians had been murdered by American ground troops at My Lai was "obviously a propaganda move to discredit the United States." Wilson continued to read from Henderson's April 24 written report to General Koster:

> No civilians were gathered and shot by United States soldiers. . . . 128 Viet Cong soldiers were killed in action. Twenty noncombatants were inadvertently killed by artillery and cross fire between United States and enemy forces. . . .

Lieutenant Colonel Glenn D. Gibson, a helicopter platoon commander at My Lai, was called to the witness stand and testified that he received no order from Henderson to poll his helicopter pilots for allegations of misconduct on the part of ground troops, and that he did not report to Colonel Henderson that he had in fact made such a poll and that the poll was negative. Henderson had sworn to the Peers Committee that he had given Gibson such an order and that he had subsequently received a negative report from Gibson.

Gibson, a tall, distinguished-looking officer, informed the court-martial jury that he received no such order from Henderson, that he made no such investigation, and that he made no such report to Colonel Henderson.

"I'm not calling Colonel Henderson a liar," he stated, "but I'm telling the truth as I saw it."

Lieutenant Colonel John Holladay, Watke's commanding officer at My Lai and one of the five officers present in Barker's operational van when General Young allegedly gave Colonel Henderson a direct order to investigate the massacre, was called as one of the final prosecution witnesses.

The witness testified that he escorted his subordinate, Major Watke, to Brigadier General Young on the day following the massacre for the purpose of making a formal complaint, and that Young was "appalled." He used the word "murder" to express his indignation, Holladay testified. Holladay stated that Watke also informed the general at this time of Thompson's threat to shoot American personnel at My Lai, and General Young, according to Holladay, expressed consternation. On March 18, two days after the massacre, Holladay testified that the entire matter was gone over again in the presence of Colonel Henderson. Young ordered Watke to repeat his allegations to Colonel Henderson, and at the conclusion of the meeting, Young ordered Henderson to investigate the massacre allegation and to report back to him orally within seventy-two hours.

Holladay also testified that he was shown a copy of Henderson's April 24 written report to General Koster, wherein Henderson reported there was no massacre of Vietnamese civilians at My Lai by American ground forces. He stated he was shown the report by the Americal Division chief of staff several days after it was submitted to General Koster.

"I said bullshit!" Holladay asserted when he read the report. He stated the chief of staff smiled when he made this remark.

While many of the witnesses who testified against Henderson had originally been charged themselves with some part of the My Lai cover-up, Tichenor's most impeccable witness was Lieutenant General William Peers, the non-West Point general who was ordered to conduct the army's investigation of the cover-up. General Peers, of course, headed the Peers Committee that took thousands of pages of testimony during its investigation. It was Henderson's testimony before this committee that resulted in two of the false testimony charges upon which he was standing trial.

General Peers was the heart of candor. On Henderson's second appearance before his committee, General Peers stated Henderson was told that his testimony showed "considerable variance" with other testimony before the committee, and that his testimony "may have been falsified." It was on Henderson's *fifth* appearance before the committee, Peers testified, that he was told that he was definitely suspected of giving false testimony to the committee, of dereliction of duty in failing to investigate the My Lai massacre as ordered to do so by General Koster and General Young, and of conspiracy to cover up the facts of the massacre.

Peers further testified that Henderson informed his committee that he knew, on the day of the massacre, that a large number of men, women, and children had been killed at My Lai. Quoting Henderson, Peers stated: "He said ground troops and air crews were shooting like a bunch of wild people all over the area. He stated there were bodies all over the village. . . . I asked him about his report that 128 V. C. were killed . . . and he insisted that the people he saw could be classified as V. C. . . . He said they were women and children. . . ."

Against this evidence defense attorney Rothblatt called a series of witnesses who testified they too were in the My Lai area following the attack, but heard no rumors of a massacre. Captain Medina (by then out of the army) testified for the defense that he had lied to Henderson when he was questioned following the attack. He stated he told Henderson there was no massacre. He also stated he told Henderson: "I have three children. I would not let anything like that happen."

Brigadier General George H. Young, former assistant division commander of the Americal Division, who allegedly gave Henderson the order to investigate the atrocity, gave surprising testimony. He swore that he had "no knowledge" of atrocities by American troops when he ordered Henderson to make his investigation of the My Lai incident. He stated that he was advised simply that a helicopter pilot had threatened American troops who refused to cease firing upon a group of civilians caught in a cross-fire. It was this allegation, he asserted, that he asked Henderson to investigate. "I have no recollection of any mention of civilian casualties mentioned at the meeting," Young asserted.

Henderson was the last defense witness.

He testified that he had relied upon his subordinates' word that no massacre occurred at My Lai. His innocence was so complete, the colonel testified, that when questioned by army investigators over a year and a half later, he still maintained that "no such massacre had occurred."

His inconsistencies to army investigators, explained Henderson, were due to his own faulty recollection, and also due to the fact that he had a genuine desire to "answer every inquiry." His meeting with General Young dealt only with an assertion of "wild shooting" by Thompson, and his threat to shoot ground troops. This was what he was ordered to investigate. "There was no discussion at all of murder," Henderson maintained, or "of reports of excessive killing." "I was making an *inquiry*, not a formal *investigation*," he complained, losing his temper from time to time on cross-examination when Tichenor seemed to indicate ulterior motives for his testimony. "I did what my judgment felt was best at the time." Although he admitted he had suspicions that Captain Medina was not telling him the truth, his doubts were finally resolved in Medina's favor when Barker submitted his report to General Koster. "At no time," Henderson emphasized, "did I have a suspicion that more than 20 noncombatants had been killed." He made "no attempt to cover up the massacre." "I made every effort to inquire into it as any commander would have done."

Henderson's defense contradicted basic common sense as well as unwritten rules of military life. Military commanders simply are kept informed on matters of common knowledge within their commands. This is a rule of survival in the army and it is followed with a vengeance by army subordinates. Furthermore, to believe Henderson's defense, one had to believe that the government's case was based on rank perjury. Yet on December 17, 1971, after only four hours of deliberation, Henderson's military jury, composed of five colonels and two generals, returned a verdict of not guilty, and Henderson was acquitted.

General Koster was reduced one grade in rank for his conduct at My Lai. Brigadier General Young was reprimanded and retired. Court-martial charges against Major Calhoun (Task Force Barker's executive officer) for failing to report the massacre were dismissed. Related charges were dropped against helicopter pilot Major Watke. Captain Kotouc, accused of cutting a finger from a prisoner's hand, was acquitted by court-martial. Sergeants Mitchell and Hutto were tried and acquitted. Murder charges were dropped against five enlisted men, and assault charges were dropped against a sixth. Cover-up charges were also dropped against seven other officers, ranging in rank from captain to full colonel. That was it, the My Lai courts-martial were completed, and in keeping with things military, the lowest officer of all, Lieutenant Calley, was singled out to bear total responsibility for the massacre.

It is in this regard that Calley is the most victimized military defendant in American history. His tragedy, standing back to back with almost two hundred years of command judicial fraud, transcends the individual and condemns the system.

15

Louis Paul Font:
West Point Honor

On March 17, 1970, page one of *The New York Times* carried a story headed "West Point Graduate Seeking Discharge over Vietnam Issue." The officer concerned, First Lieutenant Louis Paul Font, had held a press conference in the headquarters of the American Civil Liberties Union (ACLU) in New York City in order to announce his intention to seek discharge from the army as a conscientious objector. At his side was Marvin Karpatkin, general counsel of the ACLU and long-time champion of civil liberties. The incident caused the army to cringe. As a rule West Pointers don't cop out against particular wars, nor do first lieutenants denounce participation in national "causes" from the rostrum of a press conference.

Lieutenant Font, an honor graduate in the West Point class of 1968, had never been to Vietnam. He was completing his master's degree at Harvard University in the spring of 1970 when his conscience moved him to denounce the war as immoral and unjust. In a prepared statement Font attacked the genocidal nature of the Vietnam war as waged by the United States. "To me," he stated, "the United States government is destroying another country—an

undeveloped country—and in the process is destroying itself."
Font described a Christmas card. In his words "the color photograph featured Colonel [George S.] Patton standing before a pile
of dismembered Vietnamese bodies; the caption of the card read
'Colonel and Mrs. George S. Patton III—Peace on Earth.' Colonel
Patton is now a Brigadier General. Countless times I have asked
myself: Is this the American ideal or has America gone astray?"
Font continued:

> I am convinced that it makes no difference whatsoever to the
> Vietnamese who looks up into the sky and sees silver napalm
> canisters tumbling down toward him, whether the napalm falls
> because the United States government loves him or hates him
> or is liberating him or pacifying him. . . .
>
> I ask myself, how many times can a man turn his head and
> pretend that he does not see? How many deaths does it take
> before too many people have died . . . ?
>
> Were the Vietnam War, to me, a just war, I would be
> willing, and I am sure quite able, to lead men in battle. . . .
> But, for the reasons I have tried to indicate, my moral position has been so profoundly changed that I must seek discharge from the Army.

Font's story was published in newspapers across America.
Overnight he became a hero to the left. And what was worse, from
the army public relations viewpoint, Font was vocal, intelligent,
and good-looking; he was not a hippie or a long-haired dope addict. He was a former Eagle Scout, a devout Methodist, and from
the state of Kansas. His outspoken views on the Vietnam war
could affect middle America. From the beginning Font was feared
by the military, and the army was quick to respond to his application for discharge. His student days as an army officer at Harvard
University were over. The day after he submitted his application
for discharge as a conscientious objector "to the Vietnam War
only," he was assigned to Fort Meade, Maryland, to await final
action on his application. From the point of prestige, Font was

relegated to the trashcan at Meade and given a pointless, demeaning job. But he announced that he would obey all orders pending his discharge, and that he would continue to perform military duty at Fort Meade—insofar as he could. In his words: "I hope to follow the laws of the land as long as I can; then I'll have to follow the laws of conscience."

If Font was following a chart of "obedience" it was foreign to most military minds. He assuredly did not learn it at West Point. Font asserted that he did not intend to "disparage" the armed forces. But he recounted the story of his conversation with a major while he was a cadet at West Point. "How does it feel to kill?" Font asked the major. The major replied: "I feel the same elation as when I kill deer." He then asked the major if civilians were killed in Vietnam, and if so to what extent. Font stated the major responded (and these words are "etched" in his memory): "Cadet Font, it is like this. You are walking down a street after a battle and you see a six-year old girl lying there. You roll her over [a foot motion] and you say, 'How about that, the Viet Cong are now using six-year-old girls to do their dirty work.'" Font stood listening, dumfounded. Then, later, "I cannot participate in any way in a military organization where such things are being done. . . ."

At Fort Meade, Font would definitely be an oddity as well as a challenge. There he would be controlled and neutralized. He was the first West Point graduate to refuse to participate in a particular war on moral grounds. He was high profile in the eyes of the press, and the press refused to drop his story. Fort Meade authorities conducted his conscientious objector hearing in April, and the recommendation was unfavorable. This meant more months of inactivity pending final Department of the Army action on the Fort Meade recommendation. On May 4, 1970, *The Washington Post* ran a detailed story on Font, the first West Point graduate in 168 years to seek discharge because of an objection to a specific war. The *Post* further quoted Font as stating that the very thought of remaining in the army "makes me sick." On Sunday, May 24,

1970, *The Washington Post* carried a letter to the editor signed by four discharged West Point graduates strongly supporting Louis Font "in saying—No."

In June the Department of the Army ruled against Font, and on June 17 the story was carried on the wires of the Associated Press. Font and his ACLU lawyers would take the case to federal court, to the United States District Court for the District of Maryland, sitting in Baltimore. The federal judge in Baltimore ordered Font frozen in his job at Fort Meade pending final resolution of his case in federal court.

Home on leave in July, Font was quoted in the *Kansas City Star* of July 13 as stating: "While the war is going on, I object to everything in the armed forces. . . . I have no doubt that every job in the Army contributes to the Vietnam War. The entire Army is geared to it. . . . You have to draw the line someplace, and I've drawn it at the uniform." On the same day the *Chicago Daily News* carried a detailed editorial entitled "Lt. Louis Font, a Unique Man." The *Kansas City Kansan* also carried a story on Font on the same date. Three days later Font's picture was spread across half a page in the *St. Louis Dispatch*, over the heading: "No Doubt in My Mind That the Vietnam War Is Immoral and Unjust." Font also appeared on national TV on NBC's Frontiers of Faith. On July 24 the federal District Court in Baltimore rejected his claim of specific objection to only one war (conscientious-objector law requires an objection to *all* war, and not to a *specific* war), and the story was carried in scores of newspapers across America. Font's lawyers announced he would appeal.

The Washington, D.C., *Sunday Star* of August 9, 1970, quoted Lieutenant Font as stating that he would rather go to prison than remain in the army. "No matter what happens," he asserted, "I'll be a free man inside." A few days later, Lieutenant Font, anticipating that his specific objection to the Vietnam war would not be ruled upon in his favor by appellate courts, asked me to represent him in his denunciation of the military. Having all but given up hope for discharge as a conscientious objector to the Vietnam war, he resolved to speak out against that war specifically and against militarism generally, but he wished to do so within the framework of the First Amendment's guaranty of free speech insofar as possible. Thereafter Font and I conferred daily on every aspect of his case. Font had also joined a group called the Concerned Officers, and was an editor of their monthly publication. He invited me to attend one of their meetings, and I did.

On Sunday, September 27, 1970, *The New York Times* reported a news conference held by twenty-eight commissioned officers in Washington, D.C. The group called themselves the Concerned Officer Movement, and purportedly represented some 250 concerned American officers on active duty from Iceland to the Pacific. Their spokesman stated they were going to "speak out." The *Times* reported that one of their officers, First Lieutenant Louis Font, stated that "never before in United States history has there existed a group of anti-war officers." Font was further quoted:

I am many things before a military officer. . . . I am an American citizen. I am a human being. As a human being, as an American citizen and as a military officer, I reject this war. . . .

I personally refuse to participate in the Vietnam War. I simply will not go. I have asked myself time and again: "When the law becomes a crime, consensus and conformity become a crime. Am I to condone it?" My answer is no.

At Fort Meade, Lieutenant Font's hair began to grow long, and he ceased shining his shoes. His brass turned green and he reported to work late. As off-post housing coordinator, Font conducted a survey of off-post housing, and found racist practices were followed by most civilian landlords in the Fort Meade–Odenton, Maryland, area. Font reported this practice to his superiors and asked that something be done about it. He was assigned another job. He was to count the vacant barracks at Fort Meade and report their number periodically to his superiors. Instead of counting the barracks, Font inspected the barracks where antiwar, antimilitary enlisted men were quartered. On November 12, 1970, the *Baltimore News American* reported Font's findings. The barracks at Fort Meade were "an outrage to common decency." Font was told not to count any more barracks.

On November 24, 1970, Font was quoted in *The Washington Post* as asserting that Lieutenant Calley (whose trial was in progress at Fort Benning) was being scapegoated and that his trial should be halted. Font further charged in the *Post* article that the real "culprits" in Vietnam were "the generals who make military policy." My Lai, Font continued, "was not an aberration. My Lai was part of a deliberate, criminal policy." He also announced that he would co-chair a War Crimes Inquiry that would be conducted in Washington, D.C., in early December, where veterans of the Vietnam war would testify "to innumerable violations of international military conventions."

From December 1–3, 1970, the Citizens Commission of Inquiry on United States War Crimes in Vietnam held a marathon session at the Du Pont Plaza Hotel in Washington, D.C. Young veterans of the Vietnam war from all branches of service testified as to war crimes that they had witnessed or participated in, in Vietnam. The accounts were of massacres, of systematic murder and torture of Vietnamese civilians and war prisoners by American servicemen. They were startling and tragic, and they were headlined across America. It was a meeting which Louis Font and Todd Ensign of the Citizens Commission of Inquiry had originally offered to hold in Columbus, Georgia, at the height of the Calley trial. But George Latimer turned their offer down. Font had journeyed to Columbus, together with Ensign, but Latimer advised them that he didn't want to confuse the issue, and the veterans assembled in Washington, D.C.

Font's concluding remarks at the inquiry were later recorded in the *Congressional Record*:

At any rate, what I'm simply trying to get across is that the hearings are nearing an end, and yet the war crimes continue;

and that something should be done about this. And further, that what we have heard today are many incidents—different individuals, in many different places in Vietnam, but relating to the same sort of information. It seems quite obvious that a pattern emerges. And that pattern, coupled with what I learned at West Point—that a commander is responsible for *everything* that goes on in his unit—makes it quite clear to me that what is going on in Vietnam is something for which someone other than a lieutenant, such as Lieutenant Calley and others are responsible.

I feel strongly that if Lieutenant Calley is guilty of anything, then the generals, and perhaps even higher are far more responsible.

Following the December War Crimes Inquiry, Lieutenant Font returned to his job at Fort Meade. The weather was cold, and he found that the barracks where antiwar and antimilitary soldiers were billeted were just as dreadful as they were in November. Specifically, the barracks were unheated, without hot water, their urinals and toilets did not work, and there were large holes in the sides of the buildings. Many of the soldiers who lived in these buildings were also sick. Since Font was technically still assigned to the housing office at Fort Meade, he formally requested that a post medical team inspect the barracks. As usual, nothing was done.

On Thursday, December 24, the oldest newspaper in America, the *Maryland Gazette*, located only twenty miles from Washington, headlined a story across page one, together with photographs of Fort Meade barracks. The headline read: "Meade Barracks Called Deficient. Hundreds Are Living in Filth." The *Gazette* quoted a report written by First Lieutenant Louis Font, post housing officer. Font was further described as a "West Point graduate who has been at odds with other Meade officers in the past few months." Font's offer to take the *Gazette* reporters through the barracks was refused by the post, and the *Gazette* ran the story full blast.

The *Evening Capitol* in Annapolis carried the same story, and on December 29, 1970, Fort Meade officials were back on page one of the *Gazette*. Font was, in essence, called a liar and was ordered not to talk to the press any more about the condition of the barracks. A date in the future was selected for *Gazette* reporters to visit some of the barracks, thus presumably concluding the incident. But to be on the safe side, the post ordered its medical doctors to inspect the barracks. On January 12 Lieutenant Font obtained a copy of the six-page report dated January 12. It was signed by Captain Robert J. Master, M.D., Medical Corps, preventive medicine officer.

The report overwhelmingly supported Lieutenant Font's charges. The "ambient temperature" in one of the barracks was reported as 58 degrees F. Backflow from two of the toilets in another building was found to be drawn directly into the post water supply because of the absence of "siphon breakers" on the toilets. Another barracks temperature was listed as 43 degrees F., the hot water was listed as 44 degrees F. The sulfur dioxide concentration in one barracks was found dangerously high. Large holes were found in barracks. The hot water in another troop billet was found to be 38 degrees F. A pile of dirt was found in one shower room. Water was found standing on the latrine floor in another billet. A "hot" electrical outlet was lying on the floor in another barracks. One toilet in a barracks leaked when flushed and discharged large quantities of water onto the floor. Quoting from the "conclusions" section of the report:

It is the consensus of the inspectors that the barracks (particularly those in B Company) can be considered as not suitable for human habitation under the conditions observed above. It is therefore recommended that the occupants be housed in another location until such time that the basic essentials such as heat and hot water can be provided on a consistent daily basis. . . .

Lieutenant Font, meanwhile, had collected eighty-five statements from the occupants of the barracks, and on January 18, 1971, he submitted his eighty-five statements and a copy of the medical report in question to the post commander. He also mailed copies of his eighty-five statements and the post medical report to seven United States senators and congressmen.

Font also reported to the press that on the basis of his study of the verbatim report of the December War Crimes Inquiry, of which some three hundred pages of testimony were recorded, that First Army commander Lieutenant General Jonathan Seaman and Major General Samuel W. Koster, both of whom were stationed at Fort Meade, should be investigated for war-crime activity during their respective commands in Vietnam. Font's war-crime allegation was widely covered in the nation's press.

On January 21, 1971, Baltimore city's black congressman, Parren Mitchell, who had received Font's report of Fort Meade's poor barracks conditions, demanded an investigation. Many of the soldiers who lived in the worst barracks were black. Mitchell also released the entire report, including the eighty-five statements and the post medical report, to the press. The following day Lieutenant Font turned his attention to the Fort Meade barracks problem in earnest. Fearing that the First Army commander, Lieutenant General Seaman, might not have received a copy of his housing report, Font resolved to hand-carry three copies to General Seaman's office for him and his staff.

At the general's office Font announced his presence to an aide and requested a personal conference with the army commander. A few seconds later General Seaman's chief of staff, a major general, entered and began to scream at him. "I've ordered that you're not to come into this building. Why do you keep coming back?" Font tried to explain the purpose of his mission, but there was a button unbuttoned on his uniform blouse. "Button that button! That's a direct order!" Font buttoned the button.

Once again he attempted to explain his mission. He opened his briefcase to hand over a copy of his barracks report, when, according to Font, the two-star general grabbed him by the arm and propelled him toward the door. "I don't want anything of yours," the general yelled. "I order you not to leave anything—get the hell out!" Font was half shoved toward the door by the enraged general. But once at the door the general had a change of heart. He turned to several officers who witnessed the transaction.

"Call the MPs!" he screamed. "Font, you're under arrest for disobeying my order to leave this building." Nine military policemen and the deputy army staff judge advocate responded, and Font was escorted to the Fort Meade provost marshal's office where he was detained for four hours. On his release he was officially restricted to his job, his quarters, place of worship, and mess hall. Several days later formal court-martial charges were lodged against Lieutenant Font for his confrontation with the army chief of staff in General Seaman's waiting room. General Seaman, in turn, ordered the charges investigated at a formal Article 32 proceeding. The charges provided for a maximum of twenty-five years' imprisonment. Lieutenant Font promptly preferred court-martial charges of his own against the general officer involved for assault and battery.

The story of course broke in the press, and Font was once again in newsprint from coast to coast. Congressman Mitchell from Baltimore visited Fort Meade personally and inspected the barracks, which had by that time been patched up. Mitchell charged that the barracks had been "belatedly" repaired, and that the army had not acted at all "until the matter was brought to the attention of the public and a congressman." The post executive officer countercharged that the barracks were intentionally destroyed by their occupants in a plot engineered by Lieutenant Font and others. He also charged that the medical doctor who authored the medical report on the barracks was a close personal friend of Lieutenant Font's, and a part of the "conspiracy."

Lieutenant Font next preferred court-martial charges against the post commander for dereliction of duty in permitting American soldiers to live in filthy, unheated, ill-repaired buildings unfit for human habitation. The *Chicago Sun Times* reported on Sunday, January 31, 1971, that Font had been charged with five offenses, carrying a maximum sentence of twenty-five years in jail, several days *after* he had formally requested the secretary of the army to convene a board of inquiry to investigate atrocities occurring in Vietnam during operations commanded by General Seaman. The *San Francisco Sunday Examiner and Chronicle* reported that the decision whether Font was to be tried rested with Lieutenant General Jonathan O. Seaman, "one of those who Font said should be investigated in a war crimes inquiry." Reported in the same stories, and in similar stories in other newspapers, was the fact that General Seaman had only two days earlier dismissed My Lai cover-up charges against fellow West Pointer Major General Samuel Koster, the senior American officer present at the My Lai massacre (during the massacre Koster had circled over My Lai in a helicopter at two thousand feet for four hours).

Font's purpose, of course, was to escalate his charges against the military by attaching them to an item of continuing news interest. He strongly believed that the military could not stand the heat, and that they would be the first to give up. Font's defense planning in this regard was given a very able assist by the charges against Font. Of all court-martial charges that could have been leveled at Lieutenant Font, these had to be the weakest and the most absurd possible. The army promptly made them even weaker by taking five *identical,* word-for-word statements from the five officers who were present in the general's waiting room and witnessed the event.

Concerned junior officers complained that the army had falsely indicted Font just to shut him up. Congressman Mitchell called the charges against Font "blatant," and motivated solely because of his criticism of his superiors. In the *Congressional Record* of

February 4, 1971, Congressman Mikva, of Illinois, soundly condemned the army for placing Font under court-martial charges:

> . . . Lieutenant Font's superior officers have turned from petty harassment to much more serious means of silencing this man who dares to criticize their Army.
>
> This may sound like an extreme construction to place on the court-martial charges brought against Lieutenant Font by the men he criticized, but when you examine the substance of the charges it is difficult to construe them any other way.
>
> We cannot permit our Army to treat its critics in such an arrogant and arbitrary fashion. . . . If Lieutenant Font is a gadfly, then the Army needs more of them. . . .

Additional congressmen got into the fray on the side of Font. Representatives Bella S. Abzug and Ronald V. Dellums added their protest to those of Mikva and Mitchell. "Reckless repression," and "military vindictiveness," were charged by Abzug. Dellums and Mitchell demanded that the secretary of the army personally investigate the matter.

Font's request to conduct a press conference of his own to discuss possible war-crime charges against two army generals was denied. The story was carried on February 4, 1971, in *The Washington Post*. The *Post* took note that Font's present job at Fort Meade was adding up adding-machine tapes to see if the tapes were correct. Congressman Mitchell persisted in his demand for an investigation of the charges against Font. The local press reported that Fort Meade was under "siege." On February 16, 1971, Lieutenant Font requested his superiors to permit him the use of the post theater for an afternoon "rally." Font asserted that he wished to hold a rally for his local officer and enlisted supporters at Fort Meade. The request was denied.

On February 17, 1971, Lieutenant Font, in uniform and speaking at a press conference called by Congressman Parren Mitchell, calmly announced that he had that day preferred formal war-crime charges against First Army commander Lieutenant General Jonathan O. Seaman and Major General Samuel W. Koster, for conduct in contradiction to the law of land warfare in Vietnam. Taking advantage of a provision in the Uniform Code of Military Justice which permits any person on active duty to prefer court-martial charges against any other person in uniform, Font swore to his charges and submitted them to the commanding general of the Continental Army at Fort Monroe, Virginia, for investigation and appropriate action. Font handed out copies of his charges at the press conference.

General Koster, whose My Lai cover-up charges had only recently been dismissed by General Seaman, was reindicted by Font for dereliction of duty while in command of troops in Vietnam during 1967 and 1968. Font charged that Koster had permitted his troops to torture prisoners of war, to wantonly burn and destroy native homes, to indiscriminately kill Vietnamese civilians to increase unit body counts, and to turn large segments of South Vietnam into free fire zones, in contradiction to the law of land warfare. General Seaman was charged by Font in two specifications of conspiracy during 1966 and 1967 to commit war crimes in Vietnam. Seaman was charged by Font in planning the total destruction of various named Vietnamese villages and the destruction of the people living in the villages, the construction of concentration camps and the forced removal of Vietnamese population centers into these camps, and the execution of free fire zones in Vietnam. A third specification alleged that General Seaman was derelict in his duty during the same time period by failing to control troops under his command who willfully and illegally destroyed the villages of Ben Suc, Rach Bap, Bung Cong, and Rach Kien by burning all the livestock and fruit trees and gardens, by removing the civilian population to concentration camps, and by thereafter turning the land areas in question into free fire zones—all in contradiction to the law of land warfare.

Font's charges were carried in the nation's press. Neil Sheehan, writing for *The New York Times* News Service, wryly commented upon Font's purpose. Sheehan noted that Font possessed a three-hundred-page statement of atrocities compiled by Vietnam veterans at the December War Crimes Inquiry in Washington, D.C. He also noted that Seaman had only recently dismissed My Lai cover-up charges against fellow West Pointer General Koster, and that Font was still fighting for his conscientious-objector discharge in civilian courts. Sheehan then observed: "But the lieutenant, who measures his public statements carefully, had made his point."

The point was picked up by the military the same day. Font's scheduled Article 32 investigation of the court-martial charges against Font was "postponed." The same day, February 22, Font wrote a letter to Brigadier General Harold E. Parker, assistant judge advocate general of the army in charge of military justice, and asked him to read the evidence that he submitted against Generals Seaman and Koster (three hundred pages of testimony from the December War Crimes Inquiry concerning assorted war crimes by American troops in Vietnam, and two books by Jonathan Schell on the destruction of Vietnamese villages by American personnel). Font also referred Parker to Professor Richard Falk of Princeton University, one of America's foremost authorities on war crimes, with whom Font had consulted prior to his signing charges against Seaman and Koster.

Lieutenant Font then advised General Parker: "I am currently reviewing the case histories of *several more* general officers with a view toward preferring war crime charges if warranted; and I am sure that you can appreciate the difficulties that I encounter at Fort Meade in obtaining technical assistance in this regard." (Emphasis added.) Font thereupon asked Parker to provide him a judge advocate officer from the Pentagon to furnish technical assistance in his investigation. He requested the services of an officer with a background in military justice and international law, to include the law of war.

Within a week Lieutenant Font was offered a chance to resign his commission because of "substandard performance of duty." The *Maryland Gazette* reported on March 1, 1971: "It seems to be a compromise. Font will be out of the service and the Army will not have him around raising hell." The basis of the substandard performance of duty was reported in numerous newspapers, including *The New York Times* and *The Washington Post*, as reporting to work late, spending too much time on the telephone, and a general "unwillingness to expend any effort in the performance of duties." That same week, the United States Supreme Court ruled in a case involving another serviceman that a selective objection to a particular war was not legally within the definition of a conscientious objector as defined by Congress, and accordingly, a serviceman who objected to service in a particular war on moral grounds was not entitled to discharge from the armed forces as a conscientious objector. Tom Watson of the *Maryland Gazette* asked Font if the army was really throwing him out for substandard work. Watson quoted Font's answer: "The point is, I've done too good a job at Fort Meade by exposing the conditions."

But the army dragged its heels in acting on Font's resignation. Under the provisions of law which it offered Font in permitting him to resign, severance pay was required. That Font would receive an honorable discharge was never questioned, but the matter of severance pay caused the army to balk. Fort Meade officials, red-faced in the extreme, quietly called on Font at his home and asked him to sign a second resignation under another provision of law which would have authorized his honorable discharge, but without severance pay.

Lieutenant Font refused. He demanded severance pay. For days neither side budged. Then the army dismissed Font's charges of dereliction of duty against the Fort Meade post commander, relative to the failure to keep Fort Meade barracks in a livable condition. On March 31 Font joined Senator Vance Hartke in a press conference in the new Senate Office Building, announcing a proposed National Peace Action Coalition march in Washington, D.C., during the month of April. Five days later Congressman Dellums demanded that Fort Meade place Font on special travel orders which would permit him to accompany Dellums on an inspection of army bases nationwide. The request was denied.

On April 7 Font again refused to submit a resignation under regulations that would permit his discharge without severance pay. Two days later the judge advocate general of the army resolved the problem. The judge advocate general ruled that in Font's case severance pay would not be paid even though authorized by army regulations, and on April 12, 1971, Font was given his honorable discharge from the army without severance pay. The same day Harvard University reinstated Louis Font in its graduate program, tuition free.

Louis Font had won. The truth overpowered the army, and the "siege" of Fort Meade was over.

16

Michael Daley:
The Trial of a War Resister

Louis Font was a conscientious objector who gradually evolved into a war resister. Louis fought with all his energy, and his risks were tremendous. But he fought with charm, with reserved wit and humor, and he never used rough language. Michael Daley was an up-state New Yorker. He never possessed anything but hatred for the military to begin with. He barely made it through the first few months of military training before his hatred was overflowing. And his disgust with the army was undisguised. Compared to Font, Daley was a street fighter. He was an enlisted man and he used four-letter words. He could have been a conscientious objector from the start, but he refused to fill out the application. He considered it intentionally complicated and devious, something that the military devised to thwart the non-college-educated GI who might apply for conscientious objector status. A college graduate himself, Michael Daley chose other routes. When he received orders to Vietnam in the summer of 1970, he deserted.

When I first met Michael he was bitter and cynical. In appearance he was fiery, volcanic even, but frightened. In the fall of 1971, after an absence of fourteen months, he had surrendered at

Fort Devens, Massachussetts. He was processed and retained at Fort Devens to await what ordinarily would have been a routine undesirable discharge, an administrative discharge, in lieu of trial by court-martial. Technically, the military could court-martial its Michael Daleys, its dissenters, but its stockades were already filled to the breaking point, and no useful purpose was served by the court-martial of war resisters. It drew out the agony of military administrators to even greater extremes. Administrative discharges could be processed in four to six months, but court-martial and appellate judicial machinery could drag out to eighteen months or longer. This was not appealing to an already hard-pressed military, particularly to the army, which had the greatest share of dissenters. Thus army administrators leaned heavily upon the administrative process of separating war resisters from its ranks. It was a relatively inexpensive and efficient procedure. But Michael Daley's case was not routine, and the signals were changed after he had been at Fort Devens for about four months. The army resolved to court-martial Daley, and when I first met him he was under court-martial charges for being AWOL for 438 days. In my opinion he was facing certain imprisonment.

On Michael's first day out of Advanced Individual Training in August 1970 he had visited his unit's game room to play pinball. He lost a close game and broke a window in anger. He reported his act to the charge of quarters, however, and stated that he would pay for the window. Testifying at his court-martial over a year and half later, Daley brought up the window incident. Speaking in a slightly brittle New England accent, punctuated with four-letter words, he stated that after he reported the window to the charge of quarters, he turned. "This officer is behind me, and he says, 'Listen, did you just break that window in the game room?' And I turned around and told him: 'I just broke that *fucking* window in the game room.' He felt offended. . . . There's some sort of image I can't stand in officers and it's started all the way up the line. You can't talk to them because they have some medal on their shoulders. He accused me of being an SDS because I came out with that sort of an answer. He accused me of being some sort of political subversive. That was the first day I was in the Company, and I didn't, I didn't say anything except that I broke a window in the game room. . . ."

Michael always faced the issues with the military head-on.

At his trial I asked him, "Do you have any intention of being a soldier?"

He answered, "No."

"I beg your pardon?"

"No, I don't."

"Why not . . . ?"

"I believe the war is wrong. . . ."

On cross-examination, the prosecutor asked him if he ever filled out a conscientious-objector form. Michael responded that the form "favored" him as a college graduate. He stated that he could have filled it out. "I have got the credentials. I might . . . get the wording right. . . . You know, like complete the whole conscientious objector application. It's a bunch of bullshit. You have got to run an obstacle course. You have got to defend yourself. . . . I don't think it's necessary."

When I met Michael in the spring of 1972 in Baltimore, he had visited Washington, D.C., to confer with Congressman Michael Harrington, Democrat from Boston and member of the House Armed Services Committee. Harrington was at the time very ably running interference for Michael with his Fort Devens command, both in the Boston press and in Congress. Specifically, Harrington accused the Devens command of referring Michael's fourteen-month AWOL charges to trial by general court-martial (instead of separating him with an administrative discharge) because he exercised his First Amendment rights under the Constitution of the United States to criticize the United States involvement in Vietnam, and to criticize certain untoward conditions at Fort Devens. In Harrington's words, "I am seriously disturbed by concrete documentary evidence which shows that Pfc Daley is being singled out for particularly harsh treatment by the Army because of his participation in a series of entirely lawful and proper activities which focused attention on unsatisfactory living conditions at the Personnel Control Facility at Fort Devens."

The evidence that the congressman was referring to was a document written by Daley's commanding officer, a lieutenant colonel, recommending that Daley's application for an administrative discharge be denied. The colonel's reasoning was expressed in writing as follows:

> PFC Daley has been active in the Fort Devens United Front action as well as the functions of the Common Sense Bookstore and various agencies in Boston. It would be in the best interests of the U.S. Army to have this man stand trial by court-martial. It is the opinion of this command that PFC Daley should be considered for a punitive discharge by the proper judicial authority.

Harrington noted in the *Congressional Record* that the statement above "can only mean that Pfc Daley is being denied an undesirable [administrative] discharge as punishment for his participation in the activities to which [his commander] alludes." Harrington continued:

> Thus, it appears that the Army has decided to proceed with a court-martial for the offense of being AWOL based not on the merits of the case itself, but on someone's embarrassment over lawful and unrelated activities engaged in by the individual in question.
>
> . . . There can be no justification for treating him more harshly than others who have committed the same offense as he has, simply because he exercised the rights of free expression which the Constitution guarantees him.

When Michael Daley surrendered after his fourteen-month absence and his refusal to proceed to Vietnam, he was quartered in the Fort Devens Personnel Control Facility (PCF) barracks, barracks that are set aside by the army to house its dissenters who are ultimately awaiting administrative discharge. PCF barracks are not stockades. There are no bars, no guards, and the soldiers in these barracks are not in jail. But as Louis Font reported concerning Fort Meade's PCF barracks, they are generally unfit for human habitation. Devens' PCF billets were no exception. Michael Daley expressed his dissatisfaction with these barracks to his superiors at Fort Devens during the fall of 1971, following his surrender, and prior to the decision to try him by court-martial. At Daley's trial in the spring of 1972, he testified that he had made frequent complaints to PCF cadre about the poor conditions of the barracks. He had complained about the barbed wire that surrounded these barracks. He had complained because the barracks were unheated in the wintertime. He had complained because the urinals did not work and the men had to stand in urine to shave in the mornings. He had complained because there was a shortage of blankets. "A lot of people in PCF didn't have blankets during the winter months. There wasn't enough blankets to go around. . . . There was a lack of field jackets. . . . They didn't have field jackets to wear when they were on outside detail. . . ." He had also complained because of the rats and roaches that were in the barracks, and he complained because nothing was ever done about his complaints.

Michael testified that after he saw that his complaints effected no change, he had organized a soldiers' union, the United Front. He also had visited the Common Sense Bookstore in Boston and sought help from the Vietnam Veterans Against the War. Shortly afterward, in mid-December 1971, Michael had conducted his first public demonstration at Fort Devens against living conditions in the PCF barracks, against United States involvement in the Vietnam war, and against the racist tactics of the Fort Devens command in the trial of black soldiers. The demonstration, complete with placards, was conducted by about twenty to thirty off-duty soldiers, right outside the main gate at Fort Devens. Michael's fourth and last public demonstration at Fort Devens took place in mid-January 1972. This was his largest. Involving over one hundred demonstrators, it started on a Friday night, January 14, and lasted all day Saturday. The soldiers camped in pup-tents forty yards outside the main gate. Their placards denounced the Vietnam war, the racist military justice policies followed by the post, and the filthy living conditions in the PCF barracks. An angry Michael Daley was repeatedly photographed at this demonstration.

"Did you get permission to demonstrate out there?" I asked him at his trial.

"No. I didn't think it was necessary."

"Cold out there?"

"Yes."

"Was the press there?"

"Yes."

"Pictures being taken?"

"Yes."

Another item that inflamed Congressman Harrington and others who assisted in Michael Daley's defense was that on the very day of Michael Daley's biggest and most publicized demonstration at Fort Devens, the acting commander of the fort personally telephoned the chief of staff at Fort Lewis, Washington, and demanded that Daley's military records be airmailed immediately to Fort Devens. A soldier who is to be court-martialed for AWOL cannot be tried or even charged until his charging unit is in possession of his military records, which contain, among other vital documents, official morning report entries showing his AWOL. Ordinarily, if a soldier is to be court-martialed, a processing clerk in the local judge advocate office will initiate necessary correspondence to obtain missing records. Although post commanders may lawfully undertake such measures on their own, it is highly unusual and questionable conduct. Michael Daley was officially charged on the Monday following his last demonstration at Fort Devens. He was charged with a 438-day AWOL, and he was charged *before* his records arrived from Fort Lewis. So verification of the time involved had to have been obtained by someone directly from Fort Lewis, Washington, by long-distance telephone or by telegraphic means. Michael's records containing documentary evidence to support the 438-day AWOL charged against him arrived two days *later*, on January 19, 1972.

On January 24 Michael's commanding officer formally recommended that Daley's previously submitted request for discharge by administrative channels be denied. This was the document in which his commander noted that Michael had been active in the Fort Devens United Front and in the Common Sense Bookstore in Boston, and should stand trial by court-martial. In his recommendation, it was noted that Michael had surrendered at Fort Devens on October 28, 1971, and that his records were "discovered at Ft. Lewis" on January 19, 1973. It was this document, which summed up the series of circumstances leading to the decision to court-martial Michael Daley, that convinced Congressman Harrington that Daley was prosecuted for AWOL *not* because of the nature of the AWOL offense but because of his exercise of free speech at Fort Devens. And needless to say, Harrington and his New England constituents took free speech quite seriously.

After I was retained to defend Michael Daley I took stock of the case in several meetings with Michael and his defense workers in Washington. At these meetings I recommended that we up the stakes in Michael's case. I did not believe that we would win on Harrington's First Amendment issue as it currently stood, however gross it appeared. I completely agreed with Congressman Harrington's views relating to the First Amendment violation, and was completely convinced that Daley was in truth singled out for AWOL prosecution at Fort Devens because of his protest activities. But I felt we needed additional proof of the command fraud involved. So I recommended that we seek additional witnesses at Fort Devens in a *wholesale* fashion to prove further command fraud in this case. We had enough facts to work with. With a little luck we might parlay our known facts into a mountain. Not only might we gain vital additional facts, but we would also give the command an opportunity to use command force to prevent Michael Daley from gathering additional witnesses. In short, we would offer the Devens command an excellent opportunity to over-reach us in preparing our defense.

Michael thus wrote a registered letter to the Fort Devens commanding general, in longhand. The letter stated:

I respectfully notify you that beginning Friday, April 7, 1972, through Thursday, April 14, 1972, a group of friends organized in my defense plans to obtain information pertinent and crucial to my defense at my (forthcoming) general court-martial.

This will involve the distribution of the enclosed questionnaire and the statement in the *Congressional Record* of March 27, 1972, by Congressman Michael Harrington. . . .

We plan to set up a defense table in front of the Main Post Exchange so as to enable us to better distribute this questionnaire. . . . Our purpose . . . is to gather defense witnesses.

The questionnaire, which had been commercially printed in advance of Michael's letter, contained twelve questions together with several pages of material that Congressman Harrington had submitted to the *Congressional Record*. The commanding general at Ford Devens in previous answers to both Congressman Michael Harrington and to Congresswoman Bella Abzug had assured both that "at the time I made the decision to refer [Daley's] case to trial, I was completely unaware of PFC Daley's protest activities." He subsequently wrote that Michael's protest activities "although noted were not a factor" in deciding to court-martial Daley. The first question in our questionnaire, which provided space under each question for the reader's answer, asked: "Do you have any information pertaining to how [the commanding general] can state that Pfc Michael Daley's political activities 'although noted were not a factor' in . . . deciding that Pfc Daley should be court-martialed?" The next several questions related to possible knowledge on the part of the reader of the establishment and existence of military justice policies and statistics at Fort Devens pertaining to the court-martial of soldiers who absented themselves from overseas replacement stations.

In other questions we inquired if the reader had ever overheard the commanding general or his staff "make racist statements," or use "racist epithets," or tell "racist jokes," or "make a statement to the effect that Pfc Daley should be hanged for publicly advocating black rights at Fort Devens." Or if he should be hanged for "exposing substandard, disease-ridden, filthy, rat and roach infested enlisted men's barracks at Fort Devens." We asked our readers specifically if they were "satisfied with . . . living conditions" at Fort Devens. We asked Fort Devens soldiers if they had any knowledge of past racial court-martial cases at the fort. We asked if they had knowledge of "instructions" to the Fort Devens staff to hang Michael Daley for conducting protest demonstrations at Fort Devens. The readers were asked to read and answer each question and to submit the completed form, together with their names and signatures thereon, to the Michael Daley Defense Action Committee.

Under the *Canons of Professional Ethics* of the American Bar Association, either side in civil or criminal cases has the absolute, unconditional right to gather witnesses or other data pertinent to their side of the case, without resort to intermediaries of any sort. It was my belief that Fort Devens command officials would violate our rights in this regard. I did not believe that the Fort Devens' command would permit us to seek the kind of evidence our defense questionnaire sought. I did not believe that the Devens' staff judge advocate or provost marshal would permit it. In short, I felt the command would use force to prevent Michael Daley's workers from distributing the questionnaires in question, and I wished to give them that opportunity. It was for this reason that we furnished the commanding general an advance copy of the questionnaire, and advised him of the distribution date and place. Congresswoman Bella Abzug also wrote the general on this matter:

. . . But if the court-martial must go on regardless, then I am concerned that provision be made for a fair and complete defense. PFC Daley has forwarded to me a copy of a questionnaire which he desires to distribute on the post to help him gather facts and witnesses. This I consider essential to a proper defense. Therefore, I certainly hope that efforts to distribute the questionnaire will not be impeded by your command.

The day of Michael Daley's trial was drawing near when several of his co-workers first appeared to distribute the questionnaire in front of the Fort Devens main post exchange building. After several minutes they were placed in military police sedans and driven off post and told not to return. The next day between 3:00 and 4:00 p.m. two members of Michael's defense committee reported to the main PX, and started passing out questionnaires. Michael Daley and a second committeeman stood five paces to one side as witnesses. Approximately fifty questionnaires had been distributed when the agents of the Fort Devens Criminal Investigation Division and military police arrived at the scene.

The two committee members passing out the questionnaires were former First Lieut. Louis Paul Font, recently graduated from Harvard's graduate school, and Miss Amy Gwen Salzman, a seventeen-year-old high-school graduate and a member of the Common Sense Bookstore and other causes in Boston. Louis was approached first. His questionnaires were jerked from his hand. Miss Salzman was quickly accosted and relieved of her questionnaires. Louis was handcuffed, with his hands behind his back, and thrown into the rear of a military police sedan. He and Miss Salzman were then driven to the provost marshal's office, where they were separated. Louis was fingerprinted and mugged. Off and on for three hours he said he was physically harassed. He stated he was repeatedly thrown against a wall while handcuffed. Then without any charges being preferred against either of them, or without formal arrest procedures being completed or even initiated, both Font and

Salzman were returned to military police sedans, driven off post, and told not to return. Their defense questionnaires were returned to their custody at this time.

Instead of only one issue of illegal command influence in the Michael Daley case (i.e., the First Amendment issue), we now had a second—the command use of force to prevent the gathering of defense evidence at Fort Devens.

A third issue was already fast in the making, thanks to Congressman Harrington. In his effort to inquire if Daley's AWOL charges were referred to trial by general court-martial at Fort Devens for political reasons, he asked the post commander, on March 26, 1972, to provide him with information from his files as to the type of action that was taken in regard to similar AWOL cases at Fort Devens in the past. The general replied in his reply of March 30:

> There are no statistics available concerning the percentage of individuals granted administrative discharges versus those referred to trial by court-martial. These statistics are not kept. In many cases, individuals are referred to trial and then granted administrative discharges. Both the administrative and judicial actions are processed concurrently on an individual basis.

To me, a former army judge advocate officer, the general's answer was somewhat wide of the mark. True enough, statistics were probably not kept—but the *records* were kept, and it would be a simple matter to go through the records and compile whatever statistics were desired. The general's reluctance to do so prodded me to write his staff judge advocate.

On April 5, 1972, I wrote to the staff judge advocate of Fort Devens as follows:

> . . . I am interested in obtaining the number of administrative discharges issued at Fort Devens during the past 12 month period and the type of conduct involved that occasioned the

discharge—to include the number of days AWOL if AWOL was involved. I am also interested in obtaining the number of AWOL cases referred to court-martial at Fort Devens, and the number of days AWOL in each case plus the type of court-martial referred to. I feel that this information will be very pertinent to the defense, for reasons which I am sure you can appreciate.

Four days later, Captain Matt M. Railey, JAGC, assigned military defense counsel for Michael Daley at Fort Devens, began a search for all court-martial and administrative discharge records at Fort Devens for the purpose of preparing statistics in Daley's defense. These records were kept on file in the SJA's office. Before he had searched very far, the Fort Devens' SJA told him that he was not to rummage around in the files. He further advised that my written request for information pertaining to these files was denied. After giving this order, and over my demand that he be called as a witness at Michael Daley's trial to answer for this incident, the staff judge advocate placed himself on leave orders for Spain covering the period of the trial.

One more ingredient was added prior to the trial. Shortly before it was due to start, the command was placed on notice that the defense were going to challenge the Fort Devens' commanding general for his role in the infamous Phoenix Program in Vietnam, a program of "computerized assassination" of South Vietnamese civilians who were suspected of Viet Cong sympathies. At the trial I further spelled out in detail what the Phoenix Program was. The candidates for assassination were routinely identified as such by American-paid South Vietnamese agents who submitted their names to American intelligence agents (net handlers), who in turn submitted these names (in lists of four hundred or more) to Phoenix "coordinators," a committee of individuals composed of both American and South Vietnamese officials. The coordinators would go down the list in a matter of minutes, offhandedly approving those who were to be executed. This list was then turned over to execution squads, composed of paroled felons from South Vietnamese prisons, who would carry out the executions but were instructed to make their work appear that of ordinary bandits or the Viet Cong. Hence the crimes were unusually brutal and the executed man's family forced to witness it (as indicative of Viet Cong executions), or the crimes were accompanied with associated robberies and rapes, to give the appearance of an ordinary criminal event.

At the trial, arguing on the basis of the Ninth Amendment, I ultimately moved to dismiss the charges against Michael Daley because of the commanding general's alleged connection to the program.

My good friends in the Citizens Commission of Inquiry into U.S. War Crimes in Vietnam furnished me the names and services of two key former Phoenix agents, both of whom had recently been discharged from the army. I had these two witnesses flown to Boston so they would be present to testify as to the details of the Phoenix Program, how it worked, and the Fort Devens commander's connection, if any, to the program.

Shortly before my departure for Boston I submitted a detailed list of forty-eight defense witnesses, and requested government counsel to issue summonses for their appearance at the trial. Heading this list were the commanding general and his deputy post commander. Also summoned were the post SJA, and the lieutenant colonel who recommended Daley be tried because he was involved in protest demonstrations at Fort Devens and the Common Sense Bookstore. The Fort Devens provost marshal and the MPs who assaulted Daley's defense workers and a host of lesser witnesses were also requested to prove the implementation of court-martial practices and policies at Fort Devens. As always such requests in military cases must go first to the prosecutor and then to the convening authority (in this case the post commanding general) for approval. Out of the request for forty-eight subpoenas, the convening authority and his prosecutor saw fit to deny forty-six witnesses, leaving only two character witnesses from the post stockade (who even though apparently "approved" did not appear at the trial). In short, if we wished to prove command fraud at Fort Devens, we would have to do it without witnesses, a decidedly up-hill task.

At the trial itself, which took place at Fort Devens on April 13, 1972, the military judge, a judge advocate lieutenant colonel, ruled that the post commander was correct in denying the defense subpoena process. The judge listened to my requests and my motions; he read my letters from Congressman Harrington and Congresswoman Abzug, and the replies to these letters by the post commanding general. He heard testimony from Michael Daley himself as to how he conducted protest demonstrations at Fort Devens. He received evidence as to the date of his charges. He read the recommendation from Daley's commander that he was involved in political protest at Fort Devens and should be tried by court-martial. He heard the government stipulate that Colonel Pearson had personally telephoned Fort Lewis, Washington, for Daley's military records. He heard Michael Daley's military defense counsel testify that the post SJA ordered him not to search through military records at Fort Devens in a quest to gather potential defense statistics, and he heard the testimony of Louis Font and Amy Salzman as to how they were assaulted and imprisoned at Fort Devens while working to gather witnesses for Michael Daley. But the military judge steadfastly denied defense counsel the right to question anyone at Fort Devens as to their actions in the case, including the commanding general and his entire staff.

But the two witnesses I had flown to Boston to testify about the Phoenix Program were in the courtroom and ready to testify without service of subpoena process. In turn, I called the first witness, Barton Osborne, a graduate student at American University in Washington, D.C., and a former member of Army Intelligence, CIA, and Phoenix Program in Vietnam and in Washington, D.C. Osborne had testified in prior hearings on the Phoenix Program, and had cataloged its infamous details in pages of congressional testimony. He had worked with the Phoenix Program as an agent, or net handler, in Vietnam, and as a coordinator in Washington. He knew the key personnel who headed the program. He knew their code names, their cover names, and their true names. And he read and evaluated reports from the highest Phoenix officials and American general officers connected with the program. He knew how many Vietnamese were murdered monthly under this program in Vietnam by American-controlled executioners. He knew who paid the executioners and who paid the agents who collected the names for assassination. He knew where the money came from, the funds that were utilized, and he knew how the program worked. He had also seen Vietnamese agents connected with the program in Vietnam "terminated with extreme prejudice" because of their knowledge of the program and its details. Bart Osborne was perhaps guilt-ridden, for he completed his tour in Vietnam and in Army Intelligence before he spoke out. But once he spoke, he spoke with almost crushing authority, and he was a willing witness for Michael Daley. But the military judge cut Osborne off as soon as he mentioned the words "Phoenix Program."

The judge ruled that the defense could not present evidence on our constitutional objection to the Fort Devens commander's qualifications to sit as a convening authority in American court-martial cases. Thus we were not to litigate the applicability of the Ninth Amendment objection to the commanding general's right to serve as the convening authority in the case, an extremely strange ruling from the legal viewpoint. Generally, the litigation of constitutional objections are permitted in any court in the United States. But the only issue of significance which the judge saw in the trial was that pertaining to the fact of Michael Daley's AWOL. Was he AWOL for 438 days or wasn't he? On the merits, Michael Daley was convicted, for in truth he had been AWOL for 438 days, and Michael was sentenced to seven months' imprisonment and to a bad-conduct discharge and forfeiture of all pay. Long after Michael had served his time in prison and was on administrative "leave" (leave without pay) from the army, awaiting final judicial action on his appeal, I argued his case before the army's Court of Military Review, in Falls Church, Virginia. My argument on appeal was identical to that raised at the trial.

In Michael's case I expected to win on appeal. Where the abuse had been as flagrant as it had been in Michael's trial, army appellate courts have little room to hide. If the case is affirmed, it is reviewable before the Court of Military Appeals, and subsequently in federal courts. In Michael Daley's case I well knew this was not an exciting prospect for the army. The formal decision of the three-man court, composed entirely of retired judge advocate officers, was dated May 10, 1973, and it reversed Michael's conviction on a watered-down issue: that the refusal of the trial judge to call seven particular witnesses (six captains and a civilian) relating to the establishment of military-justice policies at Fort Devens was reversible error. Gone was the blood and guts of the real defense. No mention was made of the defense demand that the commanding general and his deputy and his SJA answer for alleged First Amendment violations, or for the military police assault upon defense co-workers, or for refusing defense counsel the right to inspect government files at Fort Devens. Gone was the Ninth Amendment (war-crime) objection. But the victory was nonetheless ours. It vindicated Michael Daley, and Congressman Harrington, and Congresswoman Abzug, and it vindicated the toil and countless hours of all those who worked in his behalf. But the Court of Review, composed of three military lawyers, insisted on the last word and was careful to point out:

. . . We find, as we must, that the trial judge prejudicially erred in denying the defense request for the witnesses specified in this assignment of error. By this determination, we wish to make clear that we do not purport to reach or decide the issue of command influence. Our holding here is limited to determining that the showing made by the defense at the trial level was sufficient to warrant compulsory process being issued for the attendance of the witnesses as specified in this assignment of error.

The conviction was reversed and the charges dismissed. Michael Daley was in time given full back pay and an honorable discharge from the army.

17

Captain Raymond Hopkins:
Black America in the Army

Louis Font and Michael Daley were white. Raymond Hopkins was a black army captain and, by military standards, a black militant. A product of the Detroit ghetto, Ray lived by his wits and, after graduating from high school, found a home in the army. In November 1966, while still in basic training, he was selected to attend Officers' Candidate School at Aberdeen Proving Ground, Maryland. Hopkins graduated easily and was commissioned a second lieutenant in the Ordnance Corps in May 1967. He was twenty years old at the time. He had traveled a long way from Detroit, but he could never get one foot out of the ghetto. He couldn't forget what it was like to be hungry, to live with rats and roaches, or to "catch corners." In time Ray Hopkins was assigned to Vietnam, where he earned the Army Commendation Ribbon for outstanding job performance. He was also promoted to first lieutenant and to captain. Meanwhile he had married and had a baby.

Upon returning from Vietnam, Ray was assigned to the 189th Maintenance Battalion at Fort Bragg, North Carolina. For a year and a half Captain Hopkins worked at Fort Bragg, and did his job.

One of his superiors was a white Southerner who told "nigger" jokes in an air of goodfellowship. The black officers held their tongues.

Fortunately, Ray Hopkins' tour of duty at Fort Bragg was cut short. As a reserve officer, Ray had no real chance of making a career in the army. Several months after his arrival at Bragg, in an effort to better his chances, he applied for college training at army expense. Each year the army picked a few officers from the reserve to attend college full time; if these officers were graduated, their chances of transferring into the regular army were excellent. Ray Hopkins was selected, but things began to bother him. The more he saw of the army, the more convinced he was that it was a racist organization.

When Ray and his family arrived at Hampton Institute, a black college in Virginia, Ray wore his hair short, but once on campus he let it grow long into an Afro bush, the fashion on campus at the time. But to Ray Hopkins the Afro bush hairstyle meant more than mere fashion.

After two semesters at Hampton, Ray set many of his priorities in order. He disliked college and he resolved he did not wish a career in the United States Army, and that meant he must discontinue college—for each year he spent at college he accrued two years of "pay-back" time to the army. He and his wife also had marital problems and they separated. Ray promptly visited Washington, D.C., and formally requested that he be discharged from the army. At this time Captain Hopkins expressed his feelings on racism in the military, and was advised that his college training was over, but that he would have to report to Aberdeen Proving Ground for further military duty. The army would not release him from his "pay-back" time. When Ray Hopkins arrived at Aberdeen Proving Ground in February 1971, he arrived with a chip on his shoulder and with his hair in a pronounced Afro bush.

Prior to Ray's arrival the brigade commander under whom he would eventually serve apparently had undertaken an "unofficial" policy of his own concerning the wearing of Afro hairstyles by black officers and soldiers. When Raymond reported to his colonel he was the only black officer on the base to wear an Afro bush.

The colonel interviewed Hopkins and gave him permission to look for civilian quarters in the Aberdeen-Baltimore area. Hopkins was told to take his time and get settled. Several days later he found an apartment in Baltimore. His furniture arrived and Hopkins supervised its unloading. He applied for utilities and telephone service, and while waiting for the telephone linesman to arrive and connect his telephone, some five days after his arrival at Aberdeen, there was a knock at his door. Hopkins opened the door and two white majors advised him he was under arrest for AWOL, and was promptly escorted to Aberdeen Proving Ground, to his commander's office. At this time Hopkins had an outstanding military record. He had never been subjected to military discipline of any sort.

Under usual circumstances, an officer of Hopkins' background in service who runs into trouble in the military is courteously invited to a superior's office, told to sit down and talk over his problem. He is not simply shot out of the saddle. But Hopkins was not white; he was black and he had an Afro bush haircut; and he had probably been identified by the Department of the Army as a militant black when he attempted to resign from service.

As Hopkins reported the meeting, there was no time wasted in "counseling" Hopkins. There was no friendly encouragement to get back to work. Assuming he had a "problem" there was no time spent in attempting to explore it, or even to discuss it. The colonel did not inquire why Captain Hopkins had taken four or five days to find a civilian apartment and move into it. He simply advised him that he was going to be punished, not by an intermediate commander nor by himself but by the Aberdeen commanding general himself, who would personally impose Article 15 punishment upon him for three days AWOL.

An Article 15 punishment in the army is nonjudicial punishment. Such punishment rendered upon privates and privates first class is not a very serious blemish upon their military record. But Article 15 punishment when imposed upon an officer is a very serious proceeding. It means generally that the officer will be passed over for promotion with his contemporaries. It means that a board of officers will scrutinize his records to see if he should be forced to show cause why he should not be relieved from service involuntarily. In short, an Article 15 punishment may well ruin the career of any officer unlucky enough to receive it. And the higher the rank of the officer who imposes it, the more serious the blemish upon the record of the recipient. Hence, from all outward signs, it appeared that Captain Hopkins was being set up for an early demise in the army. In addition, he was ordered to get a haircut.

Hopkins had been slated to be an instructor of live officer classes at Aberdeen prior to his arrival. But after his initial "interview," he was given another job. He was made a "non-resident" instructor, whose job was to mail correspondence courses to civilian reserve officers throughout the United States. It was here that Hopkins first met black Captain Thomas D. Boston, who explained to Hopkins the real cause of his problems at Aberdeen Proving Ground. Boston explained that widely published Department of the Army standards for Afro bush haircuts had no meaning at Aberdeen Proving Ground, and that unless Hopkins conformed to Aberdeen's more restrictive standards, he would soon find himself thrown out of the army.

Captain Boston had cut his hair, and he was getting out of the army on his own initiative, but Hopkins resolved on a different course. He resolved to seek out black enlisted men and officers at Aberdeen and encourage them to wear Afro hairstyles. To his dismay, he found that almost every black at Aberdeen wore his hair in the style of the fifties. But he found the familiar black "dap," an outlawed handshake by blacks that involved the slapping of hands and thighs and arms and shoulders as well as several hand grips. It was also something that Ray Hopkins had learned at college in Virginia. Ray soon found himself the inspirational leader of a small band of enlisted men at Aberdeen, ghetto blacks for the most part, like him, who took pride in being black and who refused to knuckle under to white bigots. They wore their hair long, in black Afro bush styles, and they dared the Aberdeen command to do something about it.

Under standard army procedures, a person who is offered punishment under Article 15 may refuse it and demand trial by court-martial. But Ray opted to accept nonjudicial punishment for his alleged AWOL, and he requested an audience with the commanding general at Aberdeen. At this conference, which took place in February 1971, Ray appeared with his Afro combed to its outermost reaches. Ray was articulate and more than ready to "rap" down his complaint for the general. He was asked if he wished to say anything. Ray felt the AWOL charge was spurious, and offered no explanation for it. Instead he discoursed on the subject of racism in the army for thirty minutes, and the general listened.

Hopkins explained to the post commander that the modern army was reeling from defeat in Vietnam; that it was raked with popular criticism; and that if it survived at all it needed members who had pride in the army as well as in themselves. He urged the general not to grind black personnel to dirt, but to recognize black pride, to encourage black soldiers to identify with things black, to seek black culture and black history. Hopkins urged the general to respond to the legitimate need of black personnel to be treated like men, to be treated equal to white soldiers, and to be permitted to be proud of the fact that they were black. He urged the general to rescind the unwritten policies at Aberdeen that permitted white first sergeants and company commanders and brigade commanders to dehumanize black soldiers who dared wear their hair in Afro bush hairstyle, a style that ostensibly was permitted by Department of the Army regulations but completely rejected by lower commanders at Aberdeen.

The general responded to Hopkins' plea for black equality at Aberdeen by finding him guilty of AWOL and imposing a thirty-day period of restriction-to-post limits. He also advised Hopkins that his "indifference" to army regulations was not in keeping with the best interest of the army. Hopkins left the office embittered. He had made a good-faith effort to explain to the general what was wrong at Aberdeen, but his plea was ignored. Thereafter Captain Hopkins was the target of repeated haircut orders.

Spring and summer came and went with no compromise, and then in the fall of 1971, unknown to Hopkins, the emphasis at Aberdeen was shifted from the length of his hair to the wearing of his hat. Like many of his contemporaries at Aberdeen and throughout the army, Hopkins often walked from his automobile parking lot to his office building with his hat in his hand. As car roofs over the years have sunk lower and lower, fewer and fewer military men wear their hats in their automobiles, and if their place of work is close to the parking lot, they often walk from the parking lot to the office building with hat in hand. On October 12 a WAC lieutenant colonel, who worked in the same building with Captain Hopkins, noticed him walking from the parking lot to the office building with his hat in his hand. She called him down about it and told him to wear his hat while in uniform when outside. Since Hopkins did not work for the colonel, and hardly knew her, he assumed her statement was more in the nature of general harassment than anything else. His superiors did not comment upon her so-called "order," nor did his unit commanders, his battalion commander, or brigade commander. No one in Hopkins' chain of command indicated to him there was the slightest problem about his wearing a hat while outdoors. The problem, as Hopkins understood it, was the length of his hair, as he still received haircut orders from his commanders during the month of October.

But in actual fact Hopkins' entire chain of command was aware of the WAC colonel's hat order to Hopkins. The word was out to keep an eye on Hopkins' hat and to note any failure to wear it. Captains and majors and lieutenant colonels, and colonels were all keeping their eyes peeled on Hopkins' headgear, and their books and pencils were at the ready in the event they saw an infraction. On October 18, 1971, Hopkins made his first slip. He was seen by the same WAC lieutenant colonel walking to his car from his office building with his hat in his hand. She called the matter to the attention of her secretary, and both ladies wrote a written report attesting to what they had seen. The WAC officer, in fact, asked that disciplinary action be taken against Hopkins for the violation.

On October 22, lightning struck again. This time *three* officers (two lieutenant colonels and a captain) at Aberdeen saw Hopkins walk from his parking lot to his office building with his hat in his hand. Written statements were obtained and in turn submitted to Hopkins' battalion commander. Once again the matter of the violation shot up and down the chain of command at Aberdeen, but again nothing was said to Hopkins until October 27, when he was told to report to his battalion commander. At this point, Hopkins was advised for the first time of the alleged order to wear his hat and of his October 18 and October 22 violations. His battalion commander advised Hopkins that the general would personally give him another Article 15, and as this was his second Article 15, he hoped it would cause his removal from the army. He then ordered Hopkins to get a haircut.

The following day, once again Hopkins was ordered to get a haircut, and then to return to his battalion commander's office for an inspection. Hopkins complied with the order. On his return to the office several officers were present. Hopkins was then stood at attention in front of the army's large haircut poster, a poster depicting photographs of soldiers with moderately long hair, including back, front, and side views of young blacks with Afro haircuts. He was given orders. "Right face." "Left face." "About face." On each movement the battalion commander and his staff studied Hopkins' appearance and compared it with the pictures on the poster. Hopkins was told to place his hat on his head. The commander conferred with his followers and then advised Hopkins: "We don't like the look of your hat on your head. The hair bunches out. It's kinky and stiff, and doesn't make a neat appearance."

It was next suggested that Hopkins buy a bigger hat. Hopkins, still at attention, responded that he had already purchased the biggest hat sold in the post exchange—which was several sizes bigger than his normal hat size. Hopkins was told to contact a tailor and have a hat specially made. Finally Hopkins was told that if he'd only get his hair cut shorter than established limits, he'd have no problem, otherwise the command was going to "help him along" in his effort to get out of the army. "So long as you look like you do, you're going to be harassed."

Captain Hopkins responded to the harassment by obtaining legal counsel at Aberdeen's local judge advocate office, and also from Fort Meade, where he obtained the only black judge advocate in the area. Ultimately, Hopkins was formally tendered a written "offer" of Article 15 punishment by the Aberdeen commanding general for his violation of the hat order. He turned down the offer and demanded trial by court-martial. His judge advocate counsel approached the special court-martial convening authority in charge of Hopkins' case at Aberdeen, and asked for a conference. This officer responded that the matter was out of his hands and suggested that counsel see the commanding general. But the general was unavailable for conference, and Hopkins and counsel requested and were granted an audience before the First Army commander at Fort Meade, a lieutenant general.

The First Army Commander listened to their appeal to halt the proceedings at Aberdeen. After hearing the entire ludicrous story, he requested that Hopkins and his counsel step out of his office while he telephoned the convening authority at Aberdeen. After the call was made Hopkins and his counsel were advised to return to the Proving Ground to see the local convening authority. This they did, and they were told that the court-martial charges against Captain Hopkins would be dropped if Hopkins would accept nonjudicial punishment administered by the commanding general at Aberdeen. Hopkins refused and the charges against him were referred to trial by special court-martial. The trial date was set for December 13, 1971, at Aberdeen Proving Ground.

Hopkins' counsel tried for more time. But time was running short, and the case ultimately was convened at Aberdeen on January 6, 1972. At this hearing Hopkins requested and was granted a continuance from the military judge for the purpose of obtaining civilian counsel. In time he was referred to me. One of my first acts in his behalf was to arrange for a Baltimore television interview. Hopkins was filmed in his apartment in Baltimore, the walls of which were covered with black-power posters.

Black Congressmen Ronald Dellums from California and Parren Mitchell from Baltimore next held a press conference for Hopkins in the House Office Building in Washington, D.C. At this conference Hopkins outlined his case against his Aberdeen commanders and against military racism in general. He explained how a bigoted first sergeant and company commander can tear to shreds any meaning in the most carefully written Pentagon racial equality directive. He explained how black soldiers are frequently worked out of their MOS (Military Occupational Specialty), and given meaningless, nonessential tasks, such as raking leaves, cleaning the post stable, or shoveling snow, and how local commanders choose not to see and not to hear of these violations. He explained how black soldiers are overcontrolled on military posts. They are overpoliced, overinspected, and overharassed. Noncommissioned officers refer to them with shorthand racist slurs, such as "you brothers," "you people," and "colored" soldiers. Hopkins stated that blacks don't get passes as easily as white soldiers; they don't get promotions as fast; and they get harsher disciplinary treatment. And they are, of course, constantly and forever threatened and harassed about the length of their hair.

The case was picked up by the local news media—and more and more witnesses came forward at Aberdeen furnishing vital details related to the command conspiracy against Hopkins. My initial action in the case also included an evaluation of Hopkins' makeup. I saw that he was both frightened and determined. He was also convinced that he was going to be convicted and sentenced to jail. As a person Hopkins was likable. Like Font and Daley and others of similar constitution, he was willing to risk his freedom to achieve a more moral society. It was my job to give him his forum, but at the same time to keep him out of jail if possible.

Hopkins and I decided to draw the lines as distinctly as possible prior to his trial. We wished to set forth the issues more clearly so that the press would have no difficulty in seeing what was involved. On January 25, 1972, several days before Hopkins' case was to convene, he took a giant step to define the issues. He signed court-martial charges of his own against the commanding general at Aberdeen, against the special court-martial convening authority, against his WAC accuser and his battalion commander and several other officers at Aberdeen who had given statements against him. Hopkins charged them with conspiracy, and alleged that they conspired:

> to commit an offense under the Uniform Code of Military Justice, to wit: the institution and processing of racially motivated non-judicial action under Article 15, UCMJ, and racially motivated court-martial charges against black Captain Raymond H. Hopkins, and the racial harassment and mal-treatment of the said Captain Hopkins, a member of the United States Army, and in order to effect the conspiracy, the said [WAC officer] did report Captain Hopkins to his superiors (and her fellow conspirators) for disciplinary action for not wearing a hat outdoors in uniform, in contradiction to her alleged oral order to Captain Hopkins to wear his hat while in uniform at all times when outdoors.

Similar charges were laid under Article 93 of the Uniform Code of Military Justice, charging each conspirator individually with mal-treatment of Captain Hopkins, and under Article 134, the "general" article of the Uniform Code.

On the same date, Hopkins swore charges against the three-star commanding general of the First Army, who had refused to intercede in his case, for dereliction of duty under Article 92 of the Uniform Code of Military Justice. Hopkins charged that the lieutenant general was derelict in his duty:

in that after being formally advised of the details of racial maltreatment of black Captain Raymond H. Hopkins, a member of his command stationed at Aberdeen Proving Ground, Maryland, by ranking officers at Aberdeen Proving Ground, Maryland, and, after being advised of the details of racially motivated non-judicial action under Article 15, UCMJ, and racially motivated court-martial charged against Captain Hopkins by the same ranking officers at Aberdeen Proving Ground, Maryland, took no action to terminate the harassment, the racially motivated non-judicial action under Article 15, UCMJ, or the racially motivated court-martial charges, as it was his duty to do.

The preferment of these charges was widely covered in the press. Captain Hopkins and I knew the army would definitely whitewash his charges (which it in fact proceeded to do) but we felt they served their purpose. They defined the issues. On one side of the coin was the government charges against Captain Hopkins —and on the other side was Hopkins' charges against the government. In the unlikely event we should win at his trial, he felt that the public would be in a better position to judge for itself the truth of his charges against the army.

On February 7 the trial convened at Aberdeen's special court-martial trial room. There was room for approximately forty spectators in the courtroom. Aberdeen command representatives, the press, and local judge advocate personnel not connected with the case sat on one side of the aisle. On the other side sat Aberdeen's black militant soldiers and WACs, each brazenly wearing Afro haircuts that matched Hopkins' in appearance. Several WACs purchased mammoth Afro wigs to wear especially for the trial.

The trial itself lasted six days. Procedurally it was divided into two parts: one which was presented to the military judge alone, and the second to the court-martial jury. The jury was composed of five officers, all white save one, and all selected by the special court-martial convening authority at Aberdeen Proving Ground and ranging in grade from captain through lieutenant colonel. On voir dire examination each juror swore he had no prejudice against black soldiers or officers, Afro haircuts or Captain Hopkins. Hopkins' charges against the Aberdeen commanding general and his staff and his charge against the First Army commanding general were read to the court-martial jury, and each member swore that such charges would have no bearing on his determination of the case against Captain Hopkins.

Former Captain Thomas Boston, an ex-infantry combat leader in Vietnam, was one of the first witnesses to testify on a defense motion to dismiss the charges because they were racially motivated and command-inspired. Boston explained the resentment he had encountered at Aberdeen when he appeared with an Afro haircut. He was told that blacks did not wear Afros at Aberdeen and was directed to cut his hair. As a former combat infantryman in Vietnam, Boston stated he was originally slated to fill a troop commander's job at Aberdeen but after his Afro hair incident he was switched to a "back-room" job, where he wrote correspondence courses and did not come into contact with the public.

Miss Shalaine Malone, a young black civilian employee at the Proving Ground, testified that she wore her hair in an Afro style to express identity with black awareness, and also because she thought her hair looked better in an Afro, since it was more consistent with the natural lie of her hair. She too testified that she had run into resentment at Aberdeen about her hairstyle. She said she was the target of dirty looks from older white employees, and that a white lieutenant colonel had stopped her in the hallway and asked if she had stuck her finger into an electric outlet to make her hair stand out on end as it did.

George Sheppard, a young Vietnam combat veteran, testified that he had run into no racial difficulty in Vietnam before coming to Aberdeen. He testified that he wore his hair in an Afro style because he felt it was beautiful and was a statement of black brotherhood. He stated that the white commanders at Aberdeen told him he looked like a wild man, and that they laughed at him.

They also ordered him to cut his hair. A black NCO testified that Aberdeen commanders had hounded him about his Afro so much that he simply cut off all his hair. A black captain who had served eighteen months in Vietnam testified that his white superiors at Aberdeen harassed him about his hairstyle; he was told by his commander that his Afro made him look like a black Lieutenant Flap in Beetle Bailey's comic strip.

All in all, some fifteen young black enlisted men and officers testified to racial harassment they received from command officials at Aberdeen Proving Ground concerning their Afro haircuts. But the prize witness for the defense was the post barber.

Mr. Huey Harris, the chief barber at Aberdeen Proving Ground and a part-time minister at a local black church, testified that he was selected by army officials to tour army posts and lecture barbers on the army way of cutting Afros. He also testified that Aberdeen officials did not follow Department of the Army Afro haircut standards. He testified that although he was a recognized army expert on Afro hairstyles, his black customers at Aberdeen were constantly ordered to return to his shop for additional haircuts immediately after he had trimmed their hair in what he deemed complete conformance with army standards. He testified that Captain Hopkins was one of those who frequently was ordered to return for additional haircuts in contradiction to applicable army standards.

The commanding general at Aberdeen had retired from the army several days before Hopkins' trial was to commence, and he was wearing civilian clothes when he testified at Hopkins' trial. For some four hours he denied all knowledge of racist activity on either his part or his staff's part, in either Hopkins' case or the cases of any other blacks at Aberdeen Proving Ground. That half of the courtroom that held black spectators actually laughed at the general, who must have wondered what had happened to army discipline at his post in the few days since his retirement.

The general's staff was called one by one, and none could account for the failure of the staff to warn Hopkins that he was under fire from the WAC lieutenant colonel; or that she was concerned over his not wearing his hat outdoors while in uniform; nor could they account for their failure to call his violation of her order to his attention on a more timely basis. They admitted that junior officers are customarily warned, and assisted by their superiors under similar circumstances. The WAC officer involved was called and, on cross-examination, admitted that she had seen other (white) officers walk about the Aberdeen Post without a hat on, and that she neither reported them for disciplinary action nor ordered them to wear their hats. She stated that she frequently had seen Hopkins' former commander outside without a hat on, and that once she had seen him walking to his parking lot without his jacket. She took no action against this officer. She admitted that the action she took against Hopkins was not fair when compared to the nonaction she had taken in other cases. Another of Hopkins' accusers admitted that he had been outside without a hat at Aberdeen some ten to fifteen times, and that no action was ever taken against him. The entire staff, in fact, admitted that they were aware of many hat violations at Aberdeen, and had taken action in only one instance—Captain Hopkins' case.

During the course of the trial I was threatened with contempt on three different occasions. I also asked the military judge three times to disqualify himself from further participation in the trial for action that I thought was prejudicial to Hopkins' rights. But after six days the case reached a stormy conclusion. The military judge denied all defense motions to dismiss the charge and the case was ultimately sent to the jury for final determination. Hopkins' only defense before the jury was that he did not consider the WAC's statement on October 12, wherein she allegedly told him to wear his hat, an order. Otherwise, he testified he could not recall whether he was without a hat while outdoors on October 18 or October 22.

The jury, which was composed of five officers, needed a majority of four to convict. I was quite certain we had the black officer on our side. I needed only one more juror, for in military law if the prosecution does not obtain the necessary majority for conviction there is an automatic acquittal. The jury closed at 3:55 p.m. to vote on its findings. One hour later it opened and announced its verdict.

Captain Hopkins was found not guilty.

Through his own efforts, and those of several congressmen, the press, a fleet of unpaid co-workers, two military lawyers, and a civilian lawyer retained at his own expense, Hopkins was thus "freed." It was an effort, of course, that far surpassed the reach of the average black GI who found himself brought up on racially motivated charges. For this reason and because the army refused to act on his own charges against his superiors, one may place a question mark on the true meaning of Hopkins' exoneration.

18

The Black Revolution:
Discipline and the Ku Klux Klan

In 1969 the black revolution appeared to be overtaking the American military establishment. In Camp Lejeune, North Carolina, a white marine died of head wounds received in a fight with black marines; and in the first seven months of that year the base recorded some 160 assaults, muggings, and robberies that had racial overtones. Hand grenades were tossed in a mess hall of the First Division in Germany. Riots occurred at Fort McClellan, Alabama, aboard naval carriers at sea, and in military installations from Germany to Washington, D.C., to Travis Air Force Base to Okinawa. Black servicemen were discontent over a host of discriminatory practices that had been smoldering in the armed services for years. While the military moved to correct the problem it also moved to silence the blacks. Blacks were arrested en masse and subjected to court-martial, but the problem didn't go away. Discontent and violence continued. Black-power handshakes, black-power jackets, and Afro bush haircuts became permanent fixtures on military installations—and the military fought back.

On November 1, 1971, at about 9:50 p.m., three black marines entered their barracks at Camp Lejeune, a barracks that was occupied predominantly by white marines. The blacks walked up and down the aisle of bunks, kicking and slapping white marines. They stopped in front of the bunk of one of the smallest, most timid men in the barracks—and one of the blacks, a large muscular youth who will be referred to as Private Smith, began to slap and punch him. Smith had a reputation among the whites as a black militant and a bully.

Smith crawled up into the top bunk with the small marine and continued to harass him. The victim began to cry. A second white marine, who occupied the bunk immediately below him, got out of his bunk and told the blacks to leave him alone. Approximately a dozen whites were in the barracks at the time and witnessed the event. Although the lights were out, there was enough illumination to see what was happening. The marine who protested the attack went to the latrine and returned in about two minutes. Smith was still harassing the smaller marine. He was lying on top of him. The blacks were again told to leave the youth alone, and within several minutes they departed the area.

The following morning the small marine told his friends that he had been raped in his rectum by Smith. His barracks mates in turn demanded that he report the matter to his first sergeant, and he made the report, formally accusing Smith of raping him the previous evening. This report culminated three days of racial friction in the unit. Smith was arrested and placed in pretrial confinement. He was charged with a series of assaults, including forcible sodomy.

At the formal pretrial investigation of the charges (the Article 32 investigation), the investigating officer did not refer to the matter of race. Nor did Smith's assigned military defense counsel. For all that appeared at the Article 32 investigation the incident could well have occurred between all-white marines or all-black marines. Racial prejudice or racial discord as a motivating factor was ignored. But the various statements submitted by the witnesses themselves did refer to the obvious racial overtone of the matter. The victim himself referred to Camp Lejeune as a "prejudiced barn," where black marines were allowed to shove white marines around. He further stated that he had been "harassed" by some of the Negroes ever since being assigned to these barracks. A second marine reported that "there had been racial tension between the whites and the blacks" ever since he had been in the barracks. Yet neither the investigating officer nor Smith's defense counsel picked up this element of the case.

Although the evidence indicated that none of the whites, except the victim himself, saw an act of sodomy committed or heard a cry of protest or scream from the victim, and although the victim did not report the act until the following day, the investigating officer recommended trial by general court-martial.

The general court convened on January 25, 1972, at Camp Lejeune, and terminated on January 27. At the trial, Smith was represented by the same attorney who represented him at the pre-trial investigation. Smith's defense counsel, his prosecutor, his judge, and his entire court-martial jury, consisting of two full colonels, three lieutenant colonels, two majors, and two captains, were white. In defense, Smith, a nineteen-year-old black youth from Baltimore, Maryland, who had an unblemished civilian and military record, admitted that he slapped and kicked his white barracks mates, including the alleged victim, but stoutly denied sexually assaulting anyone. A medical examination of the victim that took place on the day following the alleged assault failed to corroborate the sexual assault. But Smith was convicted as charged on the word of the victim, and was sentenced to be dishonorably discharged from the Marine Corps and to be confined for *ten years*.

Following the trial, but before the convening authority reviewed the conviction, I was retained on appeal. After an informal inquiry I was puzzled by the failure of counsel to inquire into the question of racial prejudice. I wondered why assigned military defense counsel dodged the issue. At the trial he had not questioned the judge or jury to ascertain possible racial bias on their part. He made no effort to ascertain if the members of the jury were aware of the pronounced degree of racial violence at Camp Lejeune that preceded this case. He made no effort to ascertain if the jurors knew what racial policies, if any, were in effect at Camp Lejeune that were designed to prevent outbreaks of racial violence, or to punish or identify offenders that were charged with such violence. He made no effort to inquire if the jury had been involved in racial confrontation themselves at Camp Lejeune, or elsewhere in the corps, or whether they had been subjected to command pressure on racial matters at Camp Lejeune. He made no effort to ascertain if the individual jurors thought it necessary to "throw the book" at a black defendant involved in a racial confrontation with a white marine simply to maintain "discipline" at the base. Nor did he inquire if the court members had been instructed by command officials at Camp Lejeune to see that Smith was "hanged" as an example to other blacks at the base.

The defense counsel made no move at the trial to expose past racial prejudices at Camp Lejeune that might have accounted for the racial confrontation that night. While witness after witness described the racial confrontation in question, the defense counsel managed to proceed through the entire trial without "raising" the issue. In an effort to ascertain what had happened, I wrote the trial defense counsel a letter. I requested him to conduct an in-depth investigation of this aspect of the case, for the purpose of submitting a posttrial brief to the convening authority before he acted on the conviction. Specifically I asked military counsel:

Has there been a general discord between the races at Lejeune? What do the *black* Marines have to say about racial relations at Lejeune? If there has been discord, when, where, and what occurred? And moreover what did the command do about it? Have there been items in the Camp papers, bulletin boards, commanders' meetings, etc. regarding race relations at Lejeune? There must be something on this subject out in the open. Under cover, I'm sure there is more, but can you dig any of this information out for me?

I then directed counsel to:

Seek out the Marines who have been the butt of racism and they can tell you what to look for—or at least some of them can. Also seek out the disorders, the confrontations, etc., that have occurred at Lejeune during the past several years between the races, and see what transpired, what happened, what was done, what the Command did and so on. Dig out all the reports made in relation to past racial troubles at Camp Lejeune. Staff members make reports on matters of this nature. Get them. See if individual commanders have been accused of racism at Lejeune, or NCOs. Get names, and dates and places, etc. Get the number of complaints. What is the haircut policy? Have there been complaints? Check out the court members on (the defendant's) case for racism. Check their units, etc. Also, please give me a full and detailed account of the several days of racial confrontation leading up to or preceding (the defendant's) offense.

I did not for one moment expect a military officer, lawyer or nonlawyer, at Camp Lejeune to undertake this investigation, because I knew the Lejeune commander simply would not permit it. My request was intentionally designed to strike close to home, and, I hoped, to strike fear into the hearts of those who had something to hide. In short, I was inviting the command to overact and to prohibit outright a legitimate inquiry of military defense counsel. In order to assure that the Lejeune commander got the bait I wrote a second letter to the base commanding general and advised him of my request for the posttrial assistance of assigned military defense counsel. I further advised the general that I was "requesting copies of all staff papers or reports, relating to racial confrontations, harmony, complaints, investigations, etc., that have taken place at Camp Lejeune in the past five years." I requested the general's "full cooperation" in this attempt to uncover facts that might possibly account for the trial and conviction of my client, Smith.

My answer was not long in coming. Four days later the general advised me in writing that the military defense counsel was "not available to undertake such an investigation." While he assured me that he did not "desire to hinder in any way the attorney-client relationship," my request for "copies of staff papers and reports must likewise be denied." A few days later I received an answer from the assigned military trial defense counsel. He advised, in part:

> As to your request for further investigation in this matter, I am in receipt of a copy of a letter from the Commanding General to you concerning that request. I hope that you can appreciate that my duties and responsibilities in this office would make further investigation on my part impossible, not to mention the impossibility of performing an investigation to the extent of which you have requested.
>
> Finally, my responsibilities do not extend to the first level of review. . . . I am unable from the standpoint of present duties and logistics to pursue any active course of assistance in the future at appellate levels.

I was satisfied that the command had been hooked, and that I had an error that would probably effect the reversal of the conviction. Military commanders are not permitted in military law to give orders to assigned military defense counsel, advising them what issues they are to investigate or not to investigate, at either the trial or the appellate level of military cases. To further develop my position in this regard, I wrote to the secretary of defense, and to the judge advocate general of the Marine Corps advising them of the illegal action that the Lejeune commander had taken in this case. I also requested the secretary of defense to appoint a board to investigate the matter of racism at Camp Lejeune and "the outrageously severe sentence that was imposed on this young black Marine." My request, of course, was ignored.

The Lejeune commander stuck by his guns and the Marine Corps and the Department of Defense stuck by the general. His orders were not countermanded—but the general lost heart on a related issue. In approving the conviction, he reduced the sentence to six years' imprisonment and the case was passed to the Court of Military Review for formal appellate review. I continued my attack on the Lejeune commander's command influence in the appellate stage of the case in a detailed brief to that court, a three-man court composed of military judge advocates. The entire story was formally presented to the court on appellate review. I expected ultimately to win on this issue before the Court of Military Appeals, the highest military court composed of three civilian judges, but the Marine Corps cut me short.

The Court of Military Review affirmed the conviction, but reduced the sentence by half. In so acting the court ruled that racism was not involved in the case at all, but reduced the sentence to three years' confinement because of the *misconception* of the assigned military defense counsel relating to the nature of his duties pending first-level appellate review. But what stopped me from further acting in the case was the administrative release of the defendant from prison, and his return to duty in the Marine Corps. Upon his release from prison, having served less than a year in jail, the defendant declined to further prosecute his appeal.

Not all cases of command fraud are winners, not even those that are publicly exposed. Smith was a loser. It would also be hard to say that Michael Daley's case, previously discussed, was a winner even though he was exonerated on appeal. He still spent seven months in military prison. Captain Hopkins, who won an acquittal at Aberdeen Proving Ground, likewise could hardly be considered a winner. Although Hopkins wanted out of service, he wanted his discharge on his own terms. But some eighteen months after his acquittal the poor efficiency reports that he received at Aberdeen during his hair ordeal served as the basis for his elimination from the army. Thus, in the final analysis, Hopkins was a loser.

There are other losers—both black and white. Specialist 5C Charles Ballentine was a college-educated black stationed at Fort Meade. He had been school-trained in the army as a veterinary technician, and for three years worked at the Fort Meade Small Animal Clinic, where he received outstanding efficiency reports and a letter of appreciation. Two months after he received the letter of appreciation he was transferred in grade to a menial labor company at Fort Meade designed to do common labor on the post. Along with stockade prisoners, this company cleaned the post stables, raked leaves, picked up trash, and did janitor work in buildings at the fort. Although Charles Ballentine was a highly trained specialist in a very select field within the army, and was a career soldier in the rank of E-5, he was utilized as a common laborer, as a rankless recruit, *for two years* within this special company at Fort Meade (a special company that was composed almost entirely of blacks). While he was in this company, contrary to army regulations, Ballentine received no efficiency reports at all, but he did receive a letter of appreciation from the educational officer for doing a good job cleaning the sixteen buildings assigned to the Education Office. Charles had been in the labor pool for over a year at the time he received this letter.

The reason for Ballentine's transfer from the Small Animal Clinic was never explained to him. However, Charles needed no explanation. He knew the reason. Several months before his transfer he noted the vast difference between the treatment he received at Fort Meade, as a college-educated black, and the treatment accorded to less educated, ghetto blacks. He resolved to assist his less fortunate brothers to better express their complaints to white superiors. Ballentine thus began to organize ghetto blacks at Fort Meade and invite them to meetings. Shortly before his transfer, Charles invited a Black Panther contingent from Baltimore to Fort Meade to address a meeting of black soldiers. The Panthers came, attired in their usual dress. It was shortly after this visit that Charles was relieved of his job at the Small Animal Clinic.

During the two-year period Charles Ballentine was worked out of his job MOS at Fort Meade, he continued to organize black soldiers. He eventually enlarged his sights and attempted to bring all minorities into his meetings, which were held weekly at the post. Various minority organizations throughout the United States, including the Congressional Black Caucus, assisted Charles in his organizing efforts. But Charles was harassed by the CID, the Military Intelligence (MI), and probably the FBI and the CIA, and he was also increasingly harassed by his military commanders. He was specifically called down for not saluting a black captain at Fort Meade and for being late to a formation. Charles accepted censure in this regard and proceeded about his business. About forty days after this incident, Ballentine's unit commander, his brigade commander, and the MI held a meeting about Ballentine. Within a few days after this meeting Charles was served court-martial charges for failing to salute the black captain and for missing formation. The charges were couched as willful disobedience of orders, and carried a maximum sentence of twenty years' imprisonment.

These charges were ultimately referred to trial by special court-martial at Fort Meade, where I represented Ballentine. At his trial the foregoing factors were proven and Charles was convicted of several of the charges and fined $100, a surprisingly low fine. The military judge, Captain Robert Bogan, a reserve judge advocate officer, explained why he adjudged such a low sentence. He stated that he felt the charges against Ballentine were exaggerated and should have been disposed of at company level via administration channels. He then commended Charles most highly for his black organizing work in the army and wished him well in this regard in the future. Much to his credit, the trial judge also *apologized* to Ballentine for his gross mal-assignment at Fort Meade for the past two years.

Ballentine was happy. He had at last been vindicated. Within days following the trial, he was advised that he was being assigned to Fort Devens, Massachusetts. Hopeful that he was being assigned to a veterinarian position, Charles drove to Fort Devens, only to learn to his dismay that once again he was being mal-assigned. But this time it was worse. It carried sinister overtones. Charles was advised that he was being assigned to a *Special Forces* unit at Fort Devens, a unit that was soon to be transferred to Europe, and he was point-blank told there were no veterinarian positions within the unit.

In this regard, I wrote the commanding general, First United States Army, Fort George G. Meade, Maryland, a letter, dated September 28, 1972. I advised the general of the facts of Ballentine's case and of his impending assignment to a Special Forces unit at Fort Devens. At this moment the First Army commanding general was serving as joint chairman of a special presidential board of inquiry into racism in the military and I had appeared as a witness at one of the many sessions conducted by this board (which was composed of both military officers and black civilians). I explained the situation as frankly as I could to the general. I advised him that Ballentine was not Special Forces–trained, and that his only training in the army had been in the veterinarian field, and as a leaf raker, stable cleaner, and building custodian at Fort Meade. I advised the general that considering Ballentine's trouble with Military Intelligence, his experience as a minority organizer at Fort Meade, his association with Black Panthers in Baltimore and other minority organizations across America, *physical harm* might come to him if he were transferred into an elite unit such as the Special Forces. I further advised the army commander that "Charles feels he might be *murdered* in his new assignment." I asked the general to stop the transfer.

On October 5, 1972, the army commander answered my letter. The general assured me that Ballentine's assignment to the Tenth Special Forces was "based upon personnel priorities and a position vacancy in that unit." However, he did not explain how Ballentine could possibly have received the necessary top-level security clearance, in view of his radical background, for assignment to a Special Forces unit, most of whose missions are highly classified, cloak-and-dagger assignments. But in view of our objection, the general advised that Ballentine was being reassigned to a "medical activity" at a U.S. Army Garrison, Fort Devens. And that ended the case.

In September 1971 a young black soldier was tried and convicted of a drug-related offense at Fort Benning, Georgia, an offense that was committed only seven days before the soldier was due to be honorably discharged from the army. The soldier had destroyed a syringe and hypodermic needle that his company commander had seized from him shortly after he was seen injecting himself in the arm with the needle. The soldier was a Vietnam combat veteran from Baltimore. His military judge, Reid Kennedy, the same judge who presided in the Calley court-martial, called it to the soldier's attention before sentencing him that the fact that he might be a drug user "may very well affect the sentence I am going to give you at this time." Judge Kennedy then sentenced the soldier to a dishonorable discharge and to a year in jail. As Kennedy suspected, the soldier was in fact a heroin addict. He had become addicted to heroin within thirty days after his arrival in Vietnam. And like countless thousands of his comrades in arms, he brought the sickness home with him.

Was this conviction just or unjust? On July 7, 1971, in Washington, D.C., Congressman Morgan F. Murphy of Illinois, testifying on the international aspects of the narcotics problem before the House Subcommittee on Europe, stated at page 19 of the subcommittee report:

In Vietnam, we discovered young American soldiers whose day to day existence depends on a $3 vial of "skag." We found men whose minds and bodies have been shattered by the effects of habit-forming drugs. . . .

At the time of our visit, the military authorities told us they estimated 10 to 15 percent of our soldiers were heroin addicts. That figure has since been lowered to a firm 10 percent labeled as users, and 5 percent as hard-core addicts.

I must admit my skepticism, gentlemen, about these revised figures as past experience shows the Department of Defense (DOD) has a tendency to deemphasize any problem which places the military in a bad light before the American taxpaying public. This time last year, for example, DOD claimed a mere 100 heroin addicts were wearing the uniform of U.S. soldiers. . . .

. . . Unofficial sources place the number [of soldier addicts] at a more realistic figure of between 30,000 to 40,000 men . . . in Vietnam.

This epidemic of drug abuse is not something which arose overnight. It has been coming for a long time—we have known about it, we urged the President to take action long ago, but nothing was done. And now we are faced with an overwhelming task—that of rehabilitating thousands of young men, not only from the strain and horrors of combat, but from the hideous specter of drug addiction as well.

In Vietnam, heroin addiction became an epidemic before action was taken. . . .

Congressman Robert H. Steele, testifying before the same subcommittee, at pages 26 and 29 of the report, stated:

In Laos, the Chief of the Laotian General Staff, General Ouane Rathikoune, is reportedly deeply involved in the heroin traffic. . . . I have learned this week that South Vietnamese military officers continue to deal in large quantities of heroin and to transport it around South Vietnam in military aircraft and vehicles, all of which were supplied by the United States. U.S. military authorities have provided Ambassador Bunker with hard intelligence that one of the chief traffickers is General Ngo Dzu, the Commander of II Corps. Dzu is one of the staunchest military backers of President Thieu, and is one of the leading strongmen in the current Saigon Government. . . . If we stopped supporting the Laotian government for one day it would fall. . . .

In *An Inquiry into Alleged Drug Abuses in the Armed Services,* dated April 23, 1971, a Special Subcommittee of the Committee on Armed Services of the House of Representatives, at pages 2161 and 2225, reported:

. . . there is a ready availability of, and amazing low price for *all* varieties of illicit drugs in Vietnam. [Emphasis in original text.]

... the heroin problem in Vietnam is increasing. ...

... the only effective drug suppression for U.S. personnel in Vietnam will come with the withdrawal of our troops from that country. ...

In Vietnam [drug] suppression is just about non-existent. ... The cold facts are that all illicit drugs in Vietnam are more plentiful than cigarettes or chewing gum.

Like the soldier sentenced at Fort Benning, thousands of American soldiers, both black and white, have been broken by drugs in Vietnam, where drug addiction was a way of life, a way of life that was conveniently ignored and hidden from the American people by the United States military until exposed in congressional reports. After this exposure, the military did its best to minimize the problem and, failing this, instituted a urine test for returning soldiers, designed to reflect if they were, at the time of the test, under the influence of drugs. The army also, of course, utilized its court-martial machinery, and hundreds of soldiers were tried for drug offenses. And hundreds of American soldiers were convicted of these offenses by compliant military jurors and judges, most of whom knew firsthand the woefully inadequate protection given to drafted American soldiers, fresh out of high school, who were rushed to defend America's interest in Vietnam—and thrust into the midst of an ongoing, raging heroin epidemic.

I represented the young black soldier from Fort Benning on appeal before the army's Court of Military Review in Washington. I advanced the foregoing factors in defense of the soldier, and asked the court, composed of three senior army judge advocate officers, to reverse his conviction and to free him—as his injury was just as surely service-connected as was that of the soldier who was shot in the head by the Viet Cong. The court listened to my argument and I departed. By the time I had reached my office in Baltimore that afternoon, I was advised by my secretary that the court clerk had telephoned prior to my arrival and advised that the conviction and sentence were affirmed.

The last case of black injustice in the armed forces that I will discuss is the case of Dwight Drewry—perhaps the most tragic of all, for he was a classic example of a southern-bred, poverty-ridden product of the black ghetto who should have made a success in the army. He had already been promoted to Specialist E-5 by the time he was assigned to Crailsheim, Germany, in June 1969.

Dwight and his wife had a child in Germany—and then the black revolution hit Crailsheim. Fist fights erupted in the mess hall between white and black troops. The fighting spread to NCO clubs and into Crailsheim proper. Tension mounted and the blacks segregated themselves. Outnumbered by ten to one, they were frightened. In August 1970 conditions further deteriorated. Approximately fifty white troops set fire to a large white cross on a hilltop overlooking Dwight Drewry's barracks at the Crailsheim military post. The next morning Dwight and several black soldiers carried the charred remains of the cross to the provost marshal's office, but nothing was done. Within days thereafter, a black soldier carried his German girl friend to the post dispensary for first aid. She had been assaulted by girl friends of white soldiers. While at the dispensary, the black soldier was shot at by a white soldier. Again nothing was done to punish the offender involved. On August 26, as explained by a government witness, Dwight Drewry and "a fairly large group of black soldiers entered the headquarters of the 1st Battalion, 51st Infantry, and proceeded up the stairwell to the second floor where they basically took over the entrance to the stairs." The white batallion commander came out of his office "and issued an order to the effect that this group was to remove themselves from the office, cease the demonstration and disburse. The order was ignored. . . ."

The purpose of the demonstration, one of many to plague the armed forces, was to complain about racial discrimination. Specifically, the Crailsheim blacks wished to complain about the burning of the cross on the hillside at their post, and about the shooting incident at the post dispensary. But the battalion commander had other ideas. He issued orders and the orders were disobeyed. The blacks, who were peaceful in their demonstration, eventually left the building and moved to the parade ground, where they were disbanded by military policemen. The leaders of the group, including Dwight Drewry, were to receive Article 15 punishment for this infraction of military discipline.

The blacks sought an audience with the corps commander in Stuttgart, but were thwarted by the "loss" of their written request. The men then took it upon themselves to visit the office of the commanding general of United States personnel in Europe, in Heidelberg, a four-star general. They were denied an audience with this officer, but were interviewed by one of his deputies, a two-star general, who assured the men that their complaints would be considered by the general. Upon their return to Crailsheim the blacks were informed that they were to receive a special court-martial for the unlawful demonstration on August 26 and that they were to be confined in the stockade awaiting trial.

Dwight Drewry and three other blacks refused to be confined. A fight ensued and military police responded. The fight spread over several barracks and eventually some twenty blacks assisted Dwight and his companions in disarming the military police. Dwight took a pistol from one of the military policemen. Four blacks, including Dwight, commandeered a German automobile and fled from Crailsheim. They were later captured crossing into Denmark and were returned to Crailsheim. Dwight now faced twenty charges, ranging from participating in an unlawful demonstration to robbery. The maximum sentence ranged upward of sixty years in jail. Broken in spirit, confined while awaiting trial, and separated from his wife and child who were shipped back to Hampton Roads by the army, Dwight resolved to plead guilty at his forthcoming general court-martial. He was sentenced to a three-year imprisonment and a bad-conduct discharge.

The convening authority reduced the sentence to one year in jail and Dwight was shipped home. After his confinement was served, he was assigned to Fort Meade, Maryland, to await final appellate

approval of his bad-conduct discharge, and ultimate release from
the army. But the army Court of Review found a technical error in
the proceedings (a military defense counsel especially requested by
Dwight was erroneously denied), and the bad-conduct discharge
was disapproved. The court also disapproved the unlawful demonstration conviction, but otherwise affirmed the remaining charges.

Dwight Drewry had been placed on administrative leave (leave
without pay) at Fort Meade while he was awaiting the Court of
Review decision. When the discharge was disapproved, he was
telephoned by Fort Meade officials and told to report to the post to
pick up an administrative discharge (under honorable conditions).
The date was early 1972. Drewry was almost penniless. He had
supported his wife and child in the traditional manner of black
common laborers. He "caught corners," that is, he and a group of
other black laborers stood on street corners in Hampton Roads
until a contractor drove by in a truck and would ask for so many
workers for a day's work, etc. Thus, when Dwight Drewry was
directed to Fort Meade to pick up his discharge he hitchhiked to
the post. He arrived in work clothes, dirty, without funds, in need
of a shave, and his hair was in an Afro bush.

He was told to get a haircut and to shave. He refused and was
physically overpowered and carried to the Fort Meade stockade.
Once again a series of court-martial charges were placed against
Dwight Drewry. Eventually I was retained to represent him at his
special court-martial at Fort Meade, a court-martial that was authorized to adjudge a maximum sentence of six months in jail and a
bad-conduct discharge. His plight was publicized in the local press.
Congressman Parren Mitchell responded and personally inter-
ceded, but to no avail. The trial proceeded. But during the course
of the trial an almost tragic event happened.

During an overnight recess in the trial, Dwight was knocked
down a flight of stairs in the post stockade, and his jaw was badly
broken. An army investigation, conducted immediately after the
event was reported, revealed that he had "slipped" and fallen
down the stairs, as indeed he himself reported. The trial was halted

for several weeks while his jaw was set. During the recess, while Dwight was in the hospital, I visited the post stockade and within five minutes learned the name of the person who had knocked him down the stairs. I reported his identity to the army, and the circumstances of the altercation. My report, of course, was ignored, but it was carried in the press. And it took the steam out of further prosecution. The army could not afford another chance injury to Dwight Drewry in the Fort Meade stockade. Dwight was accordingly transferred to the Fort Meade hospital for the remainder of his trial.

With his jaw wired tightly shut, the persecuted Dwight Drewry testified to his entire experience in Germany and to the events leading to his present court-martial. He was still convicted, but was not sentenced to a bad-conduct discharge. His sentence was only to three months in the stockade. But in the end the army lost its nerve, and Dwight was not confined at all. He was simply issued an honorable discharge and released from the army.

Under no stretch of imagination, however, could he be considered a "winner."

19

Conclusion

The Vietnam war, despite everything, did furnish an insight into the meaning and purpose of military justice. We could not win the war militarily, but more significantly, we could not maintain disciplinary control over our personnel involved in it. Yet our court-martial process, albeit bogged down by thousands of defectors, was never utilized to confront the problem. While our stockades and other AWOL "collection points" were filled to the bursting point with dissident soldiers who refused to fight, the military threw in the sponge and did not attempt to "discipline" these soldiers through the court-martial process. Even though the court-martial system was alive and functioning throughout the war, the military services opted to discharge its young defectors administratively, through nonjudicial channels, rather than to court-martial them. While this was going on in the military services, thousands and thousands of draft-eligible young Americans fled to Canada or Sweden, others went underground in the United States or participated in massive peace demonstrations, burned draft cards on the streets, or hurled bricks through the windows of FBI buildings. Yet the armed services discharged the great bulk of its own defectors

administratively—while its officers and NCOs ("lifers") slept un-
easily in their bunks in Vietnam, in fear of "fragging" attacks from
their own troops, who dropped fragmentation grenades into venti-
lation slots of their concrete bunkers.

The question is, Why? Why did the military utilize its court-
martial process so sparingly in the face of this massive discontent
among its soldiers? One reason could be that the military did not
believe it politically expedient to do so at the time. The war was
not only under fire from soldier-dissidents and draft resisters, it
was also under fire from a large segment of the American population and its Congress. Hence massive, wholesale use of its court-
martial system against soldier defectors might have only increased
the likelihood of ultimate political veto of the war by the American
people and Congress. Another reason, as powerful as the first, is
that the court-martial process was conducted in only token num-
bers during the Vietnam war simply because, under the circumstances, it *did not work* to restore "discipline." It was too slow and
cumbersome. Command control was too visible, and it gave the
dissident soldier too high a profile and too big a forum. And the
issues, or points of litigation, were not necessarily in the military
service's best interest: e.g., soldier First Amendment rights; the
right to protest the Vietnam war; the right to publish antiwar
newspapers on military bases; and the right to wear long hair.

Entwined with the foregoing reasons, one hopes, is an underlying truth to be learned from the process, a truth that might be
more overriding than political and moral dissent against the Vietnam war or against any war, and that is that the military judicial
process in reality has little if anything to do with a soldier's willingness to die in battle or to fight for a military cause. At its very
best, and in its most ideal setting, military justice vindicates respect for law and order in those members of our society who
demand punishment for those who violate our laws. But this, it is
submitted, is about as far as it goes in maintaining "discipline."
The law-abiding citizen in either the military or the civilian community obeys the law basically for the same reason. He does it

because he has an "urge" to do so, to submit to authority. He simply *feels* better when he obeys. This urge probably stems from a host of intangibles within the human spirit, and it centers perhaps on the hope that the authority figure to whom he has given his allegiance is just and honorable, and worthy of sacrifice. So long as there is an urge to obey, whatever the reason, and so long as this urge is shared by a majority of citizens, we shall have governed society. When this urge is missing, disorder will follow and conventional judicial procedures will do little if anything to force a return to obedience in either the military or the civilian community.

Military justice soothes the military ego and quiets the fear that lingers in the military breast against outright soldier mutiny—and it also, of course, provides a means of punishing soldiers who break the law. But it is submitted that it does not serve as an implement of military discipline, or of instilling discipline in troops, whatever that term implies. It has no real connection with a soldier's willingness to fight and die for a particular cause, and never did. Discipline, when used in the military sense (i.e., fear), contradicts justice. One does not effect military discipline through fair or unfair judicial procedures, not in the sense that the fear generated would drive a soldier to fight and die for a military objective. Military justice, via the court-martial process, is thus a sufficient medium to punish soldiers who break the law—but it cannot be used as a tool to break the back of entrenched soldier (or public) antipathy to the war itself. Only a more brutal, violent method of nonjudicial nature can be used to accomplish this goal —such as wholesale summary execution of soldier and civilian dissidents, or the use of concentration camps of the type utilized by dictator-led governments. But the processes involved are not dependent upon judicial forums, nor is the price paid for such processes measurable in judicial terms.

Hence it is necessary to evaluate military justice on its own merit, or lack of merit, without the usual security blanket of "discipline" that encases it from public view and criticism. It is submitted that military justice should no longer be accepted on the basis of military necessity—i.e., that it is a necessary tool through which the military commander instills "discipline" within his command. Military justice should and must be viewed for what it is—a system of law providing for the military prosecution of *people* who violate military law. It is worthy of retention in our system of government only if it measures out to be a *fair* system of law, one that is based upon the rule of law and upon no other consideration.

As a system of law, American military justice is similar to systems of justice utilized by civilian societies the world over. All systems are based on power. All are based on governing statutes or prescribed procedures, and upon the good faith of administering officials. All at times break down, and are changed or corrected to prevent future miscarriage of justice. But American military justice, it is submitted, is also quite distinct in major respects from most civilian systems. In civilian systems, one man (the convening authority) does not decide what offenses shall be covered up; what cases shall be prosecuted and what cases shall not; who shall sit upon the jury and who shall serve as judge, prosecuting attorney, and defense counsel. The chief of police in civilian communities is charged with the conduct of police investigation; but he does not select the grand jury, petty jury, prosecuting and defense counsel, and the trial judge. Nor is there a convening authority in civilian life who selects such officials from among his own employees only, over whose career he has life-and-death sway, and from whom he demands and receives complete loyalty and obedience.

Civilian systems of justice tend to separate these various functions among many agencies of government. Civilian judges, for example, are independent of police departments. They also enjoy tenure of office, and cannot be replaced at the whim of a higher official. Prosecutors are usually elected, and have no connection with the police or the judiciary. Civilian defense counsel are independent of all branches of government and cannot be stopped from advancing defense theories, regardless of the adverse effect of these theories upon government officials in any office. Nor will civilian defense counsel be required to read and initial the *Canon of Professional Ethics* because of aggressive defense tactics, or transferred to nontrial duties because they have displeased a local staff judge advocate. Civilian juries owe allegiance to no prosecuting or police official, nor are they lectured by government officials on the necessity of more convictions and heavier sentences—or given poor "efficiency reports" because of the performance of judicial duties.

Convictions in civilian systems are subjected to the highest state and federal review for compliance with the rule of law and with basic constitutional guaranties. Ideally the very purpose of civilian judicial systems is to assure both the state and every criminal defendant compliance with the rule of law at every stage of the criminal and judicial process. There is no watered-down, murky intent in civilian judicial systems to enforce "military due process" (as opposed to constitutional due process), or to instill fear in the hearts of soldiers, or to enhance the ability of a military commander to wage and win wars, or to secure his next higher promotion. There is no "under-the-table" deviation acceptable in civilian systems. Dishonest prosecutors and judges, if exposed, are prosecuted—and are sentenced to jail.

The very framework of American military justice, when compared with civilian standards, is thus warped from the beginning. It places too much trust and confidence in one man. It gives this individual, who is already burdened with the responsibility of battlefield victory, the additional duties of criminal investigation, grand jury responsibility, prosecutorial and defense responsibility, and judicial (judging) responsibility. It leads this same man to conclude that his judicial duties are closely connected with that of enforcing discipline within his command. Moreover, when the rule of law might conflict with military interest, the structure of the military system permits the same man (the convening authority) to overreach the rule of law and to resolve the case upon the dictates of "military necessity."

True, the letter of the law prohibits such action by a military commander, but the inbred nature of the system permits him to exceed the system at his whim, and to do so without real fear of prosecution even if caught. Still worse, it permits him to apply his own brand of "military necessity" to each case. It permits him to pick and choose where he will intercede and stack the jury, and tell them how to vote and what sentence to impose. It permits him to be arbitrary and unethical; and it encourages the coward, the incompetent, and the fool to manipulate his judicial processes to the same extent it encourages his counterpart, the brave, intelligent, and competent commander. And in neither situation does it provide any real counterweight to prevent the misuse of the system.

Since its creation in 1951, the United States Court of Military Appeals has made great strides in creating the beginning of a legitimate jurisprudence in the field of substantive military law. We now know the definition of most military crimes. But the court has done pitifully little to prevent the military commander from usurping the independent functions of the military court. However, the real lack of improvement in military law in this regard does not lie at the door of the Court of Military Appeals. The real failure of the Uniform Code of Military Justice lies in the simple fact that under the Uniform Code the system of military justice is in the operational control of the military department. Military commanders and military staff judge advocates are not fair-minded men in the judicial sense, and they are at best incapable of operating a system of justice along democratic lines. Their ethical motivation is command-oriented, and their integrity is indistinguishable from the principles of loyalty and obedience. They respond to the dictates of their superior without regard for ethics, logic, common sense, intelligence, morality, or the rule of law.

Military command supports the military system of justice, which includes time-honored beliefs that the military should control military courts. These same commanders are secure in the knowledge that their own superiors will wholeheartedly support them in their defiance of the rule of law in military cases, and would consider them derelict as commanders if they failed to thwart civilian control of the system. If a military defense counsel were brash enough to expose a superior's illegal efforts in the judicial area, the worst that could happen to the superior would be the loss of the particular case involved, or a series of cases if the illegality affected more than one case. But under no circumstances would the superior himself be prosecuted for jury fixing by another military commander. In other words, the "offense" of maintaining "discipline" within a military command is not recognized as criminal in the military community. While the same offense in civilian life (i.e., jury tampering) would be prosecuted with zeal, this is simply not the rule in military law. Jury tampering by military commanders in the court-martial process is perfectly acceptable in the military community and carries with it *no threat at all of prosecution if exposed.*

Military justice decisions thus involve such nonlegal issues as what is best for the military establishment, what is best for the individual commander, second-guessing superiors, fear of not being promoted, and a host of related subjects. Unfortunately, equal justice under the rule of law, mercy, moral principle, and human understanding may play no part at all when the military mind resolves to try or not to try an individual, or to convict an accused of a particular crime, whether it be simple AWOL or mass murder.

The builders of future military law, our legislators of tomorrow, should take heed of the fact that many nations following World War II moved to "civilianize" their court-martial systems. Reportedly, West Germany and Sweden essentially abolished their court-martial systems, and civilian courts in both these nations try all military offenders who violate the law. Austria and Denmark have followed the lead in this regard. Civilian control over the court-martial process was greatly enlarged in England, France, Norway, Canada, Australia, Belgium, the Netherlands, Switzerland, and

Italy. Only the United States, of all major Western nations, still clings to its long-outmoded concept of military justice.

Our legislators of tomorrow should recognize that the basis upon which the military insists upon hanging the albatross of military justice around its neck (i.e., military necessity) is, in reality, a myth, and that there is no significant relation between the state of discipline within a command and its court-martial process. If our legislators are truly interested in enhancing the state of discipline within the armed forces, not only should they recognize the inherent weakness of military morality in the field of jurisprudence, but they should take notice of the fact that American youth no longer will willingly accept military solutions to ethical problems, whether they be national or international in scope. The individual-destroying element of present-day military training should be recognized, and spirit-breaking, dehumanizing games that our military leaders have traditionally inflicted upon American youth in the name of military necessity should be reexamined.

If morality and efficiency of judicial operation are to be weighed as critical factors in the administration of military justice, change must be effected. The moving force for change must of necessity come from an enlightened American people and Congress. It is wrong and immoral on the part of our people and government to subject American servicemen and women needlessly to command-oriented, command-controlled judicial processes, where the dictates of military command, and the interests of its ruling officer caste, so greatly outweigh those of justice under the rule of law. Thus, from the viewpoint of honest administration and from the viewpoint of enforcing the rule of law, the military commander should not be permitted to operate the military judicial system—for the plain reason that he will not operate it honestly; he will manipulate it to suit his own ends as a career military officer.

It is submitted that the operation of the military judicial system should be placed in the hands of civilian administrators, preferably under the control of the attorney general of the United States. Civilian trial lawyers and civilian judges should fill the roles presently filled by military legal officers in every branch of military justice, and convening authorities who insist upon tampering with military juries should be prosecuted in United States District Courts. The investigation of criminal offenses within the military community, the preferring of court-martial charges against military defendants, and the referral of those charges to trial should be under the control of civilians. Our lesson from history in this regard is that lesser procedural reforms designed to leave the military judicial system in the operational control of military commanders are reforms in name only. Only when reform changes the very basis of the system and removes the system completely from military control will the possibility of command influence be significantly reduced in courts-martial practice.

While many forms or models of military justice can be designed to effect the foregoing principles, I endorse a system that would contain only one feature of present-day military practice—and my reason for retaining that one feature is practical rather than substantive. I do not believe, for example, that it would be practical to try courts-martial before juries composed of white farmers in southern Alabama; nor do I believe it practical to try cases in the industrial northeastern portion of the country before juries composed of blacks drawn largely from the inner-city ghetto. Also, I do not believe it would be practical to try most overseas offenses of American service personnel before civilian juries in the United States. I have found in the trial of military cases that juries composed of officers and enlisted men, when completely severed from command interests, render fair and just verdicts. Thus, in the system I recommend, the military judicial system would be staffed and operated by civilians in every respect save one: I would retain the present military jury—but I would provide that the jury be drawn by lot by civilian administrators from commands totally disconnected from that of the accused serviceman or servicewoman to be tried.

I would add one further safeguard. The present-day Court of Military Appeals should be retained, with modification. Military appellate procedure should include an appeal for good cause shown to the various United States Courts of Appeals (the circuit would depend upon the geographical location of the offense involved); and thence, again for good cause shown, to the Supreme Court of the United States for final judgment.

It is submitted that only changes of this magnitude can break the stranglehold of command control that presently exists in the military judicial system, or establish a court-martial system worthy of public trust and esteem.

Index

Index

A

Abzug, Bella S., 225, 236,
   237–38, 242, 244
Acquittals, reversing, 17, 33, 36,
   37
Adams, Sergeant Paul, 55–74
   reduced in rank, 72–73
   trial and acquittal of,
   60–74
Administrative discharge,
   140–41, 239
American Bar Association, 43,
   112, 149, 237
American Civil Liberties Union
   (ACLU), 213, 216
American common law, 22
American Revolution, 24
Annapolis *Evening Capitol*,
   220
Ansell, Brigadier General S. T.,
   33–36
Arthur, Chester, 25
Articles of War, 26–27, 41,
   42

B

Bacon, Staff Sergeant L. A., 193
Bailey, F. Lee, 184–92, 196
Ballentine, Specialist 5c Charles,
   267–70
Baltimore News American, 218
Barker, Lieutenant Colonel
   Frank, 197, 200, 201, 203,
   205, 207, 212
Barnes case, 84
Beets, Benjamin L., 40
Beets case, 40–41
Bell, Captain Charles, 143
Ben Suc, destruction of
   (Vietnam War), 225
Bernhardt, Michael, 193
Best case, 86
Billy Budd (Melville), xi
Bird, Captain Larry, 145, 149
Bish, Captain William, 144–45,
   149–50, 151
Black Panthers, 270
Black revolution, 246–77
   Afro hairstyles, 247–60

Black revolution (*cont'd*)
   black-power jackets, 261
   handshakes, 249, 261
   military injustice and,
     261–77
     Camp Lejeune, 19–20,
       261–67
     Drewry court-martial,
       274–77
     Fort Benning drug-re-
       lated charge, 270–
       271, 273
     Fort Meade, 267–70
Black soldiers, execution of
   (World War I), 30–31
Black-market cases (Korea),
   53–55
Blackmarket coffee case (West
   Germany), 1–4, 7, 10, 11
   trial and acquittal, 1–4
Bloch, Lieutenant Samuel A.,
   125–38
Board of Review Number One
   (Korean Army), 47, 48
Bogan, Captain Robert, 269
Boston, Captain Thomas D.,
   249, 257
"Boy in the box" case (Korea),
   50–53
Brisentine, Robert A., 189
Brosman, Judge, 77, 81, 82–83,
   85, 86
Brown, Eugene P., 41–43, 75
Brown case (World War II),
   41–43
Bruce, Andrew A., 23
Buchanon, Master Sergeant
   Jay A., 202
Bung Cong, destruction of
   (Vietnam War), 225

C

Calhoun, Major Charles, 203,
   204, 207, 212
Calley, First Lieutenant William
   Laws, Jr., 21, 68, 154–81,
   182–83, 184, 185, 190, 192,
   198, 206
   confined to quarters, 181
   court-martial trial and
     cover-up, 167–81, 187,
     194–95, 212, 218, 271
     final arguments,
       167–72
     "free fire zone" con-
       cept, 177–79
     instructions to the
       jury, 172–80, 181
     Medina's testimony
       and, 173
     obedience to orders
       defense, 168–69,
       173–74
     partial insanity
       defense, 172–73
     verdict and conviction,
       181
     witnesses, 168, 171,
       178–79
   pretrial hearings, 154–66
     command influence
       issue, 157–66
     Nixon's interest in,
       156, 160, 161, 162,
       163, 164
     publicity, 154–56
   sentence reduction, 187
Camp Lejeune sodomy case,
   19–20, 261–67

Canons of Professional Ethics
(American Bar Association),
112, 149, 237
Central Intelligence Agency
(CIA), 269
Chicago Daily News, 216
Chicago Sun Times, 223
Chief of military justice, duties
of, 146–47
Chilcoat, Colonel William, 160,
162
Citizens Commission of Inquiry
on United States War Crimes
in Vietnam, 178, 218–19,
221, 226, 241
Claymore Mine case, 125–38
Article 32 investigation,
132–34
background of, 125–30
charges, 125, 135
dismissal of, 138
inconspicuous-safety-
officer concept and,
129–35, 137
manufacturing process and,
127–28
Clemens case, 103
Cleveland Plain Dealer, 155
Colburn, Specialist Law-
rence M., 188, 198, 200,
206, 207
Common Sense Bookstore (Fort
Devans), 232, 233, 235, 238,
241
Concerned Officer Movement,
217
Congressional Black Caucus,
267–68
Congressional Record, 218,
223–24, 232, 236

Connor, Lieutenant General
Albert O., 186–87
Connors case, 86
Conti (witness), 168
Cooks-McGuire case, 139–53
background of, 139–144
cover-up stage, 148
strategy used in, 144–48
witnesses, 149–51
writ to Court of Military
Appeals, 151–52
Court-martial jury, selection of,
7–8
Court-martial law, concept of,
23–24
Court-of-Honor theory, 22, 25
Cowan, Sergeant Isaac, 194
Criminal Investigation Division
(CID), 1, 2
Crowder, General E. H., 31–33,
35
Culverhouse, Captain Jerry R.,
198, 206, 207, 208

D

Daley, Michael, 246, 254, 267
desertion of, 229
war resister trial, 229–45
AWOL charges, 230,
231, 232, 234, 239,
242, 243–44
Court of Military
Review on, 244–45
defense witnesses,
241–42

Daley, Michael (*cont'd*)
    public protest demon-
        strations, 233–34,
        236, 242
    questionnaire to wit-
        nesses, 235–39
    window incident,
        230–31
Daminger case, 90
Daniel, Captain Aubrey, 160,
    161, 167–70, 181
Daniel, Major General Darrell,
    109
Davis, Brigadier General Os-
    car E., 161–62
Defense counsel, right of, 22–23
Dellums, Ronald V., 225, 227,
    254
Drewry, Dwight, 274–77
Dursi, James, 168, 184, 185
Dzu, General Ngo, 272

E

Eckhardt, Major William G.,
    182, 187
Elston Act, 93–94
English common law, 22
Ensign, Todd, 178, 218
Ervin, Sam, 107

F

Fagan, Staff Sergeant Martin,
    193
Falk, Richard, 226

Federal Bureau of Investigation
    (FBI), 269, 278
Federal Power Commission, 5
Ferguson, Homer, 85, 86–87,
    89, 90–91, 98–99, 100–101,
    105, 106
First Amendment, 217, 231,
    235, 239, 279
Flores, Abel, Jr., 187
Flynn, James H., 194
Font, Louis Paul, 213–28, 229,
    233, 238–39, 246, 254
    conscientious-objection to
        Vietnam and, 213–28
    arrested, 222–23
    discharge without pay,
        227–28
    Fort Meade barracks
        report, 219–23,
        227, 233
    December War Crimes
        Inquiry, 218–19, 221,
        226
Fort Benning drug-related
    offense (1971), 270–73
Fort Bragg murder case, 109–14
Fort Devens Criminal Investi-
    gation Division, 238
Fort Devens Personnel Control
    Facility (PCF) barracks,
    232–33
Fort Devens United Front, 232,
    235
Fort Leonard Wood command-
    influence cases, 106–107
Fort Meade, 214–28
    poor barracks report, 219–
        223, 227, 233
    See also Font, Louis Paul
Forty-eighth Viet Cong Batta-
    lion, 184, 191–92

"Frontiers of Faith" (TV special), 216
Front-line soldiers, sentenced to death (World War I), 31, 32

G

General prejudice, doctrine of, 77
"German-American relations" cases, 114–24
   Claymore Mine case, 125–138
   cover-up cases, 120–21
   Mays case, 114–18
   POV accidents, 118–19
   Rankin case, 119–20
Gibson, Lieutenant Colonel Glenn D., 208–209
Gibson, Major Glenn D., 197
Glimpse, Steven R., 193
Godwin case, 87
Gonzales, Leonard, 194
Gordon case, 101–103
Grzesik (witness), 168
"Guilty plea program," 5

H

Habeas corpus, writ of, 40–41
Haeberle, Ronald L., 155, 156, 184–85
Hall (witness), 168

Hammonds, Second Lieutenant Joe W., 133
Hampton Institute, 247
Haralson, Leonard H., 191
"Harmless-error" rule (*Manual for Courts-Martial*), 76–77
Harrington, Michael, 231–32, 234, 235, 236, 239, 242, 244
Harris, Huey, 258
Hartke, Vance, 227
Harvard University, 213, 214, 228
Haywood, Elmer Glen, 193
Henderson, Colonel Oran, 21, 154
   trial of, 196–212
      Medina testimony and, 210–12
      opening statement to the jury, 200–201
      Peers Committee testimony, 197, 200, 206–207, 209
      tapes evidence, 201–202
      witnesses, 204–12
Hersh, Seymour, 154–55
Hiatt v. Brown, 75
Hicks, Captain Robert, 190
Hill, Captain William R., 163–164
Hirrlinger decision, 86
"History of Command Influence on the Military Judicial System, A" (West), xii
Holladay, Lieutenant Colonel John, 207, 209–10
Hopkins, Captain Raymond, 246–60, 267
   Afro hairstyle, trial and, 247–60

Hopkins, Capt. Raymond (cont'd)
    Article 15 punishment,
        248–49, 250, 252,
        253, 254
    AWOL charges, 248–
        249, 250
    hat wearing, 251–52,
        259
    witnesses, 254–55,
        257–58
    commissioned, 246
    plea for black equality,
        250–51
    Vietnam assignment, 246
House Armed Services Com-
    mittee, 231
Howard, Colonel Kenneth, 185,
    186, 189, 192–93
Hutto, Sergeant, 212

I

Ibbetson case, 105
Inadequate sentences, returning
    (for increased sentences), 30,
    36
Inquiry into Alleged Drug
    Abuses in the Armed Services,
    An, 272–73

J

Johnson, John A., 191
Judge Advocate General's Corps
(JAG), 4, 11, 73–74
    Basic Officers' Class, 5, 6
    trial attorney's work in, 6

K

Kansas City Kansan, 216
Kansas City Star, 216
Karen, Delmar, 24
Karpatkin, Marvin, 213
Keeffe, Arthur John, 36–37
Keller, Captain Juan, 144
Kennedy, Colonel Reid, 157,
    159–60, 164–66, 169,
    172–81, 271
Keyes v. United States, 24–25
Kilday, Judge, 98–99, 100, 105
Kim, General, 46–47
Kinch, Thomas J., 194
Ko, Colonel, 47, 48
Kotouc, Captain Eugene, 204,
    212
Korean Military Advisory
    Group headquarters
    (KMAG), 46–73
    Adams case, 55–74
        background of, 55–59
        instructions to the
            jury, 69–71
        "obedience to orders"
            defense, 68
        redrafting of charges,
            61–62
        trial and acquittal,
            64–72
    black-market cases, 53–55
    "boy in the box" case, 50–
        53

parallel between U.S.
and, 47–48
sex cases, 54–55
Koster, Brigadier General
Samuel W., 196–97, 203, 204,
205, 207, 208, 209, 212,
221, 223, 225, 226
Kraskouskas case, 94

L

LaCross, First Lieutenant
Jeffrey, 187
Laird, Melvin, 156, 159–60,
161, 165
Lamartina, Salvador, 194
Lands Division (Korean Army),
47, 48
Lathrop, Colonel Robert M.,
160, 162
Latimer, George, 76, 81, 82, 83,
85, 88, 90, 158–60, 163–64,
169–72, 178–79, 182, 190
Lee case, 97
Lemnitzer, General L. L., 95
Life (magazine), 155, 156, 184
Loudermilch, Lieutenant
Wayne, 109–14

M

MacArthur, General Douglas,
186
McCann decision, 86

McGuire, First Lieutenant
Thomas, 143–53
McKay, Lieutenant William,
144–45, 146, 147, 148
Malone, Shalaine, 257
Manual for Courts-Martial, 36,
43, 44, 47, 76, 79, 80, 107,
165
Maples (witness), 168
Marlowe, Colonel Lon, 160,
161, 163–64
Martin, Louis B., 188, 191
Maryland Gazette, 219–20, 226
Master, Captain Robert J., 220
Meadlo, Paul, 155, 160, 169
Medina, Captain Ernest, 21,
154, 168, 169, 170, 171, 172,
173, 180, 181, 201, 204
Calley's trial testimony,
173, 183
company instructions of,
193–94
Henderson trial testimony,
210–11, 212
trial and acquittal, 182–95
opening statement to
jury, 184
witnesses, 184–91
Yamashita principle
and, 185–86, 189
Michael Daley Defense Action
Committee, 237
Mikva, Congressman, 225
Military Affairs Division
(Korean Army), 47, 48
Military discipline, meaning of,
15–16
Military Intelligence (MI), 269
Military justice:
and achieving justice, 8–9
control over, 16–17

Military justice (*cont'd*)
 convening authority, 7–8, 9
 evaluation of, 280–87
 in foreign countries, 284–
  285
 introduction to, ix–xii
 Vietnam War and, 278–79
 See also Uniform Code of
  Military Justice
Military law, 15–27
 court-martial law, 23–24
 Court-of-Honor theory,
  22, 25
 defense counsel, 22–23
 denunciations of, 34–35
 execution of soldiers, 30–31
 in foreign countries, 284–
  285
 meaning of, 15
 military commanders and,
  15–22, 26–27
  Camp Lejeune racial
   discord, 19–20
  Fort Devens AWOL
   charges, 20–21
  My Lai trials, 21
  Supreme Court and, 24–26
  due process, 26
Military Law and Precedents
 (Winthrop), 38
Military Occupational Specialty
 (MOS), 254
Minimum acceptable sentences,
 establishment of (World War
 II), 37–38
Mitchell, Sergeant, 212
Mitchell, Parren, 221, 222,
 223, 225, 254, 276
Morgan, Edmund, 24, 35, 45
Moss, Tommy Lee, 194
Murphy, Morgan F., 271

My Lai cases, ix, 154–212, 223,
 225, 226
 acquittal of Medina, 182–
  195
 Calley and, 154–81
  conviction and cover-
   up, 167–81
  pretrial hearings,
   154–81
 Henderson cover-up trial,
  196–212

N

National Broadcasting Com-
 pany (NBC), 216
National Peace Action Coali-
 tion, 227
New York Times, The, 213,
 217, 225, 227
Ninth Amendment, 244
Nixon, Richard M., 156, 160,
 161, 162, 163, 164, 181
Nonjudicial punishment,
 imposition of, 52
Notre Dame Law Review, 144

O

"Obedience to orders" (de-
 fense), 68
O'Donald, Colonel, 162
Oliver, Gene, 190

Olsen, Gregory, 168, 184, 185
Osborne, Barton, 242–43
Overseas Weekly (newspaper), 120

P

Paetch, Thomas H., 194
Parker, Brigadier General Harold E., 226
Patton, Brigadier General George S., III, 214
Pearson, Colonel, 242
Peers, Lieutenant General William, 210
Peers Committee, 197, 198, 200, 206–207, 209
Pershing, General John S., 32
Personnel Control Facility (PCF), 20
Phoenix Program (Vietnam War), 240–41, 242–43
Pierce case, 90
Powell, General, 95, 98
Powell Report, 92–98
Princeton University, 226
Privately Owned Vehicle (POV) accidents, 118–19
Psychiatry in Military Law, 81–82

Q

Quinn, Chief Judge, 77, 80–81, 82, 83, 85, 90, 98, 100, 105

R

Raby, Major Kenneth, 159
Rach Bap, destruction of (Vietnam War), 225
Rach Kien, destruction of (Vietnam War), 225
Railey, Captain Matt M., 240
Rankin, Specialist 4c James C., 119–20
Rathikoune, General Ouane, 272
Resor, Stanley, 156, 159–60, 165
Reversible error, 76
Rhee, Syngman, 47
Roberts, Private Jay, 155–156
Robinson case, 83
Roden case, 86
Rothblatt, Henry B., 196, 200–201, 210–11
Rowny, Major General, 114–20, 122, 126, 135
Ruddock, Rear Admiral, 85–86
Ryukyuan-American Community Relations Advisory Council, 88–89

S

St. Louis Dispatch, 216
Salzman, Amy Gwen, 238–39
San Francisco Sunday Examiner and Chronicle, 223
Schell, Jonathan, 226
Schweiker, Richard, 156
Seaman, Lieutenant General Jonathan, 221, 222, 223, 224–225, 226

Senate Armed Services Com-
  mittee, 156
Senate Subcommittee on Con-
  stitutional Rights for Govern-
  ment Employees, 107
Sex cases (Korea), 54–55
Shapiro, Second Lieutenant
  Sidney, 39–40
Sheehan, Neil, 225–26
Sheppard, George, 257–58
Sledge (witness), 168
Smaltz, Captain, 111, 112
Staff judge advocate (SJA),
  6–7, 10, 50, 59, 72, 79, 80,
  81, 106, 119, 137, 142, 149
Steele, Robert H., 272
Stennis, John, 156
Svenson, Captain, 103–105
Swaim, Major General
  David G., 25–26
Sweden, 278, 284
Switzerland, 284

T

Talbott, Major General Orwin
  Clark, 161
Thieu, Nguyen Van, 272
Thompson, Captain Hugh, 188,
  200, 206, 208
Tichenor, Major Carroll J.,
  198–206, 207, 208, 210,
  211–12
Time (magazine), 155, 159
Torrente case, 83
Travis Air Force Base, 261
Trial judge, overruling (pro
  cedural device), 2–3

Turner (witness), 168
Twenty-fourth Infantry Division, 114–24

U

Uniform Code of Military
  Justice, 3, 61, 62, 144, 153,
  255
    Article 15, 248–49, 250,
      252, 253, 255, 275
    Article 32, 66, 115, 116,
      117, 132–33, 222, 226
    Article 37, 8–9, 11, 79, 91,
      103, 144, 153, 158
    Article 92, 255–56
    Article 93, 255
    Article 134, 95, 255
    Article 138, 72
    during 1950s and 1960s,
      75–107
        command influence
          cases, 80–84,
          106–107
        general prejudice
          doctrine, 77
        harmless-error rule,
          76–77
        navy court-martials,
          98–99
        overseas convictions,
          87–89
        Powell Report, 92–98
        precedent-setting
          cases, 75–78
        pretrial orientation of
          court members,
          79–80, 89–91

duty to prefer court-
    martial charges, 225
    enacted (1951), 8,
    17, 35, 44, 107
    failure of, 283
    reforms embodied in,
    17–18
United Front, 233
United States v. Addye, 86
United States v. Berry, 77–78,
    79
United States v. Blankenship, 84
United States v. Borner, 80
United States v. Bourchier, 82
United States v. Carter, 88
United States v. Clay, 75, 78
United States Constitution, 75,
    76, 231
United States v. Cooks, 143
United States Court of Military
    Appeals, 8, 12, 17, 35, 76,
    151, 244, 283, 286–87
    during 1950s and 1960s,
    75–107
        Powell Report, 92–98
    reversal power of, 85
United States v. Danzine, 90
United States v. Dean, 85–86
United States Department of
    State, 118
United States v. Estrada, 86
United States v. Fraser, 103
United States v. Guest, 81
United States v. Hawthorne,
    83–84
United States v. Hunter, 81
United States v. Isbell, 80–81
United States v. Johnson, 103
United States v. Kitchens, 99–
    100
United States v. Knudson, 82

United States v. Lee, 76, 78, 79
United States v. Littrice, 80
United States v. Navarre, 82–83
United States v. Olson, 89–90
United States v. Prince, 105–106
United States v. Sheppard,
    86–87
United States v. Specialist 4th
    Class James E. Mays, 114–18
United States v. Stringer, 83
United States Supreme Court,
    16, 24–26, 40, 42, 75, 170,
    186, 227
    military law and, 24–26
    See also names of cases
United States v. Walinch, 86
United States v. Wright, 106
United States v. Zagar, 83
University of California (Los
    Angeles) Law Review, xii
University of Virginia, 108

V

Vanderbilt Committee, 43–45
Vanderbilt Law Review, 45
Vietnam Veterans Against the
    War, 233
Vietnam War, 20, 21, 139, 142,
    153, 278
    drug addiction, 271–73
    "fragging" attacks, 279
    opposition to, 213–45
        war resister, 229–45
        West Point cadet,
        213–28
    Phoenix Program, 240–41,
    242–43

Vincent, Lieutenant Colonel
    Henry E., 162, 163, 164

W

Walter Reed Army Medical
    Center, 11–12, 13
War Crimes Inquiry, 218
Washington Post, The, 153,
    215–16, 218, 225, 227
Washington Sunday Star, 216
Watke, Major, 206, 207–208,
    209, 212
Watson, Tom, 227
Wells, Specialist, 110, 113
West, Sergeant Charles A., 193
Westmoreland, Major General
    William C., 95, 159–60, 162,
    163, 165, 166, 186, 201
Wicker, Captain Raymond K.,
    119, 120
Widmer, Frederick, 188–89
Williams, Captain Donald B.,
    67
Wilson, Colonel William, 160,
    208
Winthrop, Colonel William, 23,
    38
Wisconsin Law Review, 24
World War I, 8, 92, 107
    judicial cases, 28–36

at Camp Upton, 29–3
criticism of, 33–36, 3
execution of blacks,
    30–31
French death sen-
    tences, 31, 32
justification of sen-
    tences, 31–33
MP conviction, 29,
    31–32
World War II, xi, 5, 7, 8, 92,
    107, 128, 186
    judicial cases, 36–45
    Beets case, 40–41
    Brown murder case,
        41–43
    condemnation of,
        43–45
    naval injustice, 36–37
    Shapiro court-martial,
        39–40

Y

Yamashita, General, 186
Yamashita decision, 185–86,
    189
Young, Brigadier General
    George H., 197, 199, 200,
    207, 209, 211, 212
Young, Stephen, 156